D0628454

GREEK

PHRASEBOOK

Compiled by

LEXUS

www.roughguides.com

Credits

Compiled by Lexus with Costas Panayotakis
Lexus Series Editor: Sally Davies
Rough Guides Reference Director: Andrew Lockett
Rough Guides Series Editor: Mark Ellingham

First edition published in 1995.
Reprinted in 1996 and 1998.
Revised in 1999.
This updated edition published in 2006 by
Rough Guides Ltd,
80 Strand, London WC2R 0RL
345 Hudson St, 4th Floor, New York 10014, USA
Email: mail@roughguides.co.uk.

Distributed by the Penguin Group.

Penguin Books Ltd, 80 Strand, London WC2R 0RL
Penguin Putnam, Inc., 375 Hudson Street, NY 10014, USA
Penguin Group (Australia), 250 Camberwell Road, Camberwell, Victoria 3124, Australia
Penguin Books Canada Ltd, 10 Alcorn Avenue, Toronto, Ontario, Canada M4V 1E4
Penguin Group (New Zealand), Cnr Rosedale and Airborne Roads, Albany, Auckland, New Zealand

Typeset in Bembo and Helvetica to an original design by Henry Iles.
Printed in Italy by LegoPrint S.p.A

No part of this book may be reproduced in any form without permission from the publisher except for the quotation of brief passages in reviews.

© Lexus Ltd 2006
240pp.

British Library Cataloguing in Publication Data
A catalogue for this book is available from the British Library.

ISBN 13: 978-1-84353-629-1
ISBN 10: 1-84353-629-3

The publishers and authors have done their best to ensure the accuracy and currency of all information in The Rough Guide Greek Phrasebook however, they can accept no responsibility for any loss or inconvenience sustained by any reader using the book.

Online information about Rough Guides can be found at our website www.roughguides.com

CONTENTS

Introduction 5

Basic Phrases 8

Scenarios 13

English - Greek 31

Greek - English 108

Menu Reader

Food 174

Drink 204

How the Language Works

The Greek Alphabet 209

Pronunciation 211

Abbreviations 211

Nouns and Articles 212

Adjectives and Adverbs 218

Pronouns 222

Verbs 224

Questions 231

Dates 231

Days 232

Months 232

Time 233

Numbers 234

Conversion Tables 236

Introduction

The Rough Guide Greek phrasebook is a highly practical introduction to the contemporary language. Laid out in clear A-Z style, it uses key-word referencing to lead you straight to the words and phrases you want – so if you need to book a room, just look up 'room'. The Rough Guide gets straight to the point in every situation, in bars and shops, on trains and buses, and in hotels and banks.

The main part of the Rough Guide is a double dictionary: English-Greek then Greek-English. Before that, there's a section called **Basic Phrases** and to get you involved in two-way communication, the Rough Guide includes, in this new edition, a set of **Scenario** dialogues illustrating questions and responses in key situations such as renting a car and asking directions. You can hear these and then download them free from **www.roughguides.com/phrasebooks** for use on your computer or MP3 player.

Forming the heart of the guide, the **English-Greek** section gives easy-to-use transliterations of the Greek words wherever pronunciation might be a problem. Throughout this section, cross-references enable you to pinpoint key facts and phrases, while asterisked words indicate where further information can be found in a section at the end of the book called **How the Language Works**. This section sets out the fundamental rules of the language, with plenty of practical examples. You'll also find here other essentials like numbers, dates, telling the time and basic phrases. The **Greek-English** section is in two parts: a dictionary, arranged phonetically, of all the words and phrases you're likely to hear (starting with a section of slang and colloquialisms); then a compilation, arranged by subject, of various signs, labels, instructions and other basic words you may come across in print or in public places.

Near the back of the book too the Rough Guide offers an extensive **Menu Reader**. Consisting of food and drink sections (each starting with a list of essential terms), it's indispensable whether you're eating out, stopping for a quick drink, or browsing through a local food market.

καλό ταξίδι!

kalo taxithi!

have a good trip!

Basic Phrases

Basic Phrases

yes
ναί
neh

no
όχι
okhi

OK
εντάξει
endaxi

hello
χαίρετε
khereteh

good morning
καλημέρα
kalimera

good evening
καλησπέρα
kalispera

good night
καληνύχτα
kalinikhta

goodbye
αντίο
andio

hi
γειά
ya

see you
γειά, θα τα πούμε
ya, tha ta poomeh

please
παρακαλώ
parakalo

thank you
ευχαριστώ
efkharisto

yes, please
ναί, παρακαλώ
neh, parakalo

no thank you
όχι, ευχαριστώ
okhi, efkharisto

excuse me, please (to attract attention, to get past someone)
συγγνώμη, παρακαλώ
signomi, parakalo

sorry!
συγγνώμη!
signomi!

pardon? (sorry?, what did you say?)
ορίστε;
oristeh?

what did you say?
πώς είπατε;
pos **i**pateh?

I don't understand
δεν καταλαβαίνω
then katalav**e**no

do you speak English?
μιλάτε Αγγλικά;
mil**a**teh Anglik**a**?

I don't speak Greek
δεν μιλάω Ελληνικά
then mil**o** Elinik**a**

please speak more slowly
παρακαλώ, μιλάτε πιό αργά;
parakal**o**, mil**a**teh pi**o** arg**a**?

could you repeat that?
το ξαναλέτε αυτό, σας παρακαλώ;
to xanal**e**teh aft**o**, sas parakal**o**?

please write it down
μου το γράφετε, παρακαλώ;
moo to gr**a**feteh, parakal**o**?

I would like ...
θα ήθελα ...
tha **i**the**l**a ...

can I have ...?
μπορώ να έχω ...;
bor**o** na **e**kho ...?

how much is it?
πόσο κάνει;
p**o**so k**a**ni?

cheers!
εις υγείαν!
is iy**i**an!

where is/are the ...?
πού είναι ...;
poo **i**neh ...?

Scenarios

download these scenarios as MP3s from:

1. Accommodation

is there an inexpensive hotel you can recommend?
▶ υπάρχει κάποιο φτηνό ξενοδοχείο που μπορείτε να μου συστήσετε;
[iparkhi kapio ftino xenothokhio poo boriteh na moo sistiseteh?]

λυπάμαι, φαίνεται ότι είναι όλα κλεισμένα ◀
[lipameh, feneteh oti ineh ola klismena]
I'm sorry, they all seem to be fully booked

---

can you give me the name of a good middle-range hotel?
▶ μπορείτε να μου πείτε το όνομα ενός ξενοδοχείου μεσαίας κατηγορίας;
[boriteh na moo piteh to onoma enos xenothokhioo meseas katigorias?]

δώστε μου να δω; θέλετε να είστε στο κέντρο της πόλης; ◀
[thosteh moo na tho; THeleteh na isteh sto kendro tis polis?]
let me have a look; do you want to be in the centre?

---

if possible
▶ αν είναι δυνατό
[an ineh thinato]

θα σας πείραζε να είστε λίγο έξω από την πόλη; ◀
[THa sas pirazeh na isteh ligo exo apo tin poli?]
do you mind being a little way out of town?

---

not too far out
▶ όχι πολύ μακριά
[okhi poli makria]

where is it on the map?
▶ πού είναι στον χάρτη;
[poo ineh ston kharti?]

can you write the name and address down?
▶ μπορείτε να μου γράψετε το όνομα και τη διεύθυνση;
[boriteh na moo grapseteh to onoma keh ti di-efTHinsi?]

I'm looking for a room in a private house
▶ ψάχνω για ένα δωμάτιο σε πανσιόν
[psakhno ya ena thomatio seh pansion]

2. Banks

bank account	ο τραπεζικός λογαριασμός	[o trapezikos logariasmos]
to change money	αλλάζω χρήματα	[alazo khrimata]
cheque	μιά επιταγή	[mia epitayi]
to deposit	κάνω κατάθεση	[kano kataThesi]
euro	ένα ευρώ	[ena evro]
pin number	ο κωδικός	[o kothikos]
pound	η λίρα Αγγλίας	[i lira anglias]
to withdraw	κάνω ανάληψη	[kano analipsi]

can you change this into euros?
▶ μπορείτε να αλλάξετε αυτά σε ευρώ;
[boriteh na alaxeteh afta seh evro?]

πώς θέλετε τα χρήματα; ◀
[pos THeleteh ta khrimata?]
how would you like the money?

small notes
▶ χαρτονομίσματα μικρής αξίας
[khartonomismata mikris axias]

big notes
▶ χαρτονομίσματα μεγάλης αξίας
[khartonomismata megalis axias]

do you have information in English about opening an account?
▶ έχετε πληροφορίες στα Αγγλικά για να ανοίξω έναν λογαριασμό;
[ekheteh plirofories sta Anglika ya na anixo enan logariasmo?]

ναι, τί είδος λογαριασμού θέλετε; ◀
[neh, ti ithos logariasmoo THeleteh?]
yes, what sort of account do you want?

I'd like a current account
▶ θα ήθελα έναν τρέχοντα λογαριασμό
[THa iThela enan trekhonda logariasmo]

το διαβατήριό σας, παρακαλώ ◀
[to thiavatirio sas, parakalo]
your passport, please

can I use this card to draw some cash?
▶ μπορώ να κάνω ανάληψη μετρητών με αυτή την κάρτα;
[boro na kano analipsi metriton me afti tin karta?]

πρέπει να πάτε στο ταμείο ◀
[prepi na pateh sto tamio]
you have to go to the cashier's desk

I want to transfer this to my account at National Bank
▶ θέλω να μεταφέρω αυτά στον λογαριασμό μου στην Εθνική Τράπεζα
[THelo na metafero afta ston logariasmo moo stin EThniki Trapeza]

εντάξει, αλλά θα πρέπει να σας χρεώσουμε για το τηλεφώνημα ◀
[endaxi, ala THa prepi na sas khreosoomeh ya to tilefonima]
OK, but we'll have to charge you for the phonecall

download these scenarios as MP3s from:

3. Booking a room

shower	το ντους	[to doos]
telephone in the room	το τηλέφωνο στο δωμάτιο	[to tilefono sto thomatio]
payphone in the lobby	το καρτοτηλέφωνο στη ρέσεψιόν	[to kartotilefono sti resepsion]

do you have any rooms?
▸ έχετε δωμάτια;
[ekheteh thomatia?]

▸ για πόσα άτομα;
[ya posa atoma?]
for how many people?

for one/for two
▸ για ένα/για δύο
[ya ena/ya thio]

▸ ναι, έχουμε ελεύθερα δωμάτια
[neh, ekhoomeh elefTHera thomatia]
yes, we have rooms free

▸ για πόσα βράδυα;
[ya posa vrathia?]
for how many nights?

just for one night
▸ μόνο για ένα βράδυ
[mono ya ena vrathi]

how much is it?
▸ πόσο κάνει;
[poso kani?]

ενενήντα ευρώ με λουτρό και εβδομήντα ευρώ χωρίς λουτρό ◂
[enenínda evro meh lootro keh evthominda evro khoris lootro]
90 euros with bathroom and 70 euros without bathroom

does that include breakfast?
▸ αυτό περιλαμβάνει και πρωινό;
[afto perilamvani keh pro-ino?]

can I see a room with bathroom?
▸ μπορώ να δω ένα δωμάτιο με λουτρό;
[boro na tho ena thomatio meh lootro?]

ok, I'll take it
▸ εντάξει, θα το κλείσω
[endaxi, THa to kliso]

when do I have to check out?
▸ πότε πρέπει να κάνω 'check-out';
[poteh prepi na kano 'check-out'?]

is there anywhere I can leave luggage?
▸ μπορώ να αφήσω τις αποσκευές μου κάπου;
[boro na afiso tis aposkeves moo kapoo?]

4. Car hire

automatic	το αυτόματο	[to aftomato]
full tank	το γεμάτο τεπόζιτο	[to yematо tepozito]
manual	το σειριακό	[to siriako]
rented car	το νοικιασμένο αυτοκίνητο	[to nikiasmeno aftokinito]

I'd like to rent a car
▶ θα ήθελα να νοικιάσω ένα αυτοκίνητο
[THa iTHela na nikiaso ena aftokinito]

για πόσο καιρό ◀
[ya poso kero?]
for how long?

two days
▶ για δύο ημέρες
[ya thio imeres]

I'll take the ...
▶ θα πάρω το ...
[THa paro to ...]

is that with unlimited mileage?
▶ έχει απεριόριστο αριθμό χιλιομέτρων;
[ekhi aperioristo arithmo khiliometron?]

ναι ◀
[neh]
it is

παρακαλώ, μπορώ να δω την άδεια οδήγησης; ◀
[parakalo, boro na tho tin athia othiyisis?]
can I see your driving licence, please?

και το διαβατήριό σας ◀
[keh to thiavatirio sas]
and your passport

is insurance included?
▶ περιλαμβάνεται η ασφάλεια;
[perilamvaneteh i asfalia?]

ναι, αλλά πρέπει να πληρώσετε τα πρώτα εκατό ευρώ ◀
[neh, ala prepi na pliroseteh ta prota ekato evro]
yes, but you have to pay the first 100 euros

μπορείτε να δώσετε εγγύηση εκατό ευρώ; ◀
[boriteh na thoseteh engi-isi ekato evro?]
can you leave a deposit of 100 euros?

and if this office is closed, where do I leave the keys?
▶ και αν αυτό το γραφείο είναι κλειστό, πού μπορώ να αφήσω τα κλειδιά;
[keh an afto to grafio ineh klisto, poo boro na afiso ta klithia?]

τα ρίχνετε σε αυτό το κουτί ◀
[ta riKHneteh se afto to kooti]
you drop them in that box

download these scenarios as MP3s from:

5. Communications

ADSL modem	το μόντεμ ADSL	[to modem ADSL]
at	παπάκι	[papaki]
dial-up modem	το μόντεμ αναλογικής τηλεφωνίας	[to modem analo-yikis tilefonias]
dot	τελεία	[telia]
Internet	το 'Internet'	[to 'Internet']
mobile (phone)	το κινητό	[to kinito]
password	ο κωδικός	[o kothikos]
telephone socket adaptor	ο αντάπτορας για πρίζα τηλεφώνου	[o adaptoras ya priza tilefonoo]
wireless hotspot	η περιοχή για ασύρματο 'internet'	[i periokhi ya asirmato 'internet']

is there an Internet café around here?
▶ υπάρχει 'Internet café' εδώ γύρω;
[iparkhi 'Internet café' etho yiro?]

can I send email from here?
▶ μπορώ να στείλω 'email' από εδώ;
[boro na stilo 'email' apo etho?]

where's the at sign on the keyboard?
▶ πού είναι το παπάκι στο πληκτρολόγιο;
[poo ineh to papaki sto pliktrolo-yio?]

can you switch this to a UK keyboard?
▶ μπορείτε να αλλάξετε αυτό σε βρετανικό πληκτρολόγιο;
[boriteh na alaxeteh afto seh vretaniko pliktrolo-yio?]

can you help me log on?
▶ μπορείτε να με βοηθήσετε να κάνω είσοδο;
[boriteh na meh vo-iTHiseteh na kano isotho?]

can you put me through to ...?
▶ μπορείτε να με συνδέσετε με το ...;
[boriteh na meh sintheseteh meh to ...?]

I'm not getting a connection, can you help?
▶ δεν πιάνω γραμμή, μπορείτε να βοηθήσετε;
[then piano grami, boriteh na vo-iTHiseteh?]

where can I get a top-up card for my mobile?
▶ που μπορώ να πάρω μια κάρτα ανανέωσης για το κινητό μου;
[poo boro na paro mia karta ananeosis ya to kinito moo?]

zero	**five**
μηδέν	πέντε
[mithen]	[pendeh]
one	**six**
ένα	έξι
[ena]	[exi]
two	**seven**
δύο	επτά
[thio]	[epta]
three	**eight**
τρία	οχτώ
[tria]	[okhto]
four	**nine**
τέσσερα	εννιά
[tesera]	[enia]

6. Directions

hi, I'm looking for Panepistimiou Street
▶ γειά σας, ψάχνω την οδό Πανεπιστημίου
[ya sas, psakhno ya tin otho Panepistimioo]

λυπάμαι, δεν την έχω ακουστά ◀
[lipameh, then tin ekho akoosta]
sorry, never heard of it

hi, can you tell me where Panepistimiou Street is?
▶ γειά σας, μπορείτε να μου πείτε πού είναι η οδός Πανεπιστημίου;
[ya sas, boriteh na moo piteh poo ineh i othos Panepistimioo?]

είμαι και εγώ ξένος εδώ ◀
[imeh keh ego xenos etho]
I'm a stranger here too

hi, Panepistimiou Street, do you know where it is?
γειά σας, η οδός Πανεπιστημίου ξέρετε πού είναι;
[ya sas, i othos Panepistimioo xereteh poo ineh?]

where?
πού
[poo?]

which direction?
προς ποιά κατεύθυνση
[pros pia kateftHinsi?]

▶ στη γωνία
[sti gonia]
around the corner

▶ αριστερά στα δεύτερα φανάρια
[aristera sta theftera fanaria]
left at the second traffic lights

▶ κατόπιν, είναι ο πρώτος δρόμος στα δεξιά
[katopin ineh o protos thromos sta thexia]
then it's the first street on the right

αμέσως μετά
[amesos meta]
just after

απέναντι από
[apenandi apo]
opposite

στα αριστερά
[sta aristera]
on the left

εκεί
[eki]
over there

επόμενος
[epomenos]
next

ευθεία
[efTHia]
straight ahead

κοντά
[konda]
near

μετά το...
[meta to ...]
past the ...

μπροστά
[brosta]
in front of

η οδός
[i othos]
street

παραπέρα
[parapera]
further

πίσω
[piso]
back

στρίβω
[strivo]
turn off

στα δεξιά
[sta thexia]
on the right

download these scenarios as MP3s from:

7. Emergencies

accident	το ατύχημα	[to atikhima]
ambulance	το πρώτων βοηθειών	[to proton vo-iTHion]
consul	ο πρόξενος	[o proxenos]
embassy	η πρεσβεία	[i presvia]
fire brigade	η πυροσβεστική	[i pirosvestiki]
police	η αστυνομία	[i astinomia]

help!
▶ βοήθεια!
[vo-iTHia]

can you help me?
▶ μπορείτε να με βοηθήσετε;
[boriteh na meh vo-iTHiseteh?]

please come with me! it's really very urgent
▶ ελάτε, παρακαλώ, μαζί μου! είναι πραγματικά πολύ επείγον
[elateh, parakalo, mazi moo! ineh pragmatika poli epigon]

I've lost (my keys)
▶ έχασα (τα κλειδιά μου)
[ekhasa (ta klithia moo)]

(my car) is not working
▶ (το αυτοκίνητό μου) δεν λειτουργεί
[(to aftokinito moo) then litooryi]

(my purse) has been stolen
▶ έκλεψαν (το πορτοφόλι μου)
[eklepsan (to portofoli moo)]

I've been mugged
▶ με λήστεψαν
[meh listepsan]

πώς σας λένε; ◀
[pos sas leneh?]
what's your name?

χρειάζεται να δω το διαβατήριό σας ◀
[khriazeteh na tho to thiavatirio sas]
I need to see your passport

I'm sorry, all my papers have been stolen
▶ λυπάμαι, μου έκλεψαν όλα τα στοιχεία ταυτότητας
[lipameh, moo eklepsan ola ta stikhia taftotitas]

8. Friends

hi, how're you doing?
▸ γειά σου, τι κάνεις;
[ya soo, ti kanis?]

καλά, και εσύ; ◂
[kala, keh esí?]
OK, and you?

---

yeah, fine
▸ ναι, ωραία
[neh, orea]

not bad
▸ όχι άσχημα
[okhi askhima]

---

d'you know Mark?
▸ ξέρεις τον Μάρκ;
[xeris ton Mark?]

---

and this is Hannah
▸ και αυτή είναι η Χάννα
[keh aftí ineh i khana]

ναι, γνωριζόμαστε ◂
[neh, gnorizomasteh]
yeah, we know each other

---

where do you know each other from?
▸ από που γνωρίζεστε;
[apo poo gnorizesteh?]

συναντηθήκαμε στο σπίτι του Γιάννη ◂
[sinandiTHikameh sto spíti too Yani]
we met at Yanis' place

---

that was some party, eh?
▸ πολύ ωραίο πάρτυ, ε;
[poli oreo parti, eh?]

το καλύτερο ◂
[to kalitero]
the best

---

are you guys coming for a beer?
▸ έρχεστε για μιά μπύρα;
[erkhesteh ya mia bira?]

▸ 'cool', πάμε
['cool', pameh]
cool, let's go

▸ όχι, θα συναντήσω τη Μαρία
[okhi, THa sinandiso ti Maria]
no, I'm meeting Maria

---

see you at Yanis' place tonight
▸ τα λέμε στο σπίτι του Γιάννη απόψε
[ta lemeh sto spíti too Yani apopseh]

τα λέμε ◂
[ta lemeh]
see you

download these scenarios as MP3s from:

9. Health

I'm not feeling very well
▸ δεν αισθάνομαι πολύ καλά
[then esTHanomeh poli kala]

can you get a doctor?
▸ μπορείτε να φέρετε έναν γιατρό;
[boriteh na fereteh enan yatro?]

▸ πού πονάει;
[poo pona-i?]
where does it hurt?

it hurts here
▸ πονάει εδώ
[pona-i etho]

▸ πονάει συνεχώς;
[pona-i sinekhos?]
is the pain constant?

it's not a constant pain
▸ δεν πονάει συνεχώς
[then pona-i sinekhos]

---

can I make an appointment?
▸ μπορώ να κλείσω ένα ραντεβού;
[boro na kliso ena randevoo?]

can you give me something for ...?
▸ μπορείτε να μου δώσετε κάτι για ...;
[boriteh na moo thoseteh kati ya ...?]

yes, I have insurance
▸ ναι, έχω ασφάλεια
[neh, ekho asfalia]

antibiotics	το αντιβιοτικό	[to andiviotiko]
antiseptic ointment	η αντισηπτική αλοιφή	[i andisiptiki alifi]
cystitis	η κυστίτιδα	[i kistititha]
dentist	ο/η οδοντίατρος	[o/i othondiatros]
diarrhoea	η διάρροια	[i thiari-a]
doctor	ο γιατρός	[o yatros]
hospital	το νοσοκομείο	[to nosokomio]
ill	άρρωστος	[arostos]
medicine	το φάρμακο	[to farmako]
painkillers	τα παυσίπονα	[ta pafsipona]
pharmacy	το φαρμακείο	[to farmakio]
to prescribe	γράφω συνταγή	[grafo sinda-yi]
thrush	η στοματίτιδα	[i stomatitida]

10. Language difficulties

a few words	λίγες λέξεις	[liyes lexis]
interpreter	ο/η διερμηνέας	[o/i thi-ermineas]
to translate	μεταφράζω	[metafrazo]

η πιστωτική σας κάρτα δεν έγινε δεκτή
[i pistotiki sas karta then eyineh thekti]
your credit card has been refused

---

what, I don't understand; do you speak English?
τί; δεν καταλαβαίνω, μιλάτε Αγγλικά;
[ti? then katalaveno; milateh Anglika?]

αυτή δεν ισχύει
[afti then iskhi-i]
this isn't valid

---

could you say that again?
μπορείτε να το ξαναπείτε αυτό;
[boriteh na to xanapiteh afto?]

slowly
αργά
[arga]

I understand very little Greek
καταλαβαίνω πολύ λίγα Ελληνικά
[katalaveno poli liga Elinika]

I speak Greek very badly
δεν μιλάω καθόλου καλά Ελληνικά
[then milao kaTHoloo kala Elinika]

δεν μπορείτε να πληρώσετε με αυτή την κάρτα
[then boriteh na pliroseteh meh afti tin karta]
you can't use this card to pay

καταλαβαίνετε;
[katalaveneteh?]
do you understand?

sorry, no
όχι, λυπάμαι
[okhi, lipameh]

---

is there someone who speaks English?
μιλάει κανείς εδώ Αγγλικά;
[mila-i kanis etho Anglika?]

---

oh, now I understand
α, τώρα καταλαβαίνω
[ah, tora katalaveno]

is that ok now?
είναι εντάξει τώρα;
[ineh endaxi tora?]

download these scenarios as MP3s from:

11. Meeting people

hello
▸ γειά σας
[ya sas]

γειά σας, με λένε Κατερίνα ◂
[yasas, meh leneh Katerina]
hello, my name's Katerina

Graham, from England, Thirsk
▸ με λένε Graham και είμαι από το Thirsk στην Αγγλία
[meh leneh Graham keh imeh apo to Thirsk stin Anglia]

δεν το ξέρω, πού βρίσκεται; ◂
[then to xero, poo vrisketeh?]
don't know that, where is it?

---

not far from York, in the North; and you?
▸ όχι μακριά από το York στον Βορρά, και εσύ;
[okhi makria apo to York ston vora; keh esi?]

εγώ είμαι από τη Θεσσαλονίκη; είσαι εδώ μόνος σου; ◂
[ego imeh apo ti THesaloniki; iseh etho monos soo?]
I'm from Thessaloniki; here by yourself?

---

no, I'm with my wife and two kids
▸ όχι, είμαι με τη γυναίκα μου και τα δύο μου παιδιά
[okhi, imeh meh ti yineka moo keh ta thio moo pethia]

---

what do you do?
▸ τί δουλειά κάνεις;
[ti thoolia kanis?]

είμαι στους υπολογιστές ◂
[imeh stoos ipolo-yistes]
I'm in computers

---

me too
▸ κι εγώ επίσης
[ki ego episis]

here's my wife now
▸ να και η γυναίκα μου
[na keh i yineka moo]

χαίρω πολύ ◂
[khero poli]
nice to meet you

12. Post offices

airmail	αεροπορικώς	[a-eroporik**o**s]
post card	η κάρτα	[i karta]
post office	το ταχυδρομείο	[to takhithrom**io**]
stamp	το γραμματόσημο	[to gramat**o**simo]

what time does the post office close?
▶ τί ώρα κλείνει το ταχυδρομείο;
[ti **o**ra kl**i**ni to takhithrom**io**?]

τις καθημερινές στις 5 ◀
[tis kaTHimerines stis pendeh]
five o'clock weekdays

is the post office open on Saturdays?
▶ είναι ανοιχτά το ταχυδρομείο το Σάββατο;
[**i**neh anikht**a** to takhithrom**io** to S**a**vato?]

μέχρι το μεσημέρι ◀
[mekhri to mesimeri]
until midday

I'd like to send this registered to England
▶ θα ήθελα να στείλω αυτό συστημένο στην Αγγλία
[THa **i**THela na st**i**lo aft**o** sistimeno stin Angl**i**a]

βεβαίως, κάνει 10 ευρώ ◀
[veveos, kani theka evro]
certainly, that will cost 10 euros

and also two stamps for England, please
▶ και δύο γραμματόσημα για την Αγγλία, παρακαλώ
[keh th**i**o gramat**o**sima ya tin Angl**i**a, parakal**o**]

do you have some airmail stickers?
▶ έχετε αυτοκόλλητα "Αεροπορικώς";
[**e**kheteh aftok**o**lita 'a-eroporik**o**s'?]

do you have any mail for me?
▶ έχετε γράμματα για μένα;
[**e**kheteh gr**a**mata ya m**e**na?]

γράμματα	[gr**a**mata]	letters
δέματα	[th**e**mata]	parcels
εξωτερικού	[exoterik**oo**]	international
εσωτερικού	[esoterik**oo**]	domestic
ποστ-ρεστάντ	[post-rest**a**nt]	poste restante

download these scenarios as MP3s from:

13. Restaurants

bill
ο λογαριασμός
[o logariasm**o**s]

menu
ο κατάλογος
[o kat**a**logos]

table
το τραπέζι
[to trap**e**zi]

can we have a non-smoking table?
▸ μπορούμε να έχουμε ένα τραπέζι για μη-καπνιστές;
[bor**oo**meh na **e**khoomeh **e**na trap**e**zi ya m**i**-kapnist**e**s?]

there are two of us
▸ είμαστε δύο άτομα
[**i**masteh th**i**o **a**toma]

there are four of us
▸ είμαστε τέσσερα άτομα
[**i**masteh t**e**sera **a**toma]

---

what's this?
▸ τί είναι αυτό;
[ti **i**neh af**to**?]

είναι ένα είδος ψαριού ◂
[**i**neh **e**na **i**thos psar**ioo**]
it's a type of fish

είναι μιά τοπική σπεσιαλιτέ ◂
[**i**neh mi**a** topik**i** spesialit**e**h]
it's a local speciality

ελάτε μέσα και θα σας δείξω ◂
[el**a**teh m**e**sa keh THa sas th**i**xo]
come inside and I'll show you

---

we would like two of these, one of these, and one of those
▸ θα θέλαμε δύο από αυτά, ένα από αυτά και ένα από εκείνα
[THa TH**e**lameh th**i**o ap**o** af**ta**, **e**na ap**o** af**ta** keh **e**na ap**o** ek**i**na]

▸ και τί θα πιείτε;
[keh ti THa pi-**i**teh?]
and to drink?

red wine
▸ κόκκινο κρασί
[k**o**kino kras**i**]

white wine
▸ λευκό κρασί
[lef**ko** kras**i**]

a beer and two orange juices
▸ μιά μπύρα και δύο πορτοκαλάδες
[mi**a** b**i**ra keh th**i**o portokal**a**thes]

---

some more bread please
▸ ακόμη λίγο ψωμί, παρακαλώ
[ak**o**mi l**i**go psom**i**, parakal**o**]

▸ σας άρεσε το γεύμα;
[sas **a**reseh to y**e**vma?]
how was your meal?

excellent!, very nice!
▸ έξοχο!, πολύ νόστιμο!
[**e**xokho!, pol**i** n**o**stimo!]

▸ τίποτα άλλο;
[t**i**pota **a**lo?]
anything else?

just the bill thanks
▸ μόνο τον λογαριασμό, ευχαριστώ
[m**o**no ton logariasm**o**, efkharist**o**]

14. Shopping

μπορώ να σας βοηθήσω;
[boro na sas vo-iTHiso?]
can I help you?

can I just have a look around?
▶ μπορώ να κοιτάζω μόνο γύρω;
[boro na kitaxo mono yiro?]

yes, I'm looking for ...
ναι, ψάχνω για ...
[neh, psakhno ya ...]

how much is this?
▶ πόσο κάνει αυτό;
[poso kani afto?]

τριάντα δύο ευρώ
[trianda thio evro]
thirty-two euros

OK, I think I'll have to leave it; it's a little too expensive for me
▶ εντάξει, νομίζω ότι δεν θα το πάρω, είναι λίγο ακριβό για μένα
[endaxi, nomizo oti then THa to paro; ineh ligo akrivo ya mena]

αυτό πώς σας φαίνεται;
[afto pos sas feneteh?]
how about this?

can I pay by credit card?
▶ μπορώ να πληρώσω με πιστωτική κάρτα;
[boro na pliroso meh pistotiki karta?]

it's too big
▶ είναι πολύ μεγάλο
[ineh poli megalo]

it's too small
▶ είναι πολύ μικρό
[ineh poli mikro]

it's for my son – he's about this high
▶ είναι για τον γιό μου – είναι περίπου τόσο ψηλός
[ineh ya ton yo moo – ineh peripoo toso psilos]

▶ θέλετε τίποτα άλλο;
[THeleteh tipota alo?]
will there be anything else?

that's all thanks
▶ μόνο αυτό, ευχαριστώ
[mono afto, efkharisto]

make it twenty euros and I'll take it
▶ θα το πάρω αν μού το δώσετε για 20 ευρώ
[THa to paro an moo to thoseteh ya ikosi evro]

fine, I'll take it
▶ ωραία, θα το πάρω
[orea, THa to paro]

αλλαγές	[ala-yes]	to exchange
ανοιχτά	[anikhta]	open
εκπτώσεις	[ekptosis]	sale
κλειστά	[klista]	closed
ταμείο	[tamio]	cash desk

download these scenarios as MP3s from:

15. Sightseeing

art gallery	η πινακοθήκη	[i pinakoTHiki]
bus tour	η ξενάγηση με λεωφορείο	[i xenayisi meh leoforio]
city centre	το κέντρο της πόλης	[to kendro tis polis]
closed	κλειστά	[klista]
guide	ο/η ξεναγός	[o/i xenagos]
museum	το μουσείο	[to moosio]
open	ανοιχτός	[anikhtos]

I'm interested in seeing the old town
▶ θα με ενδιέφερε να δω την παλιά πόλη
[THa meh enthiefereh na tho tin palia poli]

are there guided tours?
▶ υπάρχουν ξεναγήσεις;
[iparkhoon xenayisis?]

λυπάμαι, είναι όλα κλεισμένα ◀
[lipameh, ineh ola klismena]
I'm sorry, it's fully booked

---

how much would you charge to drive us around for four hours?
▶ πόσα θα χρεώσετε για να μας πάτε βόλτα για τέσσερις ώρες;
[posa THa khreoseteh ya na mas pateh volta ya teseris ores?]

can we book tickets for the concert here?
▶ μπορούμε να κλείσουμε εδώ εισιτήρια για το κονσέρτο;
[boroomeh na klisoomeh etho isitiria ya to konserto?]

▶ ναι, σε τί όνομα;
[neh, seh ti onoma?]
yes, in what name?

▶ ποιά πιστωτική κάρτα;
[pia pistotiki karta?]
which credit card?

---

where do we get the tickets?
▶ πού θα πάρουμε τα εισιτήρια;
[poo tha paroomeh ta isitiria?]

θα τα πάρετε στην είσοδο ◀
[THa ta pareteh stin isotho]
just pick them up at the entrance

---

is it open on Sundays?
▶ είναι ανοικτά την Κυριακή;
[ineh anikta tin Kiriaki?]

how much is it to get in?
▶ πόσο κάνει η είσοδος;
[poso kani i isothos?]

---

are there reductions for groups of 6?
▶ υπάρχει έκπτωση για ομάδα έξι ατόμων;
[iparkhi ekptosi ya omatha exi atomon?]

that was really impressive!
▶ αυτό ήταν πραγματικά εντυπωσιακό!
[afto itan pragmatika endiposiako!]

16. Trains

to change trains	αλλάζω τρένο	[alazo treno]
platform	η πλατφόρμα	[i platforma]
return	ένα εισιτήριο με επιστροφή	[ena isitirio meh epistrofi]
single	ένα εισιτήριο απλό	[ena isitirio aplo]
station	ο σταθμός	[o staTHmos]
stop	η στάση	[i stasi]
ticket	ένα εισιτήριο	[ena isitirio]

how much is ...?
▸ πόσο κάνει ...;
[poso kani ...?]

a single, second class to ...
▸ ένα εισιτήριο απλό, δεύτερη θέση για ...
[ena isitirio aplo, thefteri THesi ya ...]

two returns, second class to ...
▸ δύο εισιτήρια με επιστροφή, δεύτερη θέση για ...
[thio isitiria meh epistrofi, thefteri THesi ya ...]

for today
▸ για σήμερα
[ya simera]

for tomorrow
▸ για αύριο
[ya avrio]

for next Tuesday
▸ για την άλλη Τρίτη
[ya tin ali Triti]

θέλετε να κρατήσετε θέση; ◂
[THeleteh na kratiseteh THesi?]
do you want to make a seat reservation?

πρέπει να αλλάξετε στη Λαμία ◂
[prepi na alaxeteh sti Lamia]
you have to change at Lamia

---

what time is the last train to Corinth?
▸ τι ώρα είναι το τελευταίο τρένο για την Κόρινθο;
[ti ora ineh to telefteo treno ya tin KorinTHo?]

is this seat free?
▸ είναι ελεύθερη αυτή η θέση;
[ineh elefTHeri afti i THesi?]

excuse me, which station are we at?
▸ με συγχωρείτε, σε ποιό σταθμό είμαστε;
[meh sinkhoriteh, seh pio staTHmo imasteh?]

is this where I change for Thessaloniki?
▸ εδώ πρέπει να αλλάζω τρένο για τη Θεσσαλονίκη;
[etho prepi na alaxo treno ya ti THesaloniki?]

English

Greek

A

a, an* enas, mia, ena
about: about 20 peripoo ikosi
 it's about 5 o'clock ineh yiro stis pendeh
 a film about Greece ena ergo ya tin Elatha
above pano apo
abroad sto exoteriko
absolutely! (I agree) apolitos!
accelerator to gazi
accept thekhomeh
accident to thistikhima
 there's been an accident eyineh ena thistikhima
accommodation i thiamoni
accurate akrivis
ache o ponos
 my back aches pona-i i plati moo
across: across the road apenandi sto thromo
adapter to polaplo
 (for voltage change) i briza taf
address i thi-efтhinsi
 what's your address? pia ineh i thi-efтhinsi soo?
address book i adzenda ton thi-efтhinseon
admission charge timi isothoo
adult (man/woman) o enilikos/i eniliki
advance: in advance prokatavolika
aeroplane to a-eroplano
after meta
 after you meta apo sas
 after lunch meta apo to yevma
afternoon apo-yevma
 in the afternoon kata to apo-yevma
 this afternoon afto to apo-yevma
aftershave i kolonia meta to xirisma
aftersun cream to galaktoma ya ton ilio
afterwards meta
again xana
against enandion
age i ilikia
ago: a week ago prin apo mia evthomatha
 an hour ago prin apo mia ora
agree: I agree simfono
AIDS to AIDS
air o a-eras
 by air a-eroporikos
air-conditioning o klimatismos
airmail: by airmail a-eroporikos
airmail envelope o a-eroporikos fakelos
airport to a-erothromio
 to the airport, please sto a-erothromio, parakalo
airport bus to leoforio a-erothromi-oo
aisle seat тhesi thipla sto thiathromo
alarm clock to xipnitiri
Albania i Alvania
Albanian (adj) Alvanikos
alcohol to alko-ol
alcoholic inopnevmatothis

all: all the boys ola ta agoria
all the girls ola ta koritsia
all the men oli i andres
all the women oles i yinekes
all of it olokliro
all of them ola afta
that's all, thanks afta ineh ola, efkharisto
allergic: I'm allergic to ... imeh aleryikos meh ...
allowed: is it allowed? epitrepeteh?
all right endaxi
I'm all right imeh endaxi
are you all right? (adj) iseh endaxi?
(pol) esis endaxi?
almond to amigthalo
almost skhethon
alone monos
alphabet to alfavito
see page 209
already ithi
also episis
although an keh
altogether sinolika
always panda
am*: I am imeh
am: at seven am stis efta pro mesimvrias
amazing (surprising) ekpliktikos
(very good) thavmasios
ambulance to asTHenoforo
call an ambulance! kalesteh ena asTHenoforo!
America i Ameriki
American (adj) Amerikanikos
I'm American (man/woman) imeh Amerikanos/Amerikana
among anamesa
amount to poso
(money) ta khrimata
amp: a 13-amp fuse mia asfalia thekatria amper
amphitheatre to amfiTHeatro
Ancient Greece i arkhea Elatha
Ancient Greek ta arkhea Elinika
and keh
angry THimomenos
animal to zo-o
ankle o astragalos
anniversary (wedding) i epetios too gamoo
annoy: this man's annoying me aftos o andras meh enokhli
annoying enokhlitikos
another alos, ali, alo
can we have another room? boroomeh na ekhoomeh ena alo thomatio?
another beer, please ali mia bira, parakalo
antibiotics to andiviotiko
antihistamine to andi-istaminiko farmako
antique: is it an antique? ineh antika?
antique shop to paleopolio
antiseptic to andisiptiko
any: have you got any bread/tomatoes? ekheteh psomi/domates?

dialogue

do you have any change? ekhis kaTHoloo psila?
sorry, I don't have any lipameh, then ekho kaTHoloo

anybody kanis
does anybody speak English? mila-i kanis Anglika?
there wasn't anybody there then itan kanis eki
anything otithipoteh

dialogues

anything else? tipoteh alo?
nothing else, thanks tipoteh, efkharisto

would you like anything to drink? THa THelateh na pi-iteh kati?
I don't want anything, thanks then THelo tipoteh, efkharisto

apart from ektos apo
apartment to thiamerisma
appendicitis i skoliko-ithitis
appetizer to proto piato
appetizers ta orektika
aperitif to aperitif
apology i signomi
apple to milo
appointment to randevoo

dialogue

good afternoon, sir, how can I help you? kalispera sas, kiri-eh, pos boro na sas vo-iTHiso?
I'd like to make an appointment THa iTHela na kliso ena randevoo
what time would you like? ti ora THeleteh?
three o'clock tris i ora
I'm afraid that's not possible; is four o'clock all right? fovameh oti afto then yineteh; boriteh stis teseris?
yes, that will be fine neh, poli kala
the name was ...? to onoma sas?

apricot to verikoko
April o Aprilios
archaeology i arkheoloyia
are*: we are imasteh
you are isteh
they are ineh
area i periokhi
area code o kothikos ariTHmos
arm to kheri
arrange: will you arrange it for us? THa to kanonisis ya mas?
arrival i afixi
arrive ftano
when do we arrive? poteh ftanoomeh?
has my fax arrived yet? eftaseh to fax moo?

we arrived today ftasameh simera
art i tekhni
art gallery i pinakothiki
artist (man/woman) o kalitekhnis/i kalitekhnitha
as: as big as ... megalo san ...
as soon as possible oso pio grigora yineteh
ashtray to tasaki, to stokhto-thokhio
ask roto
I didn't ask for this then zitisa afto
could you ask him to ...? boris na too pis na ...?
asleep: she's asleep kimateh
aspirin i aspirini
asthma to asthma
astonishing ekpliktikos
at: at the hotel sto xenothokhio
at the station sto stathmo
at six o'clock stis exi i ora
at Yanni's stoo Yanni
Athens i Athina
athletics o athlitismos
attractive elkistikos
aubergine i melidzana
August o Avgoostos
aunt i thia
Australia i Afstralia
Australian (adj) Afstralezikos
I'm Australian (man/woman) imeh Afstralos/Afstraleza
automatic (adj) aftomatos
(car) to aftomato aftokinito
automatic teller i mikhani ya metrita
autumn to fthinoporo
in the autumn sto fthinoporo
avenue i leoforos
average (not good) metrio
on average kata meson oro
awake: is he awake? ineh xipnios?
away: go away! fiyeh
is it far away? ineh poli makria?
awful apesios
axle o axonas

B

baby to moro
baby food i pethiki trofi
baby's bottle to bibero
baby-sitter i baby-sitter
back (of body) i plati
(back part) piso
at the back sto piso meros
can I have my money back? boro na ekho ta lefta moo piso?
to come/go back epistrefo, yirizo piso
backache ponos stin plati
bacon to bacon
bad kakos
a bad headache enas askhimos ponokefalos
badly askhima
bag i tsanda
(suitcase) i valitsa
baggage i aposkeves
baggage check o khoros filaxis aposkevon

baggage claim anazitisi aposkevon
bakery o foornaris
balcony to balkoni
a room with a balcony ena thomatio meh balkoni
bald falakros
ball (large) i bala
(small) to balaki
ballet to baleto
banana i banana
band (musical) to singrotima
bandage o epithesmos
Bandaid® to lefkoplast
bank i trapeza
bank account o trapezikos logariasmos
bar to bar
a bar of chocolate mia sokolata
barber's to koorio
basket to kalaтhi
basketball to basketball, i kalaтhosferisi
bath to banio
can I have a bath? boro na kano ena banio?
bathroom to lootro, to banio
with a private bathroom meh ithiotiko lootro
bath towel i petseta too banioo
battery i bataria
bay o kolpos
be* imeh
beach i paralia
beach mat i psaтha
beach umbrella i ombrela
beans ta fasolia
green beans ta fasolakia
runner beans ta fasolakia freska
broad beans ta kookia
beard ta yenia
beautiful oreos
because epithi
because of ... exetias ...
bed to krevati
I'm going to bed now pao ya ipno tora
bed and breakfast thomatio meh pro-ino
bedroom to ipnothomatio
beef to moskhari
beer i bira
two beers, please thio bires, parakalo
before prin
begin arkhizo
when does it begin? poteh arkhizi?
beginner (man/woman) o arkharios/i arkharia
beginning: at the beginning kat arkhas
behind piso
behind me apo piso moo
beige bez
believe pistevo
belly-dancing to tsifteteli
below apo kato
belt i zoni
bend (in road) i strofi
berth (on ship) i klini
beside: beside the ... thipla sto ...
best aristos
better kaliteros

better than ... kaliteros apo ...
are you feeling better? esthaneseh kalitera?
between metaxi
beyond pera apo
bicycle to pothilato
big megalos
too big poli megalo
it's not big enough then ineh arketa megalo
bike to pothilato
(motorbike) to mikhanaki
bikini to bikini
bill o logariasmos
(US) to khartonomisma
could I have the bill, please? boro na ekho ton logariasmo, parakalo?
bin o skoopithotenekes
bin liners i sakoola skoopithion
bird to pooli
biro® to stilo
birthday ta yenethlia
happy birthday! khronia pola!
biscuit to biskoto
bit: a little bit ligo
a big bit ena megalo komati
a bit of ... ligo apo ...
a bit expensive ligo akrivo, akrivootsiko
bite (by insect) to tsibima
(by dog) i thagonia
bitter (taste etc) pikros
black mavros
blanket i kooverta
bleach (for toilet) to Harpik®
bless you! ya soo!
blind tiflos
blinds ta pantzooria
blister i fooskala
blocked (road, pipe) frakarismenos
(sink) voolomenos
block of flats i polikatikia
blond xanthos
blood to ema
high blood pressure ipsili pi-esi ematos
blouse i blooza
blow-dry to khtenisma
I'd like a cut and blow-dry tha ithela kopsimo keh khtenisma
blue bleh
blue eyes galana matia
blusher i poothra
boarding house i pansion
boarding pass i karta epivivaseos
boat (small) to ka-iki
(for passengers) to plio
body to soma
boil (verb) vrazo
boiled egg to vrasto avgo
boiler o vrastiras
bone to kokalo
bonnet (of car) to kapo
book to vivlio
(verb) klino
can I book a seat? boro na kliso mia thesi?

dialogue

I'd like to book a table for two tha ithela na kliso ena trapezi ya thio atoma
what time would you like

it booked for? ti ora to THeleteh?
half past seven stis efta keh misi
that's fine endaxi
and your name? to onoma sas, parakalo?

bookshop to vivliopolio
bookstore to vivliopolio
boot (footwear) i bota
(of car) to port-bagaz
border (of country) ta sinora
bored: I'm bored vari-emeh
boring varetos
born: I was born in Manchester yeniTHika sto Manchester
I was born in 1960 yeniTHika to 1960 (khilia eniakosia exinda)
borrow thanizomeh
may I borrow ...? boro na thanisto ...?
both keh i thio
bother: sorry to bother you signomi poo sas enokhlo
bottle to bookali
a bottle of house red ena bookali kokino spitiko krasi
bottle-opener to anikhtiri
bottom (of person) o kolos
at the bottom of the hill sto vaTHos too lofoo
at the bottom of the road sto telos too thromoo
box to kooti
box office to tamio
boy to agori
boyfriend o filos
bra to sooti-en
bracelet to vrakhioli
brake to freno
(verb) frenaro
brandy to koniak
bread to psomi
white bread to aspro psomi
brown bread to mavro psomi
wholemeal bread to starenio psomi
break (verb) spao
I've broken the ... espasa to ...
I think I've broken my wrist nomizo oti espasa ton karpo moo
break down (car) paTHeno vlavi
I've broken down khalaseh to aftokinito moo
breakdown (car) i vlavi
breakdown service i vlaves aftokiniton
breakfast to pro-ino
break-in: I've had a break-in meh listepsan
breast to stiTHos
breathe anapneo
breeze to aeraki
bridge (over river) i yefira
brief sindomos
briefcase o khartofilakas
bright (light etc) fotinos
bright red khtipitos kokinos
brilliant (idea, person) katapliktikos
bring ferno
I'll bring it back later THa to fero piso argotera

Britain i Vretania
British Vretanikos
brochure to prospektoos
broken spasmenos
it's broken ineh spasmeno
bronchitis i vronkhititha
brooch i karfitsa
broom i skoopa
brother o athelfos
brother-in-law o gambros
brown kafeh
brown hair kastana malia
brown eyes kastana matia
bruise i melania
brush i voortsa
(for hair) i voortsa ya ta malia
(artist's) to pinelo
bucket o koovas
buffet car to boofeh
buggy (for child) to pethiko amaxaki
building to ktirio
bulb (light bulb) i lamba
Bulgaria i Voolgaria
Bulgarian (adj) Voolgarikos
bumper o profilaktiras
bunk i kooketa
bureau de change Sinalagma
burglary i thiarixi
burn (noun) to kapsimo
(verb) keo
burnt: this is burnt afto ineh kameno
burst: a burst pipe mia spasmeni solina
bus to leoforio
what number bus is it to ...? ti aritHmo ekhi to leoforio ya ...?
when is the next bus to ...? poteh ineh to epomeno leoforio ya ...?
what time is the last bus? ti ora ineh to telefteo leoforio?
could you let me know when we get there? boriteh na moo to piteh, otan ftasoomeh eki?

dialogue

does this bus go to ...? piyeni afto to leoforio sto ...?
no, you need a number ... okhi, prepi na pareteh to leoforio aritHmos ...

business i thooli-es
bus station to praktorio leoforion, o staTHmos leoforion
bus stop i stasi leoforioo
bust (sculpture) i protomi
(measurement) to stiTHos
busy (restaurant etc) polisikhnastos
I'm busy tomorrow imeh apaskholimenos avrio
but ala
butcher's o khasapis
butter to vootiro
button to koobi
buy agorazo
where can I buy ...? poo boro na agoraso ...?
by: by bus/car meh to leoforio/aftokinito
written by ... grameno apo ...

by the window thipla sto paraTHiro
by the sea konda sti THalasa
by Thursday prin apo tin Pempti
bye yasoo

C

cabbage to lakhano
cabin (on ship) i kabina
cable car to teleferik
café i kafeteria, to kafenio
cagoule to athiavrokho
cake to cake
cake shop to zakharoplastio
call fonazo
(to phone) tilefono
what's it called? pos to leneh?
he/she is called ... ton/tin leneh ...
please call a doctor seh parakalo, tilefoniseh seh ena yatro
please give me a call at 7.30 am tomorrow seh parakalo, tilefoniseh moo avrio to pro-i stis efta keh misi
please ask him to call me seh parakalo, pes too na moo tilefonisi
call back: I'll call back later THa xanarTHo argotera
(phone back) THa seh paro piso
call round: I'll call round tomorrow THa peraso avrio
camcorder i mikhani lipseos
camera i fotografiki mikhani
camera shop to katastima fotografikon ithon
camp (verb) kataskinono
can we camp here? boroomeh na kataskinosoomeh etho?
camping gas to igra-erio
campsite to kambing
can to kooti, i konserva
a can of beer mia bira seh kooti
can: can you ...? boriteh na ...?
can I have ...? boro na ekho ...?
I can't ... then boro ...
Canada o Kanathas
Canadian Kanathezikos
I'm Canadian (man/woman) imeh Kanathos/Kanatheza
canal to kanali
cancel akirono
candies i karameles
candle to keri
canoe to kano
canoeing kano kano
can-opener to anikhtiri
cap (hat) to kapelo
(of bottle) to kapaki
car to aftokinito
by car meh to aftokinito
carafe i karafa
a carafe of house white, please mia karafa aspro spitiko krasi, parakalo
caravan to trokhospito
caravan site topoTHesia ya trokhospita

carburettor to karbirater
card (birthday etc) i karta
here's my (business) card oristeh, i karta moo
cardigan i zaketa
cardphone i tilekarta
careful prosektikos
be careful! prosekheh!
caretaker o/i epistatis
car ferry to feri-bot
car hire enikiasis aftokiniton
car park to parking
carpet to khali
(fitted) i moketa
carriage (of train) to vagoni
carrier bag i sakoola
carrot to karoto
carry metafero
carry-cot to port-beh-beh
carton i koota
carwash to plindirio aftokiniton
case (suitcase) i valitsa
cash ta metrita
will you cash this for me? THA moo to exaryiroseteh?
cash desk to tamio
cash dispenser i mikhani ya metrita
cashier o/i tamias
cassette i kaseta
cassette recorder to kasetofono
castle to kastro
casualty department Protes Vo-iTHi-es
cat i gata
catch piano
where do we catch the bus to ...? apo poo THa paroomeh to leoforio?
cathedral o kaTHethrikos naos
Catholic (adj) kaTholikos
cauliflower to koonoopithi
cave i spilia
ceiling to tavani
celery to selino
cellar (for wine) to kelari
cemetery to nekrotafio
Centigrade* Kelsioo
centimetre* ena ekatosto
central kendrikos
central heating i kendriki THermansi
centre to kendro
how do we get to the city centre? pos THa pameh sto kendro?
cereal ta cornflakes
certainly sigoora
certainly not fisika okhi
chair i karekla
champagne i sampania
change (money) ta resta
(verb: money, trains) alazo
can I change this for ...? boro na alaxo afto ya ...?
I don't have any change then ekho psila
can you give me change for a 5,000 drachma note? boriteh na moo khalaseteh pendeh khiliathes thrakhmes?

dialogue

do we have to change (trains)? prepi na

alaxoomeh treno?
yes, change at Corinth/no, it's a direct train neh, alaxteh stin Korinthο/okhi, piyeni katefthian

changed: to get changed alazo rookha
chapel to eklisaki
charge i timi, i thapani
(verb) khreono
charge card i pistotiki karta
cheap ftinos
do you have anything cheaper? ekheteh tipoteh ftinotero?
check (verb) epalithevo
(US: cheque) i epitayi
see **cheque**
(US: bill) o logariasmos
see **bill**
could you check the ..., please? boriteh na elenxeteh to ..., parakalo?
checkbook to karneh epitagon
check-in to check-in
check in kano check-in
where do we have to check in? poo prepi na kanoomeh check-in?
cheek (on face) to magoolo
cheerio! yasoo!
cheers! (toast) stin iya sas!, is iyian!
cheese to tiri
chemist's to farmakio
cheque i epitayi
do you take cheques? perneteh epitayes?
cheque book to karneh epitagon
cheque card i karta epitagon
cherry to kerasi
chess to skaki
chest to stithos
chewing gum i tsikhla
chicken to kotopoolo
chickenpox i anemovloyia
child to pethi
children ta pethia
child minder i dada
children's pool i pisina ton pethion
children's portion i pethiki meritha
chin to pigooni
china i porselani
Chinese (adj) Kinezikos
chips i tiganites patates
chocolate i sokolata
milk chocolate i sokolata galaktos
plain chocolate sokolata sketi
a hot chocolate i zesti sokolata, mia sokolata rofima
choose thialego
Christian name to mikro onoma
Christmas ta khristooyena
Christmas Eve i paramoni ton khristooyenon
merry Christmas! kala khristooyena!
church i eklisia
cicada o tzitzikas
cider cider
cigar to pooro

cigarette to tsigaro
cigarette lighter o anaptiras
cinema o kinimatografos, to sinema
circle o kiklos
(in theatre) o exostis
city i poli
city centre to kendro tis polis
clean (adj) kaTharos
can you clean these for me? moo pleneteh afta?
cleaning solution (for contact lenses) to kaTharistiko thialima
cleansing lotion to galaktoma kaTharismoo
clear kaTharos
(obvious) profanis
clever exipnos
cliff o apotomos vrakhos
climbing i orivasia
cling film to na-ilon
clinic i kliniki
cloakroom i gardaroba
clock to rolo-i
close klino

dialogue

what time do you close? ti ora klineteh?
we close at 8 pm on weekdays and 6 pm on Saturdays klinoomeh stis okto to vrathi tis kaTHimerines keh stis exi to apoyevma ta Savata
do you close for lunch? klineteh ya mesimeriano fayito?
yes, between 1 and 3.30 pm neh, apo ti mia mekhri tis tris keh misi

closed klistos
cloth (fabric) to ifasma
(for cleaning etc) to pani
clothes ta rookha
clothes line i aplostra
clothes peg to mandalaki
cloud to sinefo
cloudy sinefiasmenos
clutch to debrayaz, o siblektis
coach (bus) to poolman
(on train) to vagoni
coach station o staTHmos iperastikon leoforion
coach trip to taxithi meh poolman
coast i akti
on the coast stin akti
coat (long coat) to palto
(jacket) to sakaki
coathanger i kremastra
cockroach i katsaritha
cocoa to kakao
coconut i karitha
code (for phoning) o kothikos
what's the (dialling) code for Athens? pios ineh o kothikos ya tin ATHina?
coffee o kafes
two Greek coffees, please thio Elinikoos kafethes, parakalo
coin to kerma

Coke® i koka-kola
cold krios
I'm cold kriono
I have a cold imeh kriomenos
collapse: he's collapsed katarefseh
collar o yakas
collect paralamvano
I've come to collect ... iltha ya na paro ...
collect call tilefono collect
college to koleyio
colour to khroma
do you have this in other colours? to ekheteh seh ala khromata?
colour film to enkhromo film
comb i khtena
come erkhomeh

dialogue

where do you come from?
apo poo iseh?
I come from Edinburgh
imeh apo to Ethimvoorgo

come back epistrefo
I'll come back tomorrow tha epistrepso avrio
come in beno mesa
comfortable (chair) anapaftikos
(clothes) anetos
(room, hotel) volikos
compact disc to compact disc
company (business) i eteria
compartment (on train) to koopeh
compass i pixitha
complain paraponoomeh
complaint to parapono
I have a complaint ekho ena parapono
completely telios
computer o ipolo-yistis
concert i sinavlia
concussion i thiasisi engefaloo
conditioner (for hair) to kondisioner
condom to profilaktiko
conference to sinethrio
confirm epiveveono
congratulations! sinkharitiria!
connecting flight sinthesi ptisis
connection (travel) i sinthesi
conscious sinesthanomenos
constipation i thiskiliotis
consulate to proxenio
contact erkhomeh seh epafi
contact lenses i faki epafis
contraceptive (pill) to andisiliptiko
(condom) to profilaktiko
convenient volikos
that's not convenient then meh volevi
convent to monastiri
cook (verb) ma-yirevo
not cooked misopsimeno
cooker i koozina
cookie to biskoto
cooking utensils ta ma-yirika skevi
cool throseros
Corfu i Kerkira
cork o felos
corkscrew to anikhtiri

corner: on the corner sti gonia
in the corner sti gonia
cornflakes ta cornflakes
correct (right) sostos
corridor o thiathromos
cosmetics ta kalindika
cost (verb) stikhizo
how much does it cost? poso kani?
cot i koonia
cotton to vamvaki
cotton wool to vamvaki
couch o kanapes
couchette i kooketa
cough o vikhas
cough medicine to farmako ya ton vikha
could: could you ...? boriteh na ...?
could I have ...? boro na ekho ...?
I couldn't ... then boroosa na ...
country (nation) i khora
(countryside) i exokhi
countryside i exokhi
couple (man and woman) to zevgari
a couple of ... thio apo ...
courgette to kolokithaki
courier o/i sinothos
course (main course etc) to piato
of course veveh-a
of course not fisika okhi
cousin (male/female) o xathelfos/i xathelfi
cow i a-yelatha
crab to kavoori
cracker to krakeraki
craft shop to ergastiri
crash i sigroosi
I've had a crash trakara
crazy trelos
cream (on milk, in cake) i krema
(lotion) i krema thermatos
(colour) krem
creche o pethikos stathmos
credit card i pistotiki karta

dialogue

can I pay by credit card? boro na pliroso meh pistotiki karta?
which card do you want to use? ti karta theleteh na khrisimopi-iseteh?
yes, sir endaxi, kiri-eh
what's the number? ti arithmo ekhi?
and the expiry date? keh poteh ineh i imerominia lixeos?

Crete i Kriti
crisps ta tsips
crockery ta piatika
crossing (by sea) to thalasio taxithi
crossroads to stavrothromi
crowd o kosmos
crowded yematos kosmo
crown (on tooth) i korona
cruise i krooazi-era
crutches i pateritses
cry (weep) kleo

(shout) fonazo
cucumber to agoori
cup to flidzani
a cup of ..., please ena flidzani ..., parakalo
cupboard to doolapi
cure i therapia
curly sgooros, katsaros
current to revma
curtains i koortines
cushion to maxilaraki
custom to ethimo
Customs to Telonio
cut to kopsimo
(verb) kovo
I've cut myself kopika
cutlery ta makheropiroona
cycling i pothilasia
cyclist o/i pothilatis
Cyprus i Kipros

D

dad o babas
daily kathimerina
damage (verb) katastrefo
damaged katastrafikeh
I'm sorry, I've damaged this lipameh, to khalasa
damn! na pari i oryi!
damp (adj) igros
dance o khoros
(verb) khorevo
would you like to dance? thelis na khorepsoomeh?
dangerous epikinthinos
Danish thanos
dark (adj: colour) skotinos
(hair) mavros
it's getting dark skotiniazi
date*: what's the date today? poso ekhi o minas simera?
let's make a date for next Monday as sinandithoomeh tin epomeni theftera
dates (fruit) i khoormathes
daughter i kori
daughter-in-law i nifi
dawn i avyi
at dawn tin avyi
day i mera
the day after tin epomeni mera
the day after tomorrow methavrio
the day before tin proigoomeni mera
the day before yesterday prokhtes
every day katheh mera
all day oli tin imera
in two days' time meta apo thio meres
day trip to taxithi afthimeron
dead perthamenos, nekros
deaf koofos
deal (business) i simfonia
it's a deal simfonisameh, endaxi
death o thanatos
decaffeinated coffee o kafes khoris kafe-ini
December o thekemvrios
decide apofasizo
we haven't decided yet then ekhoomeh apofasisi akoma
decision i apofasi

deck (on ship) to katastroma
deckchair i politHrona, i sez long
deduct afero
deep vatHis
definitely oposthipoteh
definitely not seh kamia periptosi
degree (qualification) to ptikhio
delay i katHisterisi
deliberately epitithes
delicatessen ta delicatessen
delicious nostimotatos
deliver thianemo
delivery (of mail) i thianomi, i parathosi
demotic i dimotiki
Denmark i thania
dental floss to othondiko nima
dentist o/i othondiatros

dialogue

it's this one here afto etho ineh
this one? afto?
no, that one okhi, ekino
here? etho?
yes neh

dentures i masela
deodorant to aposmitiko
department to tmima
department store to megalo katastima
departure i anakhorisi
departure lounge i etHoosa anakhoriseos
depend: it depends exartateh
it depends on ... exartateh apo ...
deposit (as security) i kataHesi
(as part payment) i prokatavoli
description i perigrafi
dessert to glikisma
destination o pro-orismos
develop anaptiso
(a film) emfanizo

dialogue

could you develop these films? boriteh na emfaniseteh afta ta film?
when will they be ready? poteh tHa ineh etima?
tomorrow afternoon avrio to apoyevma
how much is the four-hour service? poso kani i emfanisi seh teseris ores?

diabetic (man/woman) o thiavitikos/i thiavitiki
diabetic foods i thiavitiki trofi
dial (verb) kalo, perno ariTHmo
dialling code o kothikos ariTHmos
diamond to thiamandi
diaper i pana
diarrhoea i thiaria
diary to imerolo-yio
dictionary to lexiko
didn't see **not**
die peTHeno

diesel i dizel
diet i thi-eta
I'm on a diet kano thi-eta
I have to follow a special diet prepi na kano ithiki thi-eta
difference i thiafora
what's the difference? pia ineh i thiafora?
different thiaforetikos
this one is different afto etho ineh thiaforetiko
a different table ena alo trapezi
difficult thiskolos
difficulty i thiskolia
dinghy to zodiak®
dining room i trapezaria
dinner (evening meal) to thipno
to have dinner tro-o vrathino
direct (adj) kat-efTHian
is there a direct train? iparkhi kat-efTHian treno ya ...?
direction i katefTHinsi
which direction is it? pros ta poo ineh?
is it in this direction? ineh pros afti tin katefTHinsi?
directory enquiries i plirofori-es
dirt i vroma
dirty vromikos
disabled anapiros
is there access for the disabled? iparkhi prosvasi ya toos anapiroos?
disappear exafanizomeh
it's disappeared exafanistikeh
disappointed apogo-itevmenos
disappointing apogo-iteftiko
disaster i katastrofi
disco i diskotek
discount i ekptosi
is there a discount? kaneteh ekptosi?
disease i arostia
disgusting a-ithiastikos
dish (meal) to piato
(bowl) to bol
dishcloth i patsavoora
disinfectant to apolimandiko
disk (for computer) i thisketa
disposable diapers i khartines panes
disposable nappies i khartines panes
distance i apostasi
in the distance eki kato
distilled water apestagmeno nero
district i sinikia
disturb enokhlo
diversion (detour) i parakampsi
diving board i sanitha vootias
divorced: I'm divorced (man/woman) khorismenos/khorismeni
dizzy: I feel dizzy zalizomeh
do kano
what shall we do? ti THa kanoomeh?
how do you do it? pos to kaneteh?
will you do it for me? boriteh na moo to kaneteh?

dialogues

how do you do? ti kaneteh?
nice to meet you kharika ya ti gnorimia
what do you do? ti thoolia kaneteh?
I'm a teacher, and you? imeh thaskalos, ki esis?
I'm a student imeh fititis
what are you doing this evening? ti THA kaneteh apopseh?
we're going out for a drink; do you want to join us? THA pameh ya ena poto – THeleteh na elTHeteh mazi mas?

do you want cream? THeleteh krema?
I do, but she doesn't ego neh, ekini, omos, okhi

doctor o/i yatros
we need a doctor khriazomasteh enan yatro
please call a doctor seh parakalo, kaleseh enan yatro

dialogue

where does it hurt? poo ponateh?
right here akrivos etho
does that hurt more? sas pona-i afto pio poli?
yes neh
take this to a chemist thosteh afto seh ena farmaki-o

document to engrafo
dog o skilos
doll i kookla
domestic flight ptisi esoterikoo
donkey o ga-itharos
don't! mi!
don't do that! min to kanis afto!
(stop) stamata!
see not
door i porta
doorman o THiroros
double thiplo
double bed to thiplo krevati
double room to thiplo thomatio
doughnut to donat
down kato
down here etho kato
put it down over there valeh to eki kato
it's down there on the right vrisketeh eki kato sta thexia
it's further down the road ineh ligo parakato
downmarket (restaurant etc) ftinos
downstairs kato
dozen mia doozina
half a dozen misi doozina
drain o okhetos
draught beer varelisia bira
draughty: it's draughty kani revma
drawer to sirtari

drawing to skhethio
dreadful friktos
dream to oniro
dress to forema
dressed: to get dressed dinomeh
dressing (for cut) i gaza
(for salad) to lathoxitho
dressing gown i roba
drink to poto
(verb) pino
a cold drink to anapsiktiko
can I get you a drink? boro na seh keraso kanena poto?
what would you like (to drink)? ti тна тнelateh na piiteh?
no thanks, I don't drink okhi, efkharisto, then pino
I'll just have a drink of water тна paro monon ena potiri nero
drinking water to posimo nero
is this drinking water? ineh posimo afto to nero?
drive othiga-o
we drove here othiyisameh etho
I'll drive you home тна seh pao spiti
driver o/i othigos
driving licence i athia othiyiseos, to thiploma othiyiseos
drop: just a drop, please (of drink) poli ligo, parakalo
drug to farmako
drugs (narcotics) ta narkotika
drunk (adj) metнismenos
drunken driving methismeno othiyima
dry (adj) stegnos
(wine) xiros
dry-cleaner to stegnokaтнaristirio
duck i papia
due: he was due to arrive yesterday eprokito na ftasi khtes
when is the train due? poteh ftani to treno?
dull (pain) exasтнenimenos
(weather) moondos
(boring) vareros
dummy (baby's) i pipila
during kata ti thiarkia
dust i skoni
dusty skonismeno
dustbin o skoopithodenekes
duty-free (goods) ta aforoloyita
duty-free shop to katastima aforolo-yiton
duvet to paploma

E

each kaтнeh
how much are they each? poso ekhi to kaтнena?
ear to afti
earache: I have earache ekho pono sto afti
early noris
early in the morning noris to pro-i
I called by earlier perasa pro-

igoomenos
earrings ta skoolarikia
east i anatoli
in the east stin anatoli
Easter to Paskha
Easter Sunday i Kiriaki too Paskha
easy efkolos
eat tro-o
we've already eaten, thanks fagameh ithi, efkharisto
eau de toilette i kolonia
EC i eok
economy class tooristiki THesi
egg to avgo
hard-boiled egg avgo sfikhto
fried egg tiganito avgo
eggplant i melidzana
either: either ... or ... i ... i ...
either of them opio naneh
elastic to lastikho
elastic band to lastikhaki
elbow o angonas
electric ilektrikos
electrical appliances ilektrikes siskeves
electric fire i ilektriki somba
electrician o ilektrologos
electricity to ilektriko revma
elevator to asanser
else: something else kati alo
somewhere else kapoo aloo

dialogue

would you like anything else? THa THelateh tipoteh alo?
no, nothing else, thanks okhi, tipoteh alo, efkharisto

e-mail to e-mail
embassy i presvia
emergency i ektakti anangi
this is an emergency! ineh epigon!
emergency exit i exothos kinthinoo
empty (adj) athios
end to telos
(verb) teliono
at the end of the street sto telos too thromoo
when does it end? poteh telioni?
engaged (toilet, telephone) katilimenos
(to be married: man/woman) aravoniasmenos/aravoniasmeni
engine (car) i mikhani too aftokinitoo
England i Anglia
English ta Anglika
I'm English (man/woman) imeh Anglos/Anglitha
do you speak English? milateh anglika?
enjoy: to enjoy oneself thiaskethazo

dialogue

how did you like the film? pos soo fanikeh to ergo?
I enjoyed it very much;

did you enjoy it? moo areseh para poli; esena soo areseh?

enjoyable efkharistos
enlargement (of photo) i me-yenTHisi
enormous terastios
enough arketa
there's not enough then iparkhi arketo
it's not big enough then ineh arketa megalo
that's enough ftani, arki
entrance i isothos
envelope o fakelos
epileptic (man/woman) o epiliptikos/i epiliptiki
equipment o exoplismos
error to laTHos
especially ithika
essential vasikos, aparetitos
it is essential that ... ineh aparetito na ...
EU Evropa-iki Enosi
euro to evro
Eurocheque to Eurocheque
Eurocheque card i karta Eurocheque
Europe i Evropi
European (adj) Evropa-ikos
European Union Evropa-iki Enosi
even: even the Greeks akoma keh i Elines
even if ... akoma ki an ...
evening to vrathi
this evening simera to vrathi
in the evening to vrathi
evening meal to thipno
eventually telika
ever poteh

dialogue

have you ever been to Crete? ekheteh pa-i poteh stin Kriti?
yes, I was there two years ago neh, imoon eki prin apo thio khronia

every kaTHeh
every day kaTHeh mera
everyone oli
everything kaTHeh ti
everywhere pandoo
exactly! akrivos!
exam to thiagonisma
example to parathigma
for example parathigmatos kharin
excellent exokhos
excellent! exokha!
except ektos
excess baggage to ipervaro
exchange rate sinalagmatiki isotimia
exciting sinarpastikos
excuse me (to get past) signomi
(to get attention) parakalo
(to say sorry) meh sinkhoriteh
exhaust (pipe) i exatmisi
exhausted (tired) exandlimenos
exhibition i ekTHesi
exit i exothos
where's the nearest exit? poo ineh i plisi-esteri exothos?

expect perimeno
expensive akrivos
experienced embiros
explain exigo
 can you explain that? boris na moo to exiyisis?
express mail to katepigon
express train to treno express
extension (telephone) i sinthesi tilefonoo
 could you get me extension 221, please? meh sintheheteh meh to 221 (thiakosia ikosi ena), parakalo?
extension lead i pro-ektasi
extra: can we have an extra chair? boroomeh na ekhoomeh mia karekla akoma?
 do you charge extra for that? khreoneteh epipleon ya afto?
extraordinary asinithistos
extremely ipervolika
eye to mati
 will you keep an eye on my suitcase for me? tha moo to prosekheteh?
eyebrow pencil to molivi ya ta frithia
eye drops i stagones ya ta matia
eyeglasses (US) ta yialia
eyeliner to eyeliner
eye make-up remover to galaktoma katharismoo
eye shadow i skia mation

F

face to prosopo
factory to ergostasio
Fahrenheit* vathmi Farena-it
faint (verb) lipothimao
 she's fainted lipothimiseh
 I feel faint esthanomeh lipothimia
fair (funfair) to paniyiri
 (trade) i ektheesi
 (adj) thikeos
fairly arketa
fake i apomimisi
fall to fthinoporo
 see **autumn**
fall (verb) pefto
 she's had a fall epeseh
false pseftikos
family i iko-yenia
famous thiasimos
fan (electrical) o anemistiras
 (hand held) i ventalia
 (sports) o/i opathos
fan belt to vendilater
fantastic fandastikos
far makria

dialogue

is it far from here? ineh makria apo etho?
no, not very far okhi, okhi keh poli makria
well how far? poso makria, thilathi?
it's about 20 kilometres

ineh peripoo ikosi khiliometra

fare i timi too isitirioo
farm to agroktima
fashionable tis mothas
fast grigoros
fat (person) pakhis
(on meat) to lipos
father o pateras
father-in-law o pethe**r**os
faucet i vrisi
fault to elatoma
sorry, it was my fault signomi, itan sfalma moo
it's not my fault then fteo ego
faulty elatomatikos
favourite agapimenos
fax to fax
(verb: person) stelno fax seh ...
(document) stelno seh fax
February o Fevrooarios
feel esthanomeh
I feel hot zestenomeh
I feel unwell then esthanomeh kala
I feel like going for a walk ekho orexi na pao mia volta
how are you feeling? pos esthaneseh?
I'm feeling better esthanomeh kalitera
felt-tip pen o markathoros
fence o fraktis
fender o profilaktiras
ferry to feri bot
festival to festival
fetch pa-o na fero
I'll fetch him tha pa-o na ton fero
will you come and fetch me later? tha elthis na meh paris argotera?
feverish empiretos
few: a few liyi, liyes, liga
a few days liyes meres
fiancé o aravoniastikos
fiancée i aravoniastikia
field to khorafi
fight o agonas
figs ta sika
fill yemizo
fill in yemizo
do I have to fill this in? prepi na to yemiso?
fill up yemizo telios
fill it up, please yemisteh tin, parakalo
filling (in cake, sandwich) i yemisi
(in tooth) to sfra-yisma
film to film

dialogue

do you have this kind of film? ekheteh tetio film?
yes – how many exposures? neh – meh poses stasis?
36 trianda-exi

film processing i emfanisi too film
filter coffee o kafes filtroo
filter papers ta filtra ya kafeh
filthy vromeros

find vrisko
I can't find it then to vrisko
I've found it to vrika
find out anakalipto
could you find out for me? boris na maTHis?
fine (weather) oreos
(punishment) to prostimo

dialogues

how are you? ti kanis?
I'm fine thanks mia khara, efkharisto

is that OK? afto ineh endaxi?
that's fine thanks ineh mia khara, efkharisto

finger to thakhtilo
finish teliono
I haven't finished yet then ekho teliosi akomi
when does it finish? poteh telioni?
fire: fire! pirkaya!
can we light a fire here? boroomeh na anapsoomeh fotia etho?
it's on fire pireh fotia
fire alarm o sinayermos pirkayas
fire brigade i pirosvestiki ipiresia
fire escape i exothos pirkayas
fire extinguisher o pirosvestiras
first protos
I was first imoon protos
at first stin arkhi
the first time i proti fora
first on the left protos sta aristera
first aid i protes vo-iTHi-es
first aid kit to kooti proton vo-iTHi-on
first class (travel etc) proti THesi
first floor to proto patoma
(US) to iso-yio
first name to onoma
fish to psari
fisherman o psaras
fishing village to psarokhori
fishmonger's to psarathiko
fit (attack) i prosvoli
it doesn't fit me then moo khora-i
fitting room to thokimastirio
fix ftiakhno
(arrange) kanonizo
can you fix this? boris na to ftiaxis?
fizzy meh anTHrakiko
flag i simea
flannel to sfoogari
flash (for camera) to flas
flat (apartment) to thiamerisma
(adj) epipethos
I've got a flat tyre me epiaseh lastikho
flavour i gefsi
flea o psilos
flight i ptisi
flight number ariTHmos ptisis
flippers ta vatrakhopethila
flood i plimira
floor (of room) to patoma
(of building) o orofos

on the floor sto patoma
florist o anthopolis
flour to alevri
flower to looloothi
flu i gripi
fluent: he speaks fluent Greek mila-i aptesta elinika
fly i miga
(verb) peto
can we fly there? boroomeh na pameh eki a-eroporikos?
fly in peta-o pros
fly out peta-o apo
fog i omikhli
foggy: it's foggy ekhi omikhli
folk dancing i thimotiki khori
folk music i thimotiki mooziki
follow akolootho
follow me akolootha meh
food to fa-yito
food poisoning trofiki thilitiriasi
food shop/store to bakaliko
foot* to pothi
on foot meh ta pothia
football (game) to pothosfero
(ball) i bala
football match o pothosferirikos agonas
for ya
do you have something for ...? (headache/diarrhoea etc) ekheteh kati ya ...?

dialogues

who's the moussaka for?
ya pion ineh o moosakas?
that's for me ya mena
and this one? ki afto etho?
that's for her afto ineh ya ekini

where do I get the bus for Akropolis? apo poo tha paro to leoforio ya tin Akropoli?
the bus for Acropolis leaves from Stathiou Street to leoforio ya tin Akropoli fevyi apo tin Otho Stathioo

how long have you been here for? poso kero iseh etho pera?
I've been here for two days, how about you? vriskomeh etho pera etho keh thio meres, esi?
I've been here for a week vriskomeh etho pera etho keh mia vthomatha

forehead to metopo
foreign xenos
foreigner (man/woman) o xenos/i xeni
forest to thasos
forget xekhno
I forget xekhno
I've forgotten xekhasa
fork (for eating) to pirooni
(in road) i thiaklathosi
form (document) i etisi
formal (dress) episimos
fortnight to theka-pentimero

fortunately eftikhos
forward: could you forward my mail? boriteh na moo stileteh ta gramata moo?
forwarding address i thi-efthinsi apostolis
foundation cream krema prosopoo ya makiyaz
fountain i piyi
foyer to foyer
fracture to katagma
free elefTheros
(no charge) thorean
is it free of charge? ineh thorean?
freeway i ethniki othos
freezer i katapsixi
French (adj) galikos
(language) ta galika
French fries i tiganites patates
frequent sikhnos
how frequent is the bus to Corinth? kathеh poteh ekhi leoforio ya tin Korintho?
fresh (weather, breeze) throseros
(fruit etc) freskos
fresh orange o freskos khimos portokali
Friday i Paraskevi
fridge to psiyio
fried tiganismenos
fried egg to tiganito avgo
friend (male/female) o filos/i fili
friendly filikos
from apo
when does the next train from Patras arrive? poteh ftani to epomeno treno apo tin Patra?
from Monday to Friday apo theftera os Paraskevi
from next Thursday apo tin ali Pempti

dialogue

where are you from? apo poo iseh?
I'm from Slough imeh apo to Sla-oo

front to mbrostino meros
in front mbrosta
in front of the hotel mbrosta apo to xenothokhio
at the front sto mbrostino meros
frost i pagonia, o pa-yetos
frozen pagomenos
frozen food i katepsiymeni trofi
fruit ta froota
fruit juice o khimos frooton
fry tiganizo
frying pan to tigani
full yematos
it's full of ... ineh yemato meh ...
I'm full khortasa
full board fool pansion
fun: it was fun kala itan, kanameh kefi
funeral i kithia
funny (strange) paraxenos
(amusing) astios
furniture ta epipla
further parapera
it's further down the road ineh akoma parakato

dialogue

how much further is it to Piraeus? poso ineh akomi mekhri ton Pirea?
about 5 kilometres yiro sta pendeh khiliometra

fuse i asfalia
the lights have fused ka-ikaneh ta fota
fuse box to kooti meh tis asfali-es
fuse wire to sirma asfalias
future to melon
in future sto melon

G

gallon* ena galoni
game (cards etc) to pekhnithi
(match) o agonas
(meat) to kiniyi
garage (for fuel) to venzinathiko
(for repairs) to sineryio
(for parking) to garaz
garden o kipos
garlic to skortho
gas to gazi
gas cylinder (camping gas) i fiali gazi
gasoline i venzini
gas permeable lenses i imiskliri faki epafis
gas station to venzinathiko
gate i avloporta
(at airport) i exothos
gay (adj) omofilofilos
gay bar to gay bar
gears i takhitita
gearbox to kivotio takhititon
gear lever o levi-es takhititon
general yenikos
gents (toilet) i too-aleta ton anthron
genuine (antique etc) afTHendikos
German (adj) Yermanikos
(language) ta Yermanika
German measles i eriTHra
Germany i Yermania
get (fetch) perno
will you get me another one, please? THa moo paris alo ena, parakalo?
how do I get to ...? pos boro na pao sto ...?
do you know where I can get them? mipos xereteh poo boro na vro tetia?

dialogue

can I get you a drink? na seh keraso kanena poto?
no, I'll get this one, what would you like? okhi, ego kernao afti ti fora; ti THa iTHeles?
a glass of red wine ena potiri kokino krasi

get back (return) epistrefo
get in (arrive) ftano
get off kateveno
where do I get off? poo THa katevo?

get on (to train etc) aneveno
get out (of car etc) vyeno
get up (in the morning) sikonomeh
gift to thoro
gift shop katastima thoron, ithi thoron
gin to tzin
a gin and tonic, please ena tzin meh tonik, parakalo
girl to koritsi
girlfriend i filenatha
give thino
can you give me some change? boriteh na moo thoseteh psila?
I gave it to him to ethosa seh afton
will you give this to ...? to thinis afto ston ...?

dialogue

how much do you want for this? posa THelis ya afto?
10,000 drachmas theka khiliathes thrakhmes
I'll give you 7,000 drachmas soo thino efta khiliathes

give back epistrefo, thino piso
glad efkharistimenos
glass (material) to yali
(tumbler, wine glass) to potiri
a glass of wine ena potiri krasi
glasses ta yalia
gloves ta gandia
glue i kola
go pao
we'd like to go to the ... theloomeh na pameh sto ...
where are you going? poo pateh?
where does this bus go? poo pa-i afto to leoforio?
let's go! pameh
she's gone (left) efiyeh
where has he gone? poo piyeh aftos?
I went there last week piga eki tin perasmeni evthomatha
hamburger to go khamboorger ya to spiti
go away fevgo
go away! fiyeh!
go back (return) epistrefo
go down (the stairs etc) kateveno
go in beno
go out (in the evening) v-yeno
do you want to go out tonight? theleteh na pateh exo apopseh?
go through thiaskhizo, pao thia mesoo
go up (the stairs etc) aneveno
goat i katsika
goat's cheese to katsikisio tiri
God o THeos
goggles i maska
gold o khrisos
golf to golf
golf course to yipetho golf
good kalos
good! kala!
it's no good (product etc) afto then ineh kalo
(not worth trying) then ofeli

goodbye ya khara, adio
good evening kalispera
Good Friday i Megali Paraskevi
good morning kalimera
good night kalinikhta
goose i khina
got: we've got to ... prepi na ...
have you got any ...? ekheteh kaTHoloo ...?
government i kivernisi
gradually siga-siga
grammar i gramatiki
gram(me) ena gramario
granddaughter i egoni
grandfather o papoos
grandmother i ya-ya
grandson o egonos
grapefruit to grapefruit
grapefruit juice o khimos grapefruit
grapes ta stafilia
grass to khortari, to grasithi
grateful evgnomon
gravy o zomos too kreatos
great (excellent) poli kalo
that's great! iperokha!
it's a great success ineh megali epitikhia
Great Britain i Megali Vretania
Greece i Elatha
greedy akhortagos
Greek (adj) Elinikos
(language) ta Elinika
(man) o Elinas
(woman) i Elinitha
the Greeks i Elines
Greek coffee Elinikos kafes
Greek-Cypriot (adj) Elinokiprios
Greek Orthodox Elinikos OrTHothoxos
green prasinos
green card (car insurance) i asfalia ya othiyisi sto exoteriko
greengrocer's o manavis
grey grizos
grill i psistaria
grilled psitos sti skhara
grocer's to bakaliko
ground to ethafos
on the ground sto ethafos
ground floor to iso-yio
group to groop
guarantee i engi-isi
is it guaranteed? ineh engi-imeno?
guest (man/woman) o filoxenoomenos/i filoxenoomeni
guesthouse i pansion
guide o/i xenagos
guidebook o tooristikos othigos
guided tour i xenayisi
guitar i kiTHara
gum (in mouth) to oolo
gun (pistol) to pistoli
(rifle) to oplo
gym to yimnastirio

H

hair ta malia
hairbrush i voortsa ya malia, i khtena

haircut (man's) to **koorema**
(woman's) to **kopsimo**
hairdresser's to **komotirio**
(men's) to **koorio**
hairdryer to **pistolaki**
hair gel o **afros malion**
hairgrips ta **piastrakia malion**
hair spray to **spray** ya ta **malia**
half **misos**
half an hour **misi ora**
half a litre **miso litro**
about half that **peripoo to miso apo afto**
half board **demi-pansion**
half-bottle **miso bookali**
half fare **miso isitirio**
half price **misotimis**
ham to **zambon**
hamburger to **khamboorger**
hammer to **sfiri**
hand to **kheri**
handbag i **tsanda**
handbrake to **khirofreno**
handkerchief to **mandili**
(paper) to **khartomandilo**
handle to **kherooli**
hand luggage to **sakvooa-yaz**
hang-gliding i **anemoporia**
hangover o **ponokefalos**
I've got a hangover **ekho ponokefalo**
happen **simveni**
what's happening? ti **simveni?**
what has happened? ti **sinevi?**
happy **eftikhismenos**
I'm not happy about this then **imeh efkharistimenos meh afto**
harbour to **limani**
hard **skliros**
(difficult) **thiskolos**
hard-boiled egg to **sfikhto avgo**
hard lenses i **skliri faki**
hardly **meta vias**
hardly ever **s-khethon poteh**
hardware shop ta **ithi kingalerias**
hat to **kapelo**
hate **miso**
have* **ekho**
can I have a ...? **boro na ekho ena ...?**
do you have ...? **ekheteh ...?**
what'll you have? ti THA **piiteh?**
I have to leave now **prepi na piyeno tora**
do I have to ...? **prepi na ...?**
can we have some ...? **boroomeh na ekhoomeh merika ...?**
hayfever **aler-yia sti yiri**
hazelnuts to **foondooki**
he* **aftos**
is he here? **ineh etho?**
head to **kefali**
headache o **ponokefalos**
headlights i **provolis**
headphones ta **akoostika**
health food shop **katastima iyi-inon trofon**
healthy **iyi-is**
hear **akoo-o**

dialogue

can you hear me? meh akoos?
I can't hear you, could you repeat that? then seh akoo-o, boris na to epanalavis?

hearing aid ta akoostika
heart i karthia
heart attack i karthiaki prosvoli
heat i zesti
heater i thermansi
(radiator) to kalorifer
heating i thermansi
heavy varis
heel (of foot) i fterna
(of shoe) to takooni
could you heel these? boriteh na moo valeteh kenooryia takoonia safta?
heelbar o tsagaris
height to ipsos
helicopter to elikoptero
hello ya sas
(familiar) ya soo
(answer on phone) ebros
helmet (for motorcycle) to kranos
help i vo-ithia
(verb) vo-itho
help! vo-ithia!
can you help me? boriteh na meh vo-ithiseteh?
thank you very much for your help efkharisto ya ti vo-ithia sas
helpful exipiretikos
hepatitis i ipatititha
her*: I haven't seen her then tin ekho thi
to her saftin
with her mazi tis
for her yaftin
that's her afti ineh
that's her towel afti ineh i petseta tis
herbal tea tsa-i too voonoo
herbs ta votana
here etho
here is/are ... na ...
here you are (offering) oristeh
hers* thiko tis
that's hers afto ineh thiko tis
hey! eh!
hi! (hello) ya soo
hide (something) krivo
(oneself) krivomeh
high psilos
highchair to kareklaki moroo
highway i ethniki othos
hill o lofos
him*: I haven't seen him then ton ekho thi
to him safton
with him mazi too
for him yafton
that's him aftos ineh
hip o gofos
hire niki-azo
for hire eniki-azonteh
where can I hire a bike? poo boro na niki-aso ena pothilato?
his*: it's his car ineh to aftokinito too
that's his ineh thiko too

hit khtipao
hitch-hike kano otostop
hobby to khobi
hold kratao
hole i tripa
holiday i thiakopes
 on holiday seh thiakopes
Holy Week i Megali Evthomatha
home to spiti
 at home (in my house etc) sto spiti
 (in my country) stin patritha moo
 we go home tomorrow piyeno stin patritha moo avrio
honest timios
honey to meli
honeymoon o minas too melitos
hood (US) to kapo
hope elpizo
 I hope so etsi elpizo
 I hope not elpizo pos okhi
hopefully meh kali tikhi
horn (of car) to klaxon
horrible friktos
horse to alogo
horse riding i ipasia
hospital to nosokomio
hospitality i filoxenia
 thank you for your hospitality sas efkharisto ya ti filoxenia sas
hot zestos
 (spicy) kafteros, kaftos
 I'm hot zestenomeh
 it's hot today kani poli zesti simera
hotel to xenothokhio
hotel room: in my hotel room sto thomatio too xenothokhioo
hour i ora
house to spiti
house wine to krasi too magazioo
hovercraft to hovercraft, o a-erolisTHitiras
how pos
 how many? posi?
 how do you do? khero poli

dialogues

how are you? pos iseh?
fine, thanks, and you? poli kala, efkharisto; ki esi?

how much is it? poso kani afto?
5000 drachmas pendeh khiliathes thrakhmes
I'll take it THa to paro

humid igros
humour to khioomor
hungry pinasmenos
 are you hungry? pinas?
hurry (verb) viazomeh
 I'm in a hurry viazomeh
 there's no hurry then iparkhi via
 hurry up! viasoo!
hurt travmatizomeh
 it really hurts pona-i poli
husband o sizigos
hydrofoil to iptameno thelfini

I

I ego
ice o pagos
with ice meh pago
no ice, thanks khoris pago, efkharisto
ice cream to pagoto
ice-cream cone to pagoto khonaki
iced coffee to frapeh
ice lolly to pagoto xilaki
idea i ithea
idiot o vlakas
if an
ignition i miza
ill arostos
I feel ill imeh arostos
illness i arostia
imitation (leather etc) i apomimisi
immediately amesos
important spootheos
it's very important ineh poli simandiko
it's not important then ineh spootheo
impossible athinaton
impressive endiposiakos
improve veltiono
I want to improve my Greek THelo na kaliterepso ta Elinika moo
in: it's in the centre ineh sto kendro
in my car mesa sto aftokinito moo
in Athens stin Athina
in two days from now seh thio meres apo tora
in May sto Ma-io
in English sta Anglika
in Greek sta Elinika
is he in? ineh eki?
in five minutes seh pendeh lepta
inch* i intsa
include perilamvano
does that include meals? afto perilamvani keh fayito?
is that included in the price? perilamvaneteh stin timi?
inconvenient akatalilos, avolos
incredible apiTHanos
Indian (adj) Inthikos
indicator to flas, o thiktis
indigestion i thispepsia
indoor pool i esoteriki pisina
indoors mesa
inexpensive ftinos
see cheap
inner tube (for tyre) i sabrela
infection i molinsi
infectious kolitikos
inflammation i anaflexi
informal anepisimos
information i plirofori-es
do you have any information about ...? ekheteh tipoteh plirofori-es skhetika meh ...?
information desk i plirofori-es
injection i enesi
injured travmatismenos
she's been injured khtipiseh
in-laws ta peTHerika
innocent aTHo-os

insect to endomo
insect bite to tsibima endomoo
do you have anything for insect bites? ekheteh tipoteh ya tsibimata apo endoma?
insect repellent to AUTAN®
inside mesa
inside the hotel mesa sto xenothokhio
let's sit inside as katsoomeh mesa
insist epimeno
I insist epimeno
insomnia i a-ipnia
instant coffee to neskafeh
instead andi
give me that one instead thosteh moo afto sti THesi too aloo
instead of ... sti THesi too ...
insulin i insoolini
insurance i asfalia
intelligent exipnos
interested: I'm interested in ... enthiaferomeh poli ya ...
interesting enthiaferon
that's very interesting ineh poli enthiaferon
international thi-ethnis
internet to Internet
interpret thi-erminevo
interpreter o/i thi-ermineas
intersection to stavrothromi
interval (at theatre) to thi-alima
into mesa
I'm not into ... then moo aresi ...
introduce sistino
may I introduce ...? boro na sas sistiso ton ...?
invitation i prosklisi
invite proskalo
Ionian Sea to I-onio pelagos
Ireland i Irlanthia
Irish Irlanthos
I'm Irish (man/woman) imeh Irlanthos/Irlantheza
iron (for ironing) to ilektriko sithero
can you iron these for me? boriteh na moo ta sitheroseteh?
is* ineh
island to nisi
it afto
it is ... ineh ...
is it ...? ineh ...?
where is it? poo ineh?
it's him ineh aftos
it was ... itan ...
Italian (adj) Italos
(language) ta Italika
Italy i Italia
itch: it itches meh tro-i

J

jack (for car) o grilos
jacket to sakaki
jar to vazaki
jam i marmelatha
jammed: it's jammed ineh frakarismeno
January o I-anooarios
jaw to sagoni
jazz i tzaz

jealous ziliaris
jeans ta tzins
jellyfish i tsookhtra
jersey to fanelaki
jetty o molos
Jewish Evra-ikos
jeweller's to khrisokho-io
jewellery ta kosmimata
job i thoolia
jogging to jogging
 to go jogging pao ya jogging
joke to astio
journey to taxithi
 have a good journey! kalo taxithi!
jug i kanata
 a jug of water mia kanata nero
juice o khimos
July o I-oolios
jump pithao
jumper to poolover
jump leads ta kalothia batarias
junction i thiastavrosi
June o I-oonios
just (only) monon
 just two mono thio
 just for me mono ya mena
 just here akrivos etho
 not just now okhi tora
 we've just arrived molis ftasameh

K

keep krato
 keep the change krata ta resta
 can I keep it? boro na to kratiso?
 please keep it kratisteh to, sas parakalo
ketchup to ketsap
kettle i booyota, o vrastiras
key to klithi
 the key for room 201, please to klithi ya to 201 (thiakosia ena), parakalo
key ring to brelok
kidneys ta nefra
kill skotono
kilo* ena kilo
kilometre* ena khiliometro
 how many kilometres is it to ...? posa khiliometra ineh mekhri to ...?
kind (generous) evyenikos
 that's very kind ineh poli evyeniko

dialogue

which kind do you want? ti ithos THeleteh?
I want this/that kind THelo afto/ekino to ithos

king o vasilias
kiosk to periptero
kiss to fili
 (verb) filao
kitchen i koozina
kitchenette i koozinoola
Kleenex® ta khartomandila
knee to gonato
knickers i kilota
knife to makheri

knitwear plekta rookha
knock khtipo
knock down khtipo
he's been knocked down khtipithikeh
knock over (object) anapothoyirizo
(pedestrian) khtipo
know (somebody) gnorizo
(something, a place) xero
I don't know then xero
I didn't know that then to ixera
do you know where I can find ...? mipos xereteh poo boro na vro ...?

L

label i etiketa
ladies' (toilets) i too-aleta ton yinekon
ladies' wear yinekia ithi
lady i kiria
lager i bira
lake i limni
lamb (meat) to arni
lamp i lamba
lane (on motorway) i loritha
(small road) i parothos
language i glosa
language course mathimata xenis glosas
large megalos
last telefteos
last week i perasmeni evthomatha
last Friday tin perasmeni Paraskevi
last night kh-thes vrathi
what time is the last train to Salonika? ti ora ineh to telefteo treno ya tin thesaloniki?
late arga
sorry I'm late meh sinkhoriteh poo aryisa
the train was late to treno ikheh kathisterisi
we must go – we'll be late prepi na piyenoomeh – tha aryisoomeh
it's getting late nikhtoni
later argotera
I'll come back later tha yiriso argotera
see you later adio, tha ta xanapoomeh
later on argotera
latest o pi-o prosfatos
by Wednesday at the latest tin Tetarti to argotero
laugh yelo
launderette to plindirio rookhon
laundromat to plindirio rookhon
laundry (clothes) i boogatha, ta aplita
(place) to katharistirio
lavatory i too-aleta
law o nomos
lawn to grasithi
lawyer o/i thikigoros
laxative to kathartiko
lazy tebelis
lead (electrical) o agogos

(verb) othigo
where does this lead to? poo othiyi afto?
leaf to filo
leaflet to thiafimistiko
leak i thiaro-i
(verb) stazo
the roof leaks i steyi stazi
learn maTHeno
least: not in the least katholoo
at least toolakhiston
leather to therma
leave (bag etc) afino
(go away) fevgo
(forget) xekhnao
I am leaving tomorrow fevgo avrio
he left yesterday efiyeh kh-THes
may I leave this here? boro nafiso afto etho?
I left my coat in the bar afisa tin tsanda moo sto bar
when does the bus for Athens leave? poteh fevyi to leoforio ya tin ATHina?
leeks ta prasa
left aristera
on the left pros ta aristera
to the left pros ta aristera
turn left stripseh aristera
there's none left then emineh tipoteh
left-handed aristerokhiras
left luggage (office) o khoros filaxis aposkevon
leg to pothi
lemon to lemoni
lemonade i lemonatha
lemon tea tsai meh lemoni
lend thanizo
will you lend me your ... ? THa moo thanisis to thiko soo ...?
lens (of camera) o fakos
lesbian i lesvia
less ligotero
less than ligotero apo
less expensive ligotero akrivo
lesson to maTHima
let (allow) epitrepo
will you let me know? THa moo to pis?
I'll let you know THa soo po
let's go for something to eat pameh na fameh kati
let off katevazo
will you let me off at ...? THa meh katevaseteh sto ...?
letter to grama
do you have any letters for me? ekho kanena grama?
letterbox to gramatokivotio
lettuce to marooli
lever o levi-es
library i vivlioTHiki
licence i athi-a
lid to kapaki
lie (tell untruth) leo psemata
lie down xaplono
life i zo-i
lifebelt i zoni asfalias
lifeguard o navagosostis
life jacket to sosivio
lift (in building) to asanser
could you give me a lift? boriteh na meh pateh?

would you like a lift? THeleteh na sas pao?
light to fos
(not heavy) elafros
do you have a light? (for cigarette) ekhis fotia?
light green anikhto prasino
light bulb i lamba, o glombos
I need a new light bulb khriazomeh mia kenoorya lamba
lighter (cigarette) o anaptiras
lightning i astrapi
like (verb) moo aresi
I like it moo aresi afto
I like going for walks moo aresi na piyeno peripato
I like you moo aresis
I don't like it then moo aresi afto
do you like it? soo aresi afto?
I'd like to go swimming THa iTHela na pao ya kolimbi
I'd like a beer THa iTHela mia bira
would you like a drink? THa iTHeles ena poto?
would you like to go for a walk? THa iTHeles na pameh mia volta?
what's it like? meh ti miazi?
I want one like this THelo ena san ki afto
lime to moskholemono
lime cordial to lime
line (on paper) i grami
(phone) i tilefoniki grami
could you give me an outside line? THa moo thoseteh grami?
lips ta khilia
lip salve to vootiro kakao
lipstick to krayon
liqueur to liker
listen akoo-o
litre* ena litro
a litre of white wine ena litro aspro krasi
little mikros
just a little, thanks ligo mono, efkharisto
a little milk ligo gala
a little bit more ligo akomi
live zo
we live together sizoomeh

dialogue

where do you live? poo menis?
I live in London meno sto Lonthino

lively thrastirios
liver to sikoti
loaf i fradzola
lobby (in hotel) to saloni
lobster o astakos
local dopios
can you recommend a local wine/restaurant? boriteh na mas sistiseteh ena dopio krasi/estiatorio?
lock i klitharia
(verb) klithono
it's locked ineh klithomeno
lock in klithono mesa
lock out klithono apo exo
I've locked myself out

klithoтнika apexo
locker (for luggage etc) i тнiritha
lollipop to glifidzoori
London to Lonтнino
long makris
how long will it take to fix it? poso kero тна pari ya na to ftiaxeteh?
how long does it take? posi ora kani?
a long time polis keros, poli ora
one day/two days longer mia mera/thio meres parapano
long-distance call to iperastiko tilefonima
look: I'm just looking, thanks efkharisto, vlepo mono
you don't look well then feneseh kala
look out! prosexe!
can I have a look? boro na tho?
look after prosekho, frondizo
look at kitazo
look for psakhno
I'm looking for ... psakhno ya ...
look forward to perimeno meh khara
I'm looking forward to it to perimeno pos keh pos
loose (handle etc) khalaros
lorry to fortigo
lose khano
I've lost my way ekho khaтнi
I'm lost, I want to get to ... ekho khaтнi, тнelo na pao sto ...
I've lost my (hand)bag ekhasa tin tsanda moo
lost property (office) to grafio apolesтнendon
lot: a lot, lots pola
not a lot okhi pola
a lot of people poli anтнropi
a lot bigger poli megalitero
I like it a lot moo aresi poli
lotion i losion
loud thinatos
lounge to saloni
love i agapi
(verb) agapo
I love Greece latrevo tin Elatha
lovely oreos
low khamilos
luck i tikhi
good luck! kali tikhi!
luggage i aposkeves
luggage trolley to karotsaki ya tis aposkeves
lump (on body) to priximo
lunch to yevma
lungs o pnevmonas
luxurious (hotel, furnishings) politelis
luxury politelias

M

Macedonia i Makethonia
machine i mikhani
mad (insane) trelos
(angry) trelos apo тнimo
magazine to periothiko
maid (in hotel) i servitora

maiden name to patronimo
mail ta gramata, to takhithromio
(verb) takhithromo
is there any mail for me? ekho kanena grama?
mailbox to gramatokivotio
main kirios
main course to kirio piato
Mainland Greece i Ipirotiki Elatha
main post office kendriko takhithromio
main road (in town) o kendrikos thromos
(in country) o aftokinito-thromos
main switch o kendrikos thiakoptis
make (brand name) i marka
(verb) kano
I make it 500 drachmas ipoloyizo oti kani pedakosi-es thrakhmes
what is it made of? apo ti ineh ftiagmeno?
make-up to make-up
man o andras
manager o thi-efthindis, o manager
can I see the manager? boro na tho ton thi-efthindi?
manageress i thi-efthindria
manual to aftokinito meh kanonikes takhitites
many pola
not many liga, okhi pola
map o khartis
March o Martios
margarine i margarini
market i agora
marmalade i marmelatha
married: I'm married (said by a man/woman) imeh pandremenos/pandremeni
are you married? (said to a man/woman) isteh pandremenos/pandremeni?
mascara i maskara
match (football etc) to mats, o agonas
matches ta spirta
material (fabric) to ifasma
matter: it doesn't matter then pirazi
what's the matter? ti simveni?
mattress to stroma
May o Ma-ios
may: may I have another one? tha ithela ki alo ena?
may I come in? boro na bo?
may I see it? boro na to tho?
may I sit here? boro na kathiso etho?
maybe isos
mayonnaise i ma-yoneza
me* emena
that's for me afto ineh ya mena
send it to me stilteh to seh mena
me too ki ego episis
meal to fa-yito

dialogue

did you enjoy your meal?
sas areseh to fayito?

it was excellent, thank you itan poli nostimo, efkharisto

mean: what do you mean? ti eno-iteh?

dialogue

what does this word mean? ti simeni afti i lexi?
it means ... in English simeni ... sta Anglika

measles i ilara
meat to kreas
mechanic o mikhanikos
medicine to farmako
Mediterranean i Meso-yios
medium (adj: size) metrios
medium-dry imixiro krasi
medium-rare misopsimeno
medium-sized metrio meyethos
meet sinandao
nice to meet you kharika poo sas gnorisa
where shall I meet you? poo tha sas sinandiso?
meeting i sinandisi
meeting place to meros sinandisis
melon to peponi
men i anthres
mend thiorthono
could you mend this for me? boriteh na moo to ftiaxeteh?
menswear ta anthrika ithi
mention anafero
don't mention it parakalo
menu to menoo
may I see the menu, please? boro na tho to menoo, parakalo?
see Menu Reader page 174
message to minima
are there any messages for me? iparkhi kanena minima ya mena?
I want to leave a message for ... thelo nafiso ena minima ya ...
metal to metalo
metre* to metro
microwave (oven) o foornos mikrokimaton, to microwave
midday to mesimeri
at midday to mesimeri
middle: in the middle sti mesi
in the middle of the night arga ti nikhta
the middle one to meseo
midnight ta mesanikhta
at midnight ta mesanikhta
might: I might tha boroosa
I might not then tha boroosa
I might want to stay another day bori na thelo na mino akomi mia mera
migraine i imikrania
mild (weather) ethrios
(taste) elafros
mile* ena mili
milk to gala
milkshake to milkshake
millimetre* ena khiliosto
minced meat o kimas
mind: never mind then pirazi

I've changed my mind alaxa gnomi

dialogue

do you mind if I open the window? seh pirazi an anixo to paraTHiro?
no, I don't mind okhi, then meh pirazi

mine*: it's mine ineh thiko moo
mineral water to emfialomeno nero
mint (sweet) i menda
minute to lepto
in a minute seh ena lepto
just a minute ena lepto
mirror o kaTHreftis
Miss thespinis
miss khano
I missed the bus ekhasa to leoforio
missing lipi
one of my ... is missing lipi ena ...
there's a suitcase missing lipi mia valitsa
mist i katakhnia
mistake to laTHos
I think there's a mistake nomizo oti iparkhi ena laTHos etho
sorry, I've made a mistake meh sinkhoriteh, ekana laTHos
misunderstanding i parexiyisi
mix-up: sorry, there's been a mix-up meh sinkhoriteh, iparkhi ena berthema
modern modernos
modern art gallery i galeri modernas tekhnis
Modern Greek ta Nea Elinika
moisturizer i ithatiki krema
moment: I won't be a moment mia stigmi parakalo
monastery to monastiri
Monday i theftera
money ta lefta
month o minas
monument to mnimio
moon to fengari
moped to mikhanaki
more* perisoteros
can I have some more water, please? akomi ligo nero, parakalo
more expensive/interesting pio akrivo/enthiaferon
more than 50 perisotero apo peninda
more than that pio poli ap afto
a lot more poli perisotero

dialogue

would you like some more? THa THelateh ligo akomi?
no, no more for me, thanks okhi, okhi alo ya mena, efkharisto
how about you? ki esis?
I don't want any more, thanks then THelo alo, efkharisto

morning to pro-**i**
this morning simera to pro-**i**
in the morning to pro-**i**
mosquito to koon**oo**pi
mosquito repellent to fithaki ya ta koon**oo**pia
most: I like this one most of all afto moo aresi pio poli apo ola
most of the time sinithos
most tourists i perisoteri tooristes
mostly kirios
mother i mitera
motorbike i motosikleta
motorboat i varka meh mikhani
motorway i ethniki othos
mountain to voono
in the mountains pano sta voona
mountaineering i orivasia
mouse to pondiki
moustache to moostaki
mouth to stoma
mouth ulcer pliyi sto stoma
move metakino
he's moved to another room piyeh seh alo thomatio
could you move your car? boriteh na metakiniseteh to aftokinito sas?
could you move up a little? boriteh na metakinithiteh ligo?
where has it moved to? poo metaferthikeh?
movie to film
movie theater o kinimatografos, to sinema
Mr kiri-eh
Mrs kiria
Ms thespinis
much poli
much better/worse poli kalitera/khirotera
much hotter poli pio zesta
not much okhi poli
not very much okhi para poli
I don't want very much then thelo para poli
mud i laspi
mug (for drinking) i koopa
I've been mugged meh listepsan
mum i mama
mumps i parotititha
museum to moosio
mushrooms ta manitaria
music i moosiki
musician o/i moosikos
Muslim (adj) Moosoolmanikos
mussels ta mithia
must: I must ... prepi na ...
I mustn't drink alcohol then prepi na pio alko-ol
mustard i moostartha
my* o/i/to ... moo
myself: I'll do it myself tha to kano o ithios
by myself apo monos moo

N

nail (finger) to nikhi
(metal) to karfi
nailbrush i voortsa ya ta nikhia

nail varnish to mano
name to onoma
my name's John meh leneh John
what's your name? pos seh leneh?
what is the name of this street? pos leneh afto to thromo?
napkin i petseta
nappy i pana
narrow (street) stenos
nasty (person) apesios
(weather, accident) askhimos
national ethnikos
nationality i ethnikotita
natural fisikos
nausea i naftia
navy (blue) ble maren
near konda
is it near the city centre? ineh konda sto kendro tis polis?
do you go near the Acropolis? pernateh apo tin Akropoli?
where is the nearest ...? poo ineh to plisi-estero ...?
nearby etho konda
nearly skhethon
necessary aparetitos, anangeos
neck o lemos
necklace to koli-e
necktie i gravata
need: I need ...
khriazomeh ...
do I need to pay? khriazeteh na pliroso?
needle i velona
negative (film) to arnitiko
neither: neither (one) of them
kanenas apo aftoos
neither ... nor ... ooteh ... ooteh ...
nephew o anipsios
net (in sport) to thikhti
network map o khartis othikoo thiktioo
never poteh

dialogue

have you ever been to Athens? ekheteh pa-i poteh stin Athina?
no, never, I've never been there okhi, poteh, then ekho pa-i poteh eki

new neos, kenooryos
news (radio, TV etc) ta nea
newsagent's to praktorio efimerithon
newspaper i efimeritha
newspaper kiosk to periptero meh efimerithes
New Year to neo etos
Happy New Year! eftikhismenos o kenooryos khronos!
New Year's Eve i protokhronia
New Zealand i Nea Zilanthia
New Zealander: I'm a New Zealander (man/woman) imeh Neozilanthos/Neozilantheza
next epomenos
the next turning on the left i epomeni strofi sta aristera
the next street on the left

o epomenos thromos sta aristera
at the next stop stin epomeni stasi
next week tin ali evthomatha
next to thipla apo
nice (food) nostimos
(looks, view etc) oreos
(person) kalos
niece i anipsia
night i nikhta
at night to vrathi
good night kalinikhta

dialogue

do you have a single room for one night? ekheteh ena mono thomatio ya mia nikhta?
yes, madam malista, kiria moo
how much is it per night? poso kani ti mia nikhta?
it's 5000 drachmas for one night ineh pendeh khiliathes thrakhmes ya mia nikhta
thank you, I'll take it efkharisto, THa to kliso

nightclub to nait-klab
nightdress to nikhtiko
night porter o nikhterinos THiroros
no okhi
I've no change then ekho psila
there's no ... left then emineh kaTHoloo ...
no way! apokli-eteh!
oh no! (upset) okh!, o okhi!
nobody kanenas
there's nobody there then ineh kanis eki
noise i fasaria
noisy: it's too noisy ekhi poli fasaria
non-alcoholic khoris alko-ol
none kanis
non-smoking compartment o khoros ya mi kapnizondes
noon to mesimeri
no-one kanenas
nor: nor do I ooteh kego
normal fisiolo-yikos
north o voras
in the north sta vori-a
north of Athens vori-a tis ATHinas
northeast o vorio-anatolikos
northwest o vorio-thitikos
northern vorios
Northern Ireland i Vorios Irlanthia
Norway i Norviyia
Norwegian (adj) Norviyikos
nose i miti
nosebleed i emorayia sti miti
not* then
no, I'm not hungry okhi, then pina-o
I don't want any, thank you efkharisto, then THelo
it's not necessary then ineh aparetito

I didn't know that then to ixera
not that one – this one okhi afto – to alo
note (banknote) to kharto-nomisma
notebook to blokaki, to simiomatario
notepaper (for letters) to kharti alilografias
nothing tipoteh
nothing for me, thanks tipoteh ya mena, efkharisto
nothing else tipoteh alo
novel to miTHistorima
November o No-emvrios
now tora
number* o ariTHmos
I've got the wrong number pira laTHos noomero
what is your phone number? pio ineh to tilefono soo?
number plate i pinakitha
nurse (man/woman) o nosokomos/i nosokoma
nursery slope i pista ekmaTHisis
nut (for bolt) to paximathi
nuts to karithi

O

o'clock* i ora
occupied (toilet) katilimenos
October o Oktovrios
odd (strange) paraxenos
of* too
off (lights) klisto
it's just off Omonia Square ligo pio eki apo tin Omoni-a
we're off tomorrow fevgoomeh avrio
offensive (language, behaviour) prosvlitikos
office (place of work) to grafio
officer (said to policeman) astinomeh
often sikhna
not often okhi sikhna
how often are the buses? kaTHeh poteh ekhi leoforia?
oil (for car) ta lathia
(for salad) to lathi
ointment i alifi
OK endaxi
are you OK? iseh kala?
is that OK with you? iseh efkharistimenos etsi?
is it OK to ...? pirazi na ...?
that's OK thanks (it doesn't matter) ineh endaxi, efkharisto
I'm OK (nothing for me) tipoteh ya mena
(I feel OK) imeh mia khara
is this train OK for ...? afto ineh to treno ya ...?
I said I'm sorry, OK? soo ipa signomi, endaxi?
old (person) yeros
(thing) palios

dialogue

how old are you? poso khronon iseh?
I'm twenty-five imeh ikosi-pendeh khronon
and you? ki esi?

old-fashioned demodeh
old town (old part of town) i palia poli
in the old town stin palia poli
olive oil to eleolatho
olives i eli-es
omelette i omeleta
on pano
(lights) anikhto
on the street/beach sto thromo/stin paralia
is it on this road? ineh safto to thromo?
on the plane mesa sto a-eroplano
on Saturday to Savato
on television stin tileorasi
I haven't got it on me then to ekho mazi moo
this one's on me (drink) ego kernao afti ti fora
the light wasn't on to fos then itan anikhto
what's on tonight? ti pezi simera?
once (one time) mia fora
at once (immediately) amesos
one* enas, mia, ena
the white one to aspro
one-way ticket: a one-way ticket to ... ena aplo ya ...
onion to kremithi
only mono
only one mono ena
it's only 6 o'clock ineh mono exi i ora
I've only just got here molis eftasa
on/off switch o thiakoptis
open (adj) aniktos
(verb: door, shop) anigo
when do you open? poteh aniyeteh?
I can't get it open then boro na to anixo
in the open air stin ipeTHro
opening times ores litooryias
open ticket isitirio meh anikhti epistrofi
opera i opera
operation (medical) i enkhirisi
operator (telephone: man/woman) o tilefonitis/i tilefonitria
opposite: the opposite direction stin anditHeti kateftHinsi
the bar opposite to bar apenandi
opposite my hotel apenandi apo to xenothokhio moo
optician o optikos
or i
orange (fruit) to portokali
(colour) portokali
orange juice i portokalatha
orchestra i orkhistra
order: can we order now? (in restaurant) boroomeh na paragiloomeh tora?
I've already ordered, thanks ekho ithi paragili, efkharisto
I didn't order this then paragila afto
out of order then litooryi
ordinary kanonikos
other alos, ali, alo
the other one to alo
the other day tis pro-ales

I'm waiting for the others
perimeno toos aloos
do you have any others?
ekheteh tipoteh ala?
otherwise thiaforetika
our* o/i/to ... mas
ours* thikos mas
out: he's out then ineh etho
three kilometres out of town
tria khiliometra exo apo tin poli
outdoors exo
outside ... exo ...
can we sit outside?
borroomeh na kaTHisoomeh exo?
oven o foornos
over: over here etho
over there eki, eki pera
over 500 pano apo pendakosia
it's over teliosa
overcharge: you've overcharged me meh khreosateh parapano
overcoat to palto
overlook: I'd like a room overlooking the courtyard
THa iTHela ena thomatio meh THea stin avli
overnight (travel) oloniktio
overtake prosperno
owe: how much do I owe you?
poso sas khrostao?
own: my own ... thiko moo ...
are you on your own? iseh monos soo?
I'm on my own imeh monos moo
owner (man/woman) o ithioktitis/i ithioktitria

P

pack (verb) ftiakhno tis valitses
a pack of ... ena paketo ...
package (parcel) to paketo
package holiday i organomeni ekthromi
packed lunch to etimo mesimeriano
packet: a packet of cigarettes ena paketo tsigara
padlock to looketo, i klitharia
page (of book) i selitha
could you page Mr ...?
boriteh na fonaxeteh ton kirio ...?
pain o ponos
I have a pain here
esTHanomeh ena pono etho
painful othiniros
painkillers to pafsipono
paint i boya
painting o pinakas zografikis
pair: a pair of ... ena zevgari ...
Pakistani (adj) Pakistanikos
palace to palati
pale khlomos
pale blue galazios
pan to tapsi
panties to slip, i kilotes
pants (underwear: men's) to sovrako
(women's) to slip, i kilotes
(US: trousers) to pandaloni

pantyhose to kalson
paper to kharti
(newspaper) i efimeritha
a piece of paper ena komati kharti
paper handkerchiefs ta khartomandila
parcel to thema
pardon (me)? (didn't understand/hear) signomi?
parents: my parents i gonis moo
parents-in-law ta petherika
park to parko
(verb) parkaro
can I park here? boro na parkaro etho?
parking lot to parking
part to meros
partner (boyfriend, girlfriend) o filos, i fili
party (group) i omatha
(celebration) to parti
pass (in mountains) to perasma
passenger o/i epivatis
passport to thiavatirio
past: in the past sto pareltthon
just past the information office amesos meta to grafio pliroforion
path to monopati
pattern to s-khethio
pavement to pezothromio
on the pavement sto pezothromio
pavement café kafenio sto thromo
pay plirono
can I pay, please? boro na pliroso, parakalo?
it's already paid for ineh ithi pliromeno

dialogue

who's paying? pios tha plirosi?
I'll pay ego tha pliroso
no, you paid last time, I'll pay okhi, esi pliroses tin teleftea fora, ego tha pliroso

payphone to tilefono meh kermata
peaceful irinikos
peach to rothakino
peanuts fistikia arapika
pear to akhlathi
peas ta bizelia
peculiar (taste, custom) paraxenos
pedestrian crossing i thiavasi pezon
pedestrian precinct o pezothromos
peg (for washing) to mandalaki
(for tent) to palooki
pen to stilo
pencil to molivi
penfriend (male/female) o filos thi' alilografias/i fili thi' alilografias
penicillin i penikilini
penknife o soo-yias
pensioner o/i sindaxiookhos
people i anthropi
the other people in the hotel

i ali anTHropi sto xenothokhio
too many people ipervolika poli anTHropi
pepper (spice) to piperi
(vegetable) i piperia
peppermint (sweet) i menda
per: per night tin vrathia
how much per day? poso tin imera?
per cent tis ekato
perfect telios
perfume to aroma
perhaps isos
perhaps not isos okhi
period (time, menstruation) i periothos
perm i permanand
permit i athia
person to atomo
personal stereo to walkman®
petrol i venzini
petrol can ena thokhio venzinis
petrol station to venzinathiko
pharmacy to farmakio
phone to tilefono
(verb) perno tilefono, tilefono
phone book o tilefonikos katalogos
phonecard i tilekarta
phone number o ariTHmos tilefonoo
photo i fotografia
excuse me, could you take a photo of us? meh sinkhoriteh, THa boroosateh na mas pareteh mia fotografia?
phrase book to vivlio thialogon
piano to piano
pickpocket o portofolas
pick up: will you be there to pick me up? THa iseh eki na meh paris?
picnic to piknik
picture i ikona
pie i pita
(meat) i kreatopita
(fruit) i frootopita
piece to komati
a piece of ... ena komati ...
pill to khapi
I'm on the pill perno antisiliptika khapia
pillow to maxilari
pillow case i maxilaroTHiki
pin i karfitsa
pineapple o ananas
pineapple juice o khimos anana
pink roz
pipe (for smoking) i pipa, to tsibooki
(for water) o solinas
pipe cleaners kaTHaristis pipas
Piraeus o Pireas
pistachio nuts fistiki-a Eyinis
pity: it's a pity ineh krima
pizza i pitsa
place to meros
is this place taken? ineh piasmeni afti i THesi?
at your place sti THesi soo
at his place sti THesi too
plain (not patterned) monokhromo

plane to a-eroplano
by plane meh to a-eroplano
plant to fito
plaster cast o yipsos
plasters to lefkoplast
plastic plastikos
(credit cards) i pistotiki karta
plastic bag i plastiki sakoola
plate to piato
plate-smashing spasimo pi-aton
platform i platforma
which platform is for Patras, please? pia platforma ya tin Patra, parakalo?
play (in theatre) to тheatriko ergo
(verb) pezo
playground to yipetho
pleasant efkharistos
please parakalo
yes please neh, parakalo
could you please ...? тha boroosateh, parakalo, na ...?
please don't stamata, seh parakalo
pleased to meet you kharika poli
pleasure: i efkharistisi
my pleasure efkharistisi moo
plenty: plenty of ... poli/pola ...
there's plenty of time iparkhi arketi ora
that's plenty, thanks efkharisto, arki
pliers i pensa
plug (electrical) i briza
(for car) to boozi
(in sink) i tapa
plumber o ithravlikos
pm* meta mesimvrias
poached egg to avgo poseh
pocket i tsepi
point: two point five thio koma pendeh
there's no point then iparkhi logos
points (in car) i platines
poisonous thilitiriothis
police i astinomia
call the police! kalesteh tin astinomia!
policeman o astifilakas
police station to astinomiko tmima
policewoman i astinomikos
polish to verniki
polite evgenikos
polluted molismenos
pony to poni
pool (for swimming) i pisina
poor (not rich) ftokhos
(quality) kakos
pop music i moosiki pop
pop singer o tragoothistis pop, i tragoothistria pop
population o pliтhismos
pork to khirino
port (for boats) to limani
(drink) i mavrothafni
porter (in hotel) o akh-тhoforos
portrait to portreto
posh (restaurant) akrivos
(people) kiriles

possible thinatos
is it possible to ...? ineh thinaton na ...?
as ... as possible oso to thinaton ...
post (mail) ta gramata
(verb) takhithromo
could you post this for me? boriteh na moo to takhithromiseteh?
postbox to gramatokivotio
postcard i kartpostal
postcode o takhithromikos kothikos
poster (for room) to poster
(in street) i afisa
post office to takhithromio
poste restante post restand
pots and pans (cooking implements) katsaroles keh tigania
potato i patata
potato chips ta tsips
pottery ta keramika
pound* (money) i lira
(weight) i libra
power cut i thiakopi revmatos
power point o revmatothotis
practise: I want to practise my Greek THelo na exaskiso ta Elinika moo
prawns i garithes
(larger) i karavitha
prefer: I prefer ... protimo ...
pregnant engios
prescription (for chemist) i sindayi
present (gift) to thoro
president (of country) o pro-ethros
pretty (beautiful) omorfos, oreos
(quite) arketa
it's pretty expensive ineh arketa akrivo
price i timi
priest o papas
prime minister o proTHi-poorgos
printed matter ta endipa
priority (in driving) i protereotita
prison i filaki
private ithiotikos
private bathroom to ithiotiko banio
probably piTHanon
problem to provlima
no problem! kanena provlima!
program(me) to programa
promise: I promise iposkhomeh
pronounce: how is this pronounced? pos to proferis afto?
properly (repaired, locked etc) opos prepi
protection factor (of suntan lotion) o vaTHmos prostasias
Protestant o thiamartiromenos
public convenience i kinokhristi tooaleta
public holiday i thimosia aryia
pudding (dessert) to glikisma
pull travao
pullover to poolover
puncture to foo-it
purple mov

purse (for money) to portofoli
(US: handbag) i tsanda
push sprokhno
pushchair to karotsaki
put vazo
where can I put ...? poo boro na valo ...?
could you put us up for the night? boriteh na mas filoxeniseteh ya ena vrathi?
pyjamas i pitzames

Q

quality i piotita
quarantine i karantina
quarter to tetarto
quayside: on the quayside stin provlita
question i erotisi
queue i oora
quick grigora
that was quick afto itan grigoro
what's the quickest way there? pios ineh o pio grigoros thromos?
fancy a quick drink? ekhis orexi ya ena poto sta grigora?
quickly grigora
quiet (place, hotel) isikhos
quiet! siopi!
quince to kithoni
quite (fairly) arketa
(very) telios
that's quite right poli sosta
quite a lot arketa

R

rabbit o lagos
race (for runners, cars) i koorsa
racket i raketa
radiator (in room) to kalorifer
(of car) to psiyio aftokinitoo
radio to rathiofono
on the radio sto rathiofono
rail: by rail sithirothromikos
railway o sithirothromos
rain i vrokhi
in the rain mes tin vrokhi
it's raining vrekhi
raincoat i kabardina, to athiavrokho
rape o viasmos
rare (steak) okhi poli psimeno
rash (on skin) to exanthima
raspberry to vatomooro
rat o arooreos
rate (for changing money) i timi sinalagmatos
rather: it's rather good ineh malon kalo
I'd rather ... tha protimoosa na ...
razor (dry) to xirafaki
(electric) i xiristiki mikhani
razor blades to xirafaki
read thiavazo
ready etimos
are you ready? (to man/woman) iseh etimos/etimi?
I'm not ready yet then imeh etimos akomi

dialogue

when will it be ready? poteh THA ineh etimo?
it should be ready in a couple of days THA prepi na ineh etimo seh mia-thio meres

real pragmatikos
really pragmatika
(very) poli
really! (surprise, doubt) psemata!
really? (interest) aliTHia?
rearview mirror o kaTHreftis aftokinitoo
reasonable (prices etc) loyikos
receipt i apothixi
recently prosfata
reception (in hotel) i resepsion
(for guests) i thexiosi
at reception stin paralavi
reception desk to grafio ipothokhis
receptionist i/o resepsionist
recognize anagnorizo
recommend: could you recommend ...? boriteh na moo sistiseteh ...?
record (music) o thiskos
red kokinos
red wine to kokino krasi
refund i epistrofi khrimaton
can I have a refund? moo epistrefondeh khrimata?
region i periokhi
registered: by registered mail sistimeno
registration number o ariTHmos kikloforias
relative o/i singenis
religion i THriskia
remember: I don't remember then THimameh
I remember THimameh
do you remember? THimaseh?
rent (for apartment etc) to enikio
(verb) niki-azo
to/for rent eniki-azonteh
rented car to enikiasmeno aftokinito
repair i episkevi
can you repair it? boriteh na to episkevaseteh?
repeat epanalamvano
could you repeat that? boriteh na to epanalaveteh?
reservation (train, bus) to klisimo THesis

dialogue

I have a reservation ekho kani mia kratisi
yes sir, what name please? malista, kiri-eh; seh ti onoma, parakalo?

reserve krato

dialogue

can I reserve a table for tonight? boro na kliso ena trapezi ya apopseh?
yes madam, for how many

people? malista, kiria moo; ya posa atoma?
for two ya thio
and for what time? keh ya ti ora?
for eight o'clock ya tis okhto
and could I have your name please? to onoma sas, parakalo?
see alphabet page 209 for spelling

rest: I need a rest khriazomeh xekoorasi
the rest of the group to ipolipo groop
restaurant to estiatorio
rest room i too-aleta
retired: I'm retired imeh seh sindaxi
return: a return to ... ena isitirio met epistroftis ya to ...
reverse charge call to tilefonima kolekt
reverse gear i opisTHen
revolting apesios
Rhodes i Rothos
rib to plevro
rice to rizi
rich (person) ploosios
(food) varis
ridiculous yelios
right (correct) sostos
(not left) thexia
you were right ikhes thikio
that's right sosta
this can't be right afto then bori na ineh sosto
right! endaxi!
is this the right road for ...? ineh aftos o sostos thromos ya ...?
on the right sta thexia
turn right stripseh thexia
right-hand drive meh thexio timoni
ring (on finger) to thaktilithi
I'll ring you THa soo tilefoniso
ring back THa seh paro piso
ripe (fruit) orimos
rip-off: it's a rip-off ineh listia
rip-off prices astronomikes times
risky ripsokinthinos
river to potami
road (country) o thromos
(in town) i othos
is this the road for ...? ineh aftos o thromos ya ...?
down the road parakato
road accident to aftokinitistiko thistikhima
road map o othikos khartis
roadsign i pinakitha
rob: I've been robbed meh listepsan
rock o vrakhos
(music) i rok moosiki
on the rocks (with ice) meh pagakia
roll (bread) to psomaki
roof i orofi, i steyi
(flat) i taratsa
roof rack i s-khara aftokinitoo
room to thomatio
(space) to meros

in my room sto thomatio moo
room service to servis thomatioo
rope to skhini
rosé (wine) to rozeh
roughly (approximately) pano-kato
round: it's my round ineh i sira moo
roundabout (for traffic) o kikloforiakos komvos, i platia
round trip ticket: a round trip ticket to ... ena isitirio met epistrofis ya to ...
route i poria
what's the best route for ...? pios ineh o kaliteros thromos ya ...?
rubber (material) lastikho (eraser) i svistra, i goma
rubber band to lastikhaki
rubbish (waste) ta skoopithia (poor quality goods) kaki piotita
rubbish! (nonsense) trikhes!
rucksack to sakithio
rude a-yenis
ruins ta eripia, i arkheotites
rum to roomi
rum and coke ena roomi meh koka kola
run (person) trekho
how often do the buses run? poso sikh-na pernoon ta leoforia?
I've run out of money moo teliosan ta khrimata
rush hour ora ekhmis

S

sad lipimenos
saddle i sela
safe (not in danger) asfalis (not dangerous) akinthinos, avlavis
safety pin i paramana
sail to pani
sailboard to windsurf
sailboarding to windsurf
salad i salata
salad dressing to lathoxitho
sale: for sale politeh
salmon o solomos
Salonika i THesaloniki
salt to alati
same: the same o ithios
the same as this to ithio opos afto
the same again, please to ithio xana, parakalo
it's all the same to me to ithio moo kani
sand i amos
sandals ta santhalia
sandwich to sandwich
sanitary napkins i servi-etes
sanitary towels i servi-etes
sardines i sartheles
Saturday to Savato
sauce i saltsa
saucepan i katsarola
saucer to piataki
sauna i sa-oona
sausage to lookaniko
say: how do you say ... in Greek? pos to leneh ... sta

Elinika?
what did he say? ti ipeh?
I said ... ipa ...
he said ... ipeh ...
could you say that again? boriteh na to xanapiteh?, boriteh na to epanalaveteh?
scarf (for neck) to kaskol
(for head) to mandili
scenery to topio
schedule (US) to programa
scheduled flight i programatismeni ptisi
school to skholio
scissors: a pair of scissors to psalithi
scotch to skots whisky
Scotch tape® to sellotape®
Scotland i Skotia
Scottish Skotsezikos
I'm Scottish (man/woman) imeh Skotsezos/Skotseza
scrambled eggs ta khtipita avga
scratch i gratzoonia
screw i vitha
screwdriver to katsavithi
scuba diving i anapnefstiki siskevi katathiti
sea i THalasa
by the sea konda sti THalasa
seafood ta THalasina
seafood restaurant i psaro-taverna
seafront i paralia
on the seafront stin paralia
seagull o glaros
search psakh-no
seashell i akhivaTHa
seasick: I feel seasick esthanomeh naftia
I get seasick meh piani i THalasa
seaside: by the seaside konda stin paralia
seat i THesi
is this anyone's seat? ineh kanenos afti i THesi?
seat belt i zoni asfalias
sea urchin o akhinos
seaweed ta fikia
secluded apomeros
second (of time) to theftero-lepto
(adj) thefteros
just a second! mia stigmi!
second class (travel) thefteri THesi
second floor o thefteros orofos
(US) o tritos orofos
second-hand apo theftero kheri
see vlepo, kitazo
can I see? boro na tho?
have you seen ...? ekhis thi ...?
see you! ta xanalemeh!
I see (I understand) katalava
I saw him this morning ton itha simera to pro-i
self-catering apartment to anexartito thiamerisma
self-service self-servis
sell poolo
do you sell ...? poolateh ...?
Sellotape® to sellotape®
send stelno
I want to send this to England

thelo na stilo afto stin Anglia
senior citizen o/i sindaxi-ookhos
separate (adj) khoristos
separated: I'm separated (man/woman) imeh khorismenos/khorismeni
separately (pay, travel) xekhorista
September o Septemvrios
septic siptikos
serious sovaros
service charge (in restaurant) to filothorima
service station to venzinathiko
serviette i hartopetseta, i petseta
set menu to tabl-dot
several arketi
sew ravo
could you sew this back on? boriteh na to rapseteh pali sti THesi too?
sex to sex
shade: in the shade sti skia
shake: let's shake hands as thosoomeh ta kheria
shallow (water) rikha nera
shame: what a shame! ti krima!
shampoo to samboo-an
a shampoo and set ena loosimo meh mizampli
share (verb: room, table etc) mirazomeh
sharp (knife etc) kofteros
(taste, pain) thinatos
shattered (very tired) exandlimenos
shaver i xiristiki mikhani
shaving foam o afros xirismatos
shaving point i priza xiristikis mikhanis
she* afti
is she here? ineh etho?
sheet (for bed) to sendoni
shelf to rafi
shellfish ta ostraka
sherry to seri
ship to plio
by ship meh plio
shirt to pookamiso
shit! skata!
shock to sok
I got an electric shock from the ... ilektristika meh ...
shock-absorber to amortiser
shocking (behaviour, prices) exofrenikos
shoe to papootsi
a pair of shoes ena zevgari papootsia
shoelaces ta korthonia papootsion
shoe polish to verniki papootsion
shoe repairer o tsangaris
shop to magazi
shopping: I'm going shopping pao ya psonia
shopping centre to emboriko kendro
shop window i vitrina
shore i akti
short (person) kondos
(time) ligos

(journey) sindomos
shortcut o sindomos thromos
shorts to sorts
should: what should I do? ti prepi na kano?
he shouldn't be long then prepi na aryisi
you should have told me eprepeh na moo to ikhes pi
shoulder o omos
shout (verb) fonazo
show (in theatre) to ergo
could you show me? boriteh na moo thixeteh?
shower (in bathroom) to doos
(rain) i bora
with shower meh doos
shower gel to afrolootro
shut (verb) klino
when do you shut? poteh klineteh?
when do they shut? poteh klinoon?
they're shut ineh klista
I've shut myself out klistika apexo
shut up! skaseh!
shutter (on camera) to thiafragma
(on window) to exofilo, to pandzoori
shy dropalos
sick (ill) arostos
see **ill**
I'm going to be sick (vomit) ekho tasi pros emeto
side i plevra
the other side of town i ali akri tis polis
side lights ta khamila fota
side salad i salata ya garnitoora
side street to thromaki
sidewalk to pezothromio
sight: the sights of ... ta axioTHeata too ...
sightseeing: we're going sightseeing pameh na thoomeh ta axioTHeata
sightseeing tour i xenayisi sta axioTHeata
sign (roadsign etc) to sima
signal: he didn't give a signal then ekaneh sima
signature i ipografi
signpost i pinakitha, i tabela
silence i siopi
silk to metaxi
silly ano-itos
silver to asimi
silver foil to aloominokharto
similar omios
simple (easy) aplos
since: since yesterday apo kh-THes
since I got here apo toteh poo irTHa etho
sing tragootho
singer (man/woman) o tragoothistis/i tragoothistria
single (man/woman) monos
a single to ... ena aplo ya ...
I'm single imeh elefTHeros/elefTHeri
single bed to mono krevati
single room to mono thomatio
sink (in kitchen) o nerokhitis
sister i athelfi

sister-in-law (brother's wife) i nifi (wife's sister) i kooniatha
sit: can I sit here? boro na kaTHiso etho?
is anyone sitting here? kaTHeteh kanis etho?
sit down kaTHomeh
sit down! katseh kato!
site to axioTHeato (archaeological) arkheoloyikos khoros
size to meh-yeTHos
skin to therma
skindiving i katathisis
skinny kokaliaris
skirt i foosta
sky o ooranos
sleep (verb) kimameh
did you sleep well? kimiTHikes kala?
I need a good sleep khriazomeh ena kalo ipno
sleeper (on train) i kooketa
sleeping bag to sleeping bag
sleeping car i klinamaxa, i kooketa
sleeping pill to ipnotiko khapi
sleepy: I'm feeling sleepy nistazo
sleeve to maniki
slide (photographic) to slide
slip (under dress) to misofori
slippery glisteros
slow argos
slow down! pio arga
slowly siga-siga
could you say it slowly? boriteh na to piteh arga-arga?
very slowly poli arga
small mikros
smell: it smells (smells bad) vroma-i
smile (verb) khamo-yelo
smoke o kapnos
do you mind if I smoke? sas pirazi an kapniso?
I don't smoke then kapnizo
do you smoke? kapnizeteh?
snack: I'd just like a snack THa iTHela na fao kati prokhiyo
snake to fithi
sneeze to ftarnisma
snorkel o anapnefstiras
snow to khioni
so: it's so good ineh poli kalo
not so fast okhi toso grigora
so am I keh ego to ithio
so do I keh ego episis
so-so etsi ki etsi
soaking solution (for contact lenses) igro sindirisis fakon epafis
soap to sapooni
soap powder to aporipandiko
sober xemeTHistos
socks i kaltses
socket (electrical) i priza
soda (water) i sotha
sofa o kanapes
soft (material etc) apalos
soft-boiled egg to melato avgo
soft drink to anapsiktiko
soft lenses i malaki faki
sole i sola
could you put new soles on these? boriteh na moo valeteh kenooryi-es soles safta?

some: can I have some water/ rolls? moo thineteh ligo nero?/liga psomakia?
can I have some? boro na paro ligo?
somebody, someone kapios
something kati
something to drink kati na pi-iteh
sometimes merikes fores
somewhere kapoo
son o yos
song to tragoothi
son-in-law o gambros
soon sindoma
I'll be back soon THA yiriso sindoma
as soon as possible oso to thinaton grigorotera
sore: it's sore ineh ereTHismeno
sore throat pona-i o lemos moo
sorry: (I'm) sorry signomi
sorry? (didn't understand/hear) pardon?, signomi?
sort: what sort of ...? ti ithos ...?
soup i soopa
sour (taste) xinos
south notos
south of noti-a
in the south sto noto
to the south noti-a
South Africa i Noti-os Afriki
South African (adj) Notio-afrikanos
I'm South African (man/woman) imeh Notio-afrikanos/ Notio-afrikana
southeast notio-anatolikos
southwest notio-thitikos
souvenir to enTHimio
Spain i Ispania
Spanish (adj) ispanikos
(language) ta ispanika
spanner to klithi
spare part ta andalaktika
spare tyre i rezerva
spark plug to boozi
speak: do you speak English? milateh Anglika?
I don't speak ... then milo ...

dialogue

can I speak to Costas? boro na miliso ston Kosta, parakalo?
who's calling? pios ton zita-i?
it's Patricia i Patricia
I'm sorry, he's not in, can I take a message? lipameh, then ineh etho, boro na too thoso kapio minima?
no thanks, I'll call back later okhi, efkharisto, THA xanaparo argotera
please tell him I called parakalo, piteh too pos tilefonisa

speciality i spesialiteh
spectacles ta yali-a
speed i takhitita
speed limit to orio takhititas
speedometer to konder

spell: how do you spell it? pos to grafeteh?
see **alphabet** page 209
spend xothevo
spider i arakhni
spin-dryer to stegnotirio
splinter i agitha
spoke (in wheel) i aktina
spoon to kootali
sport to spor
sprain: I've sprained my ... straboolixa to ...
spring (season) i anixi
(in seat etc) to elatirio
square (in town) i platia
stairs ta skalopatia, i skales
stale (bread, taste) bayatikos
stall: the engine keeps stalling i mikhani sinekhos stamata
stamp to gramatosimo

dialogue

a stamp for England, please ena gramatosimo ya Anglia, parakalo
what are you sending? ti tha stileteh?
this postcard afti tin karta

star to asteri
(in film) o/i star
start i arkhi, to xekinima
(verb) arkhizo
when does it start? poteh arkhizi?
the car won't start to aftokinito then xekina
starter (of car) i miza
(food) to proto piato
starters ta orektika
starving: I'm starving petheno tis pinas
state (in country) i politia
the States (USA) i Inomenes Politi-es
station o stathmos
statue to agalma
stay: where are you staying? poo meneteh?
I'm staying at ... meno sto ...
I'd like to stay another two nights tha ithela na mino ales thio nikhtes
steak i brizola
steal klevo
my bag has been stolen klepsaneh tin tsanda moo
steep (hill) apotomos
steering to timoni
step: on the steps sta skalopati-a
stereo to stereofoniko singrotima
sterling i lira sterlina
steward (on plane) o a-erosinothos
stewardess i a-erosinothos
sticking plaster to lefkoplast
still: I'm still waiting akoma perimeno
is he still there? ineh akoma eki?
keep still! stasoo akinitos!
sting: I've been stung by ... meh tsibiseh ...
stockings i na-ilon kaltses
stomach to stomakhi

stomach ache o ponos sto stomakhi, o stomakhoponos
stone (rock) i petra
stop stamatao
please, stop here (to taxi driver etc) parakalo, stamatisteh etho
do you stop near ...? stamatateh konda ...?
stop doing that! stamata na to kanis afto!
stopover i stasi
storm i THi-ela
straight: it's straight ahead ineh olo efTHia
a straight whisky ena sketo whisky
straightaway amesos
strange (odd) paraxenos
stranger (man/woman) o xenos/i xeni
I'm a stranger here imeh xenos etho
strap to loori
strawberry i fraoola
stream to rema, to potamaki
street o thromos
on the street sto thromo
streetmap o othikos khartis
string (cord) o spangos
(guitar etc) i khorthi
strong thinatos
stuck frakarismenos
the key's stuck koliseh to klithi
student o fititis, i fititria
stupid vlakas
suburb ta pro-astia
subway (US: railway) o ipo-yios
suddenly xafnika
suede to kastori
sugar i zakhari
suit (man's) to koostoomi
(woman's) to ta-yer
it doesn't suit me (jacket etc) then moo pa-i
it suits you soo pa-i
suitcase i valitsa
summer to kalokeri
in the summer to kalokeri
sun o ilios
in the sun ston ilio
out of the sun sti skia
sunbathe kano ilioTHerapia
sunblock (cream) to andiliako
sunburn to kapsimo apo ton ilio
sunburnt kamenos apo ton ilio
Sunday i Kiriaki
sunglasses ta yalia ilioo
sun lounger i shez long
sunny: it's sunny ekhi liakatha
sun roof (in car) i tzamenia skepi
sunset i thisi too ilioo
sunshade i ombrela ilioo
sunshine i liakatha
sunstroke i ili-asi
suntan to mavrisma
suntan lotion to lathi mavrismatos
suntanned iliokamenos
suntan oil to lathi mavrismatos
super katapliktikos
supermarket to supermarket
supper to thipno
supplement (extra charge) epipleon, to prosTHeto
sure: are you sure? iseh

sigooros?
sure! veveos!
surname to epiTHeto
swearword i vrisia
sweater to poolover
sweatshirt i fanela
Sweden i Soo-ithia
Swedish (adj) Soo-ithikos
sweet (taste) glikos
(dessert) to gliko
sweets i karameles
swelling to priximo
swim kolimbao
I'm going for a swim pao ya kolibi
let's go for a swim pameh ya kolibi
swimming costume to ma-yo
swimming pool i pisina
swimming trunks to ma-yo
switch o thiakoptis
switch off (engine) svino
(TV, lights) klino
switch on (engine) anavo
(TV, lights) anigo
swollen prismenos

T

table to trapezi
a table for two ena trapezi ya thio
tablecloth to trapezomandilo
table tennis to ping-pong
table wine to epitrapezio krasi
tailback (of traffic) i oora
tailor o raftis
take (lead) perno
(accept) thekhomeh
can you take me to the airport? boriteh na meh pateh sto a-erothromio?
do you take credit cards? thekhesteh pistotikes kartes?
fine, I'll take it endaxi THa to paro
can I take this? (leaflet etc) boro na paro afto?
how long does it take? posi ora THa pari?
it takes three hours perni tris ores
is this seat taken? ineh piasmeni i THesi?
hamburger to take away khamboorger ya to spiti
can you take a little off here? (to hairdresser) boriteh na pareteh ligo apo etho?
talcum powder i poothra talk
talk (verb) milo
tall psilos
tampons ta tampax®, ta tabon
tan to mavrisma
to get a tan mavrizo
tank (of car) to depozito
tap i vrisi
tape (cassette) i kaseta
(sticky) i tenia
tape measure to metro
tape recorder to magnitofono
taste i yefsi
can I taste it? boro na to thokimaso?
taxi to taxi
will you get me a taxi? THa moo kaleseteh ena taxi?

where can I find a taxi? poo boro na vro ena taxi?

dialogue

to the airport/to the Hilton Hotel please
sto a-erothromio/sto xenothokhio Khilton, parakalo
how much will it be? poso THa stikhisi?
1,500 drachmas khili-es pendakosi-es thrakmes
that's fine, right here, thanks endaxi, etho pera ineh, efkharisto

taxi-driver o taxidzis
taxi rank o staTHmos taxi
tea to tsa-i
tea for one/two please tsa-i ya enan/thio parakalo
teabags ta fakelakia tsa-i
teach: could you teach me? boris na meh maTHis?
teacher (man/woman) o thaskalos/i thaskala
team i omatha
teaspoon to kootalaki
tea towel i petseta koozinas
teenager o neos, i nea
telephone to tilefono
television i tileorasi
tell: could you tell him ...? boriteh na too piteh ...?
temperature (weather) i THermokrasia
(fever) o piretos
temple (church) o na-os
tennis to tennis
tennis ball i bala too tennis
tennis court to yipetho tennis
tennis racket i raketa tennis
tent i skini
term (at university, school) i s-kholiki periothos
terminus (rail) to terma
terrible foveros
terrific exeretikos
text (message) to minima sto kinto
than* apo
smaller than mikroteros apo
thanks, thank you efkharisto
thank you very much efkharisto para poli
thanks for the lift efkharisto poo meh pirateh
no thanks okhi efkharisto

dialogue

thanks efkharisto
that's OK, don't mention it parakalo, then kani tipoteh

that ekinos, ekini, ekino
that one ekino
I hope that ... elpizo oti ...
that's nice ti orea!
is that ...? afto ineh ...?
that's it (that's right) akrivos
the* o, i, to; (pl) i, i, ta
theatre to THeatro
their* o/i/to ... toos
theirs* thiki toos
them* toos, tis, ta

for them ya ekinoos
with them maftoos
I gave it to them to ethosa saftoos
who? – them pi-i? – afti
then (at that time) toteh
(after that) katopin
there eki
over there eki pera
up there eki pano
is there ...? iparkhi ...?
are there ...? iparkhoon ...?
there is ... iparkhi ...
there are ... iparkhoon ...
there you are (giving something) oristeh
thermometer to THermometro
Thermos flask® to THermos
these afti, aftes, afta
can I have these? boro na ekho afta?
Thessaly i THesalia
they* afti, aftes, afta
thick pakhis
(stupid) khazos
thief (man/woman) o kleftis/i kleftra
thigh to booti
thin leptos
(person) athinatos
thing to pragma
my things ta pragmata moo
think skeptomeh
(believe) nomizo
I think so etsi nomizo
I don't think so then nomizo
I'll think about it THa to skepto
third party insurance asfalia ya khrisi apo tritoos
thirsty: I'm thirsty thipso
this aftos, afti, afto
this one afto etho
this is my wife apo etho i yineka moo
is this ...? ineh ...?
those ekini, ekines, ekina
which ones? – those pi-a? – afta
Thrace i THraki
thread i klosti
throat o lemos
throat pastilles pastili-es lemoo
through thiamesoo
does it go through ...? (train, bus) perna-i apo to ...?
throw (verb) rikhno
throw away (verb) peto
thumb o andikhiras
thunderstorm i kateyitha
Thursday i Pempti
ticket to isitirio

dialogue

a return to Athens ena isitirio epistrofis ya tin ATHina
coming back when? poteh ineh i epistrofi?
today/next Tuesday simera/tin epomeni Triti
that will be 2,000 drachmas thio khiliathes thrakhmes, parakalo

ticket office (bus, rail) i THiritha
tide i paliri-a
tie (necktie) i gravata

tight (clothes etc) stenos
it's too tight ineh poli steno
tights to kalson
till mekhri
time* o khronos
(occasion) i fora
what's the time? ti ora ineh?
this time afti ti fora
last time tin perasmeni fora
next time tin epomeni fora
four times teseris fores
timetable to programa
tin (can) i konserva
tinfoil to asimokharto
tin-opener to anikhtiri
tiny mikroskopikos
tip (to waiter etc) to filothorima
tired koorasmenos
I'm tired imeh koorasmenos
tissues ta khartomandila
to: to Salonica/London ya tin Thesaloniki/to Lonthino
to Greece/England ya tin Elatha/Anglia
to the post office sto takhithromio
toast (bread) to tost
today simera
toe to thakhtilo too pothioo
together mazi
we're together (in shop etc) imasteh mazi
can we pay together? boroomeh na plirosoomeh mazi?
toilet i too-aleta
where is the toilet? poo ineh i too-aleta?
I have to go to the toilet prepi na pao stin too-aleta
toilet paper kharti iyias
tomato i domata
tomato juice to domatozoomo, o domatokhimos
tomato ketchup to ketsap
tomorrow avrio
tomorrow morning avrio to pro-i
the day after tomorrow methavrio
toner (cosmetic) to tonotiko
tongue i glosa
tonic (water) to tonik
tonight apopseh
tonsillitis i amigthalititha
too (excessively) poli
(also) episis
too hot poli kafto
too much para poli
me too kego episis
tooth to thondi
toothache o ponothondos
toothbrush i othondovoortsa
toothpaste i othondokrema
top: on top of ... pano apo ...
at the top stin korifi
top floor to retire
topless yimnostiTHi
torch o fakos
total to sinolo
tour i peri-iyisi, i xenayisi
is there a tour of ...? iparkhi peri-iyisi ya ...?
tour guide o/i xenagos
tourist (man/woman) o tooristas/ i tooristria
tourist information office Grafio Pliroforion E-OT

tour operator to taxithiotiko grafio
towards pros
towel i petseta
town i poli
 in town stin poli
 just out of town akrivos exo apo tin poli
town centre to kendro tis polis
town hall to thimarkhio
toy to pekh-nithi
track (US) i platforma
 see **platform**
tracksuit i aTHlitiki forma
traditional parathosiakos
traffic i kikloforia
traffic jam i kikloforiaki simforisi
traffic lights ta fanaria tis trokheas
trailer (for carrying tent etc) i rimoolka
 (US: caravan) to trokhospito
trailer park topoTHesia ya trokhospita
train to treno
 by train meh treno

dialogue

> **is this the train for ...?** afto ineh to treno ya ...?
> **sure** neh
> **no, you want that platform there** okhi, THa pateh seh ekini tin platforma eki

trainers (shoes) ta aTHlitika papootsia
train station o sithiro-thromikos staTHmos
tram to tram
translate metafrazo
 could you translate that? boriteh na metafraseteh afto?
translation i metafrasi
translator o/i metafrastis
trashcan o skoopithodenekes
travel taxithevo
 we're travelling around taxithevoomeh triyiro
travel agent's to taxithiotiko grafio
traveller's cheque i taxithiotiki epitayi
tray o thiskos
tree to thendro
tremendous tromeros
trendy modernos
trim: just a trim please (to hairdresser) ligo konditera, parakalo
trip (excursion) to taxithi
 I'd like to go on a trip to ... THa iTHela na pao ena taxithi stin ...
trolley to trolley, to karotsaki
trolleybus to trolley
trouble o belas
 I'm having trouble with ... ekho provlimata meh ...
 sorry to trouble you meh sinkhoriteh poo sas vazo seh mbela
trousers to pandaloni
true aliTHinos
 that's not true then ineh aliTHia

trunk (US: of car) to port-bagaz
trunks (swimming) to mayo
try prospaTHo, thokimazo
 can I have a try? boro na thokimaso?
try on provaro
 can I try it on? boro na to thokimaso pano moo?
T-shirt to bloozaki
Tuesday i Triti
tuna o tonos
tunnel i siraga
Turkey i Toorkia
Turkish (adj) Toorkikos
Turkish coffee Toorkikos kafes, Elinikos kafes
Turkish-Cypriot (adj) Toorkiko-Kipriakos
turn: turn left/right stripseh aristera/thexia
 where do I turn off? poo strivo?
turn off: can you turn the heating off? boris na klisis ti THermansi/to kalorifer?
turn on: can you turn the heating on? boris na anixis ti THermansi/to kalorifer?
turning (in road) i strofi
TV i tileorasi
tweezers to tsimbithaki
twice thio fores
 twice as much ta thipla
twin beds thio krevatia
twin room to thomatio meh thio krevatia
twist: I've twisted my ankle stramboolixa ton astragalo moo
type to ithos
 a different type of ... ena alo ithos apo ...
typical kharaktiristikos
tyre to lastikho

U

ugly askhimos
UK to Inomeno Vasili-o
ulcer to elkos
umbrella i ombrela
uncle o THios
unconscious anesTHitos
under apo kato
 (less than) ligotero apo
underdone (meat) misop-simenos
underground (railway) o ipo-yios
underpants to sovrako, to slip
understand: I understand katalaveno
 I don't understand then katalaveno
 do you understand? katalavenis?
unemployed anergos
United States i Inomenes Politi-es
university to panepistimio
unleaded petrol i amolivthi venzini
unlimited mileage aperiorista khiliometra
unlock xeklithono
unpack anigo tis valitses
until mekhri

unusual asiniTHistos
up pano
(upwards) pros ta pano
up there eki pano
he's not up yet (not out of bed) then sikoTHikeh akomi
what's up? (what's wrong?) ti yineteh?
upmarket (restaurant etc) akrivos
upset stomach o stomakhoponos
upside down ta pano kato
upstairs pano
urgent epigon
us* mas
with us meh mas
for us ya mas
use khrisimopi-o
may I use ...? boro na khrisimopi-iso ...?
useful khrisimos
usual siniTHismenos
the usual (drink etc) to siniTHismeno

V

vacancy: do you have any vacancies? (hotel) ekheteh elefTHera thomatia?
vacation i thiakopes
see **holiday**
vaccination o emvoliasmos
vacuum cleaner i ilektriki skoopa
valid (ticket etc) engiros
how long is it valid for? ya poso is-khi-i?
valley i kilatha
valuable (adj) politimos
can I leave my valuables here? boro na afiso ta timalfi moo etho?
value i axia
van to trokhospito
vanilla i vanilia
a vanilla ice cream ena pagoto vanilia
vary: it varies metavaleteh
vase to vazo
veal to moskhari
vegetables ta lakhanika
vegetarian o/i khortofagos
vending machine o aftomatos politis
very poli
very little for me poli ligo ya mena
I like it very much moo aresi para poli
vest (under shirt) to fanelaki
via thia mesoo
video (film) i video-tenia
(video recorder) to video
view i THea
villa i vila
village to khorio
vinegar to xithi
vineyard to ambeli
visa i viza
visit (verb) episkeptomeh
I'd like to visit ... THa iThela na episkefto ...
vital: it's vital that ... ineh vasiko na ...
vodka i votka
voice i foni

volleyball to volley-ball, i khirosferisi
voltage i tasis
vomit (verb) kano emeto

W

waist i mesi
waistcoat to yileko
wait perimeno
wait for me perimeneh meh!
don't wait for me mi meh perimenis
can I wait until my wife gets here? boro na paragilo otan eltHi i yineka moo?
can you do it while I wait? na perimeno na to kaneteh?
could you wait here for me? boriteh na meh perimeneteh na yiriso?
waiter o servitoros
waiter! garson!
waitress i garsona, i servitora
waitress! sas parakalo!
wake: can you wake me up at 5.30? boriteh na meh xipniseteh stis pendeh keh misi?
wake-up call tilefonima ya xipnima
Wales i Oo-alia
walk: is it a long walk? ineh poli perpatima?
it's only a short walk ekhi ligo perpatima
I'll walk THa perpatiso
I'm going for a walk pao ena peripato
Walkman® to walkman®
wall o tikhos
wallet to portofoli
wander: I like just wandering around moo aresi na khazevo triyiro
want: I want a ... THelo ena ...
I don't want any ... then THelo ...
I want to go home THelo na pao spiti moo
I don't want to then THelo
he wants to ... THeli na ...
what do you want? ti THelis?
ward (in hospital) o THalamos
warm zestos
I'm so warm zestenomeh arketa
was*: I was ... imoon ...
he/she/it was ... itan ...
wash (verb) pleno
(oneself) plenomeh
can you wash these? boriteh na plineteh afta?
washer (for bolt etc) i rothela
washhand basin o niptiras
washing (clothes) i boogatha
washing machine to plindirio
washing powder i skoni plindirioo, to aporipandiko
washing-up liquid to sapooni piaton
wasp i sfinga
watch (wristwatch) to rolo-i
will you watch my things for me? boriteh na prosekheteh

ta pragmata moo?
watch out! prosekheh!
watch strap to looraki roloyioo
water to nero
may I have some water? moo thineteh ligo nero?
waterproof (adj) athi-avrokhos
waterskiing to THalasio ski
wave (in sea) to kima
way: could you tell me the way to ...? boriteh na moo piteh pos THa pa-o sto ..?
it's this way apo etho ineh
it's that way apo eki ineh
is it a long way to ...? ineh makri-a ya to ...?
no way! apokli-eteh!

dialogue

could you tell me the way to ...? boriteh na moo thixeteh to thromo ya ...?
go straight on until you reach the traffic lights piyeneteh olo isia mekhri na ftaseteh sta fanaria
turn left stripsteh aristera
take the first on the right parteh ton proto thromo sta thexia
see where

we* emis
weak athinatos
weather o keros

dialogue

what's the weather forecast? ti ipeh to theltio keroo?
it's going to be fine THa ineh kalos keros
it's going to rain THa vrexi
it'll brighten up later THa anixi o keros argotera

wedding o gamos
wedding ring i vera
Wednesday i Tetarti
week i evthomatha
a week (from) today seh mia evthomatha apo simera
a week (from) tomorrow seh mia evthomatha apo avrio
weekend to Savatokiriako
at the weekend to Savatokiriako
weight to varos
weird paraxenos
weirdo o trelaras
welcome: welcome to ... kalos ilTHateh sto ...
you're welcome (don't mention it) parakalo
well: I don't feel well then esTHanomeh kala
she's not well ekini then ineh kala
you speak English very well milateh poli kala Anglika
well done! bravo
this one as well ki afto episis
well well! (surprise) ya thes!

dialogue

how are you? ti kanis?
very well, thanks poli kala, efkharisto
and you? ki esi?

well-done (meat) kalopsimenos
Welsh Oo-alos
I'm Welsh (man/woman) imeh Oo-alos/Oo-ali
were*: we were imasteh
you were isasteh/isteh
they were itan
west thitikos
in the west sta thitika
West Indian (adj) apo tis thitikes Inthi-es
wet vregmenos
what? ti?
what's that? ti ineh ekino?
what should I do? ti prepi na kano?
what a view! ti THea!
what bus do I take? ti leoforio prepi na paro?
wheel i rotha
wheelchair i anapiriki poliTHrona
when? poteh?
when we get back otan yirisoomeh
when's the train/ferry? poteh fevyi to treno/to karavi?
where? poo?
I don't know where it is then xero poo ineh

dialogue

where is the cathedral? poo ineh o kaTHethrikos naos?
it's over there ineh eki pera
could you show me where it is on the map? boriteh na moo thixeteh sto kharti poo ineh?
it's just here ineh akrivos etho
see way

which: which bus? pio leoforio?

dialogue

which one? pio?
that one ekino
this one? afto?
no, that one okhi, ekino

while: while I'm here oso imeh etho
whisky to whisky
white aspros
white wine to aspro krasi
who? pios?
who is it? pios ineh?
the man who ... o anTHropos poo ...
whole: the whole week oli tin evthomatha
the whole lot ola
whose: whose is this? pianoo ineh afto?
why? yati?

why not? yati okhi?
wide platis
wife: my wife i sizigos moo
will: will you do it for me? THA moo to kanis afto?
wind o anemos
window to paraTHiro
near the window konda sto paraTHiro
in the window (of shop) sti vitrina
window seat i THesi sto paraTHiro
windscreen to parbriz
windscreen wiper o ialokaTHaristiras
windsurfing to windsurfing
windy: it's so windy ekhi poli a-era
wine to krasi
can we have some more wine? boroomeh na ekhoomeh ligo krasi akoma?
wine list o katalogos ton krasion
winter o khimonas
in the winter ton khimona
winter holiday i khimerines thiakopes
wire to sirma
(electric) to ilektriko kalothio
wish: best wishes poles efkhes
with meh
I'm staying with ... meno meh ...
without khoris
witness o/i martiras
will you be a witness for me? THA iseh martiras moo?
woman i yineka
wonderful THavmasios
won't*: it won't start then THA xekinisi
wood (material) to xilo
woods (forest) to thasos
wool to mali
word i lexi
work i thoolia
it's not working then thoolevi
I work in ... ergazomeh seh ...
world o kosmos
worry: I'm worried stenokhoriemeh
worry beads to kombolo-i
worse: it's worse ineh khirotera
worst o khiroteros
worth: is it worth a visit? axizi mia episkepsi?
would: would you give this to ...? boriteh na thoseteh afto ston ...?
wrap: could you wrap it up? boriteh na to tilixeteh?
wrapping paper to kharti peritiligmatos
(for presents) kharti ya thora
wrist o karpos
write grafo
could you write it down? boriteh na moo to grapseteh?
how do you write it? pos to grafeteh?
writing paper to kharti alilografias
wrong: it's the wrong key afto

ineh lathos klithi
the bill's wrong o logariasmos ineh lathos
sorry, wrong number signomi, lathos noomero
sorry, wrong room signomi, lathos thomatio
there's something wrong with ... iparkhi kapio lathos meh ...
what's wrong? ti simveni?

X

X-ray i aktinografia

Y

yacht to yot
yard* i yartha
(courtyard, backyard) i avli
year o khronos
yellow kitrinos
yes neh
yesterday kh-thes
yesterday morning kh-thes to pro-i
the day before yesterday prokh-thes
yet akomi

dialogue

has it arrived yet? akomi then eftaseh?
no, not yet okhi, okhi akomi
you'll have to wait a little longer yet tha prepi na perimeneteh akomi ligo

yoghurt to ya-oorti
you* (fam) esi
(pl or polite) esis
I'll see you later tha seh tho argotera
this is for you afto ineh ya sas
with you mazi sas
young neos
your* (fam) o/i/to ... soo
(pl or polite) o/i/to ... sas
your camera i fotografiki mikhani soo/sas
yours (fam) thiko soo
(pl or polite) thiko sas
youth hostel o xenonas neon

Z

zero mithen
zip to fermoo-ar
could you put a new zip in? boriteh na valeteh ena kenoor-yio fermoo-ar?
zip code o takhithromikos kothikos
zoo o zo-oloyikos kipos

Greek

English

Colloquial Greek

The following are words or expressions you might well hear. You shouldn't be tempted to use any of the stronger ones unless you are sure of your audience.

άντε γαμήσου [andeh gamisoo] fuck off!
βλάκα [vlaka] idiot, blockhead
βρωμο... [vromo] bloody ...
γαμώ το! [gamo to] fuck!
γκόμενα [gomena] bird, chick
γουστάρω [goostaro] I feel like it
δεν πειράζει [den pirazi] it doesn't matter
είσαι; [iseh] do you want to?
έλα [ela] come on!, move!
θαυμάσια! [THavmasia] great!
in [in] fashionable
καμάκι [kamaki] stud, Don Juan
κερατάς [keratas] bastard
μαλάκα [malaka] wanker
μου τα'πρηξες [moo taprixes] you're getting on my tits, you're getting up my nose
μπάτσος [batsos] cop
Παναγία μου [Panayia moo] my God!
πούστης [poostis] faggot, poofter
πουτάνα [pootana] whore
πώ πώ! [po po] bloody hell!
ρε Κώστα [reh Kosta] Kostas, my old pal
ρε μαλάκα [reh malaka] you stupid wanker
σκάσε! [skaseh] shut up!
σκατά! [skata] shit!
στ'αρχίδια μου [starkhidia moo] I don't give a fuck
τζάμπα [tzamba] dirt cheap
τί γίνεται; [ti yineteh] how is it going?
τί νά κάνουμε; [ti na kanoomeh] what can you do?
τύφλα στο μεθύσι [tifla sto meTHisi] pissed (drunk)

A

αγάπη (η) [agapi (i)] love
αγαπημένος [agapimenos] favourite
αγαπώ [agapo] love (verb)
αγγίζω [angizo] touch (verb)
ΑΓΓΛΙΑ Αγγλία (η) [Anglia (i)] England
Αγγλίδα (η) [Anglitha (i)] Englishwoman
ΑΓΓΛΙΚΑ Αγγλικά (τα) [Anglika (ta)] English
ΑΓΓΛΙΚΟΣ Αγγλικός [Anglikos] English
άγγλος (ο) [Anglos (o)] Englishman
αγελάδα (η) [ayelatha (i)] cow
αγενής [ayenis] rude
άγκυρα (η) [angira (i)] anchor
αγκώνας (ο) [angonas (o)] elbow
ΑΓΝΟ ΠΑΡΘΕΝΟ ΜΑΛΛΙ αγνό παρθένο μαλλί pure new wool
ΑΓΟΡΑ αγορά (η) [agora (i)] market
αγοράζω [agorazo] buy (verb)
αγόρι (το) [agori (to)] boy
άγριος [agrios] wild, fierce
αγρόκτημα (το) [agroktima (to)] farm
αγρότης (ο) [agrotis (o)] farmer
αγώνας (ο) [agonas (o)] fight, struggle; game
άδεια (η) [athia (i)] licence; permission
άδεια οδηγήσεως (η) [athia othiyiseos (i)] driving licence
άδειος [athios] empty, vacant
αδελφή (η) [athelfi (i)] sister
ΑΔΕΛΦΟΙ αδελφοί brothers
αδελφός (ο) [athelfos (o)] brother
ΑΔΙΕΞΟΔΟ αδιέξοδο cul-de-sac, dead end
αδύνατος [athinatos] impossible; weak
Α.Ε. public limited company
ΑΕΡΑΝΤΛΙΑ αεραντλία (η) air pump
αέρας (ο) [aeras (o)] air; wind; choke
ΑΕΡΟΔΡΟΜΙΟ αεροδρόμιο (το) [aerothromio (to)] airport
ΑΕΡΟΛΙΜΗΝ αερολιμήν (ο) [aerolimin (o)] airport
αεροπλάνο (το) [aeroplano (to)] plane
αεροπορική εταιρεία (η) [aeroporiki eteria (i)] airline
ΑΕΡΟΠΟΡΙΚΩΣ αεροπορικώς [aeroporikos] by air; by air mail
ΑΕΡΟΣΥΝΟΔΟΣ αεροσυνοδός (ο/η) [aerosinothos (o/i)] steward, stewardess
ΑΘΗΝΑ Αθήνα (η) [ATHina (i)] Athens
αθλητής (ο) [aTHlitis (o)] athlete
ΑΘΛΗΤΙΚΑ αθλητικά (τα) [aTHlitika (ta)] sports shop
αθλητικά παπούτσια (τα) [aTHlitika papootsia (ta)] trainers
ΑΘΛΗΤΙΚΕΣ ΕΓΚΑΤΑΣΤΑΣΕΙΣ αθλητικές εγκαταστάσεις sporting facilities
αθλητική φόρμα (η) [aTHlitiki forma (i)] tracksuit
ΑΘΛΗΤΙΚΟ ΚΕΝΤΡΟ αθλητικό

κέντρο (το) [aTHlitiko kendro (to)] sports centre
αθώος [aTHoos] innocent
ΑΙΓΑΙΟ Αιγαίο (το) [E-yeo (to)] Aegean
ΑΙΘΟΥΣΑ ΤΡΑΝΖΙΤ αίθουσα τράνζιτ transit lounge
αίμα (το) [ema (to)] blood
αιμορραγώ [emoragO] bleed
αισθάνομαι [esTHanomeh] feel (verb)
ΑΙΤΗΣΗ αίτηση (η) [etisi (i)] application form; application
αιτία (η) [etia (i)] cause; reason
εξ αιτίας ... [exetias ...] because of ...
αιώνας (ο) [eonas (o)] century
ΑΚΑΤΑΛΛΗΛΟ ακατάλληλο adults only
Α΄ ΚΑΤΗΓΟΡΙΑΣ Α΄ κατηγορίας first class
ακολουθώ [akolooTHO] follow
ακόμα, ακόμη [akoma, akomi] still, yet; even; also
ακουστικά (τα) [akoostika (ta)] hearing aid; headphones
ΑΚΟΥΣΤΙΚΟ ακουστικό (το) [akoostiko (to)] receiver
ακούω [akoo-o] hear; listen
άκρη (η) [akri (i)] edge; end; tip
ΑΚΡΙΒΕΣ ΑΝΤΙΤΙΜΟ ΜΟΝΟ ακριβές αντίτιμο μόνο exact fare only
ακριβός [akrivos] expensive
ακροατήριο (το) [akroatirio (to)] audience
ΑΚΡΥΛΙΚΟ ακρυλικό [akriliko] acrylic
ΑΚΤΗ ακτή (η) [akti (i)] beach; coast, shore
ακυρώνω [akirono] cancel
ΑΛΒΑΝΙΑ Αλβανία (η) [Alvania (i)] Albania
αληθινός [aliTHinos] true; real
αλλά [alla] but
ΑΛΛΑΓΗ ΛΑΔΙΩΝ αλλαγή λαδιών oil change
αλλάζω [allazo] change (verb)
αλλάζω ρούχα [allazo rookha] change one's clothes
ΑΛΛΕΡΓΙΑ αλλεργία (η) [alleryia (i)] allergy
ΑΛΛΕΡΓΙΑ ΣΤΗ ΓΥΡΗ αλλεργία στη γύρη [alleryia sti yiri] hay fever
αλλεργικός σε [alleryikos seh] allergic to
άλλη [ali] other; else
άλλη μία [ali mia] another
άλλο [alo] other; else; another
όχι άλλο [okhi alo] no more
άλλο ένα [alo ena] another
άλλος [alos] other; else
άλλος ένας [alos enas] another
αλλού [aloo] elsewhere
αλμυρός [almiros] salty
άλογο (το) [alogo (to)] horse
ΑΛΟΙΦΗ αλοιφή (η) [alifi (i)] ointment
αλουμινόχαρτο (το) [aloominokharto (to)] aluminium foil
ΑΛΣΟΣ άλσος (το) [alsos (to)] wooded park, grove
αλτ! [alt!] stop!
αλυσίδα (η) [alisitha (i)] chain
ΑΜΑΞΑ άμαξα (η) [amaxa (i)] coach, car (on train)

ΑΜΑΞΙ αμάξι (το) [amaxi (to)] car (on train)
ΑΜΑΞΟΣΤΟΙΧΙΑ αμαξοστοιχία (η) [amaxostikhia (i)] train
Αμερικανίδα (η) [Amerikanitha (i)] American (woman)
Αμερικανικός [Amerikanikos] American (adj)
Αμερικανός (ο) [Amerikanos (o)] American (man)
ΑΜΕΡΙΚΗ Αμερική (η) [Ameriki (i)] America
ΑΜΕΣΟΣ ΔΡΑΣΙΣ άμεσος δράσις emergencies
αμέσως [amesos] immediately
αμμόλοφοι (οι) [amolofi (i)] sand dunes
άμμος (η) [amos (i)] sand
αμορτισέρ (το) [amortiser (to)] shock-absorber
αμπέλι (το) [ambeli (to)] vineyard
αμπέρ (το) [amper] amp
ΑΜΠΟΥΛΕΣ αμπούλες ampoules
αν [an] if
ΑΝΑΒΡΑΖΟΝΤΑ ΔΙΣΚΙΑ αναβράζοντα δισκία effervescent tablets
ανάβω [anavo] light (verb)
αναγκαίος [angeos] necessary
ανάγκη [angi] need
αναγνωρίζω [anagnorizo] recognize, acknowledge, admit
ανακατεύω [anakatevo] mix (verb)
ΑΝΑΚΟΙΝΩΣΗ ανακοίνωση (η) [anakinosi (i)] announcement
ΑΝΑΚΛΗΣΙΣ ανάκλησις (η) [anaklisis (i)] withdrawal
ΑΝΑΛΗΨΗ ανάληψη withdrawal(s) (of money)
αναμείνατε στο ακουστικό [anaminateh sto akoostiko] hold the line please
ανάμεσα [anamesa] among; between
αναπαύομαι [anapavomeh] rest, relax
ανάπαυση (η) [anapafsi (i)] rest
αναπαυτικός [anapaftikos] comfortable
αναπηρική πολυθρόνα (η) [anapiriki poliTHrona (i)] wheelchair
ανάπηρος [anapiros] disabled
αναπνέω [anapneo] breathe
αναποδογυρίζω [anapothoyirizo] knock over
αναπτήρας (ο) [anaptiras (o)] lighter
αναπτύσσω [anaptiso] develop; explain
ανατολή (η) [anatoli (i)] east; dawn
ανατολή του ήλιου (η) [anatoli too ilioo (i)] sunrise
ΑΝΑΧΩΡΕΙ ΚΑΘΗΜΕΡΙΝΑ ΓΙΑ ... αναχωρεί καθημερινά γιά ... departs daily to ...
ΑΝΑΧΩΡΗΣΕΙΣ αναχωρήσεις departures
ΑΝΑΧΩΡΗΣΗ αναχώρηση (η) [anakhorisi (i)] departure
ΑΝΑΨΥΚΤΗΡΙΟ αναψυκτήριο refreshments
άνδρας (ο) [anthras (o)] man
ΑΝΔΡΙΚΑ ανδρικά (τα) [anthrika

(ta)] menswear
ΑΝΔΡΙΚΑ ΕΙΔΗ ΚΑΙ ΑΞΕΣΟΥΑΡ **ανδρικά είδη και αξεσουάρ** men's fashions and accessories
ΑΝΔΡΙΚΑ ΕΝΔΥΜΑΤΑ **ανδρικά ενδύματα** [anthrika enthimata] menswear
ΑΝΔΡΙΚΑ ΕΣΩΡΟΥΧΑ **ανδρικά εσώρουχα** [anthrika esorookha] men's underwear
ΑΝΔΡΙΚΑΙ ΚΟΜΜΩΣΕΙΣ **ανδρικαί κομμώσεις** [anthrikeh komosis] men's hairdresser
ΑΝΔΡΙΚΑ ΥΠΟΔΗΜΑΤΑ **ανδρικά υποδήματα** [anthrika ipothimata] men's footwear
ΑΝΔΡΙΚΑ ΥΠΟΚΑΜΙΣΑ **ανδρικά υποκάμισα** [anthrika ipokamisa] men's shirts
ΑΝΔΡΩΝ **ανδρών** gents' (toilet), men's room
ανεβαίνω [aneveno] get in (car); get up; go up
ΑΝΕΛΚΥΣΤΗΡΑΣ **ανελκυστήρας (ο)** [anelkistiras (o)] lift, elevator
ΑΝΕΜΙΣΤΗΡΑΣ **ανεμιστήρας (ο)** [anemistiras (o)] fan
άνεμος (ο) [anemos (o)] wind
ΑΝΕΞΑΡΤΗΤΟ ΔΙΑΜΕΡΙΣΜΑ **ανεξάρτητο διαμέρισμα (το)** [anexartito thiamerisma (to)] self-catering apartment
ανεξάρτητος [anexartitos] independent
άνεργος [anergos] unemployed
ανήκω [aniko] belong
ανησυχώ [anisikho] be anxious, be worried
ανησυχώ για [anisikho ya] worry about
ανηψιά (η) [anipsia (i)] niece
ανηψιός (ο) [anipsios (o)] nephew
ΑΝΘΟΠΩΛΕΙΟ **ανθοπωλείο (το)** [anThopolio (to)] florist's
άνθρωποι (οι) [anThropi (i)] people
αν και [an keh] although
ΑΝΟΔΟΣ **άνοδος (η)** [anothos (i)] ascent, way up
ανοίγω [anigo] open (verb); switch on
ανοίγω τις βαλίτσες [anigo tis valitses] unpack
ΑΝΟΙΚΤΑ **ανοικτά** [anikta] open
ΑΝΟΙΚΤΟ ΑΠΟ ... ΩΣ ... **ανοικτό από ... ως ...** [anikto apo ... os ...] open from ... to ...
ΑΝΟΙΚΤΟΝ **ανοικτόν** [anikton] open (adj)
ανοικτός [aniktos] open (adj); on (light)
άνοιξη (η) [anixi (i)] spring (season)
ανοιχτήρι (το) [anikhtiri (to)] tin opener; corkscrew
ΑΝΟΙΧΤΟ **ανοιχτό** [anikhto] open; light (colour)
ΑΝΤΑΛΛΑΚΤΙΚΑ **ανταλλακτικά (τα)** spare parts
ΑΝΤΑΛΛΑΚΤΙΚΑ ΑΥΤΟΚΙΝΗΤΩΝ **ανταλλακτικά αυτοκινήτων (τα)** auto spares
ανταλλάσω [andalaso] exchange (verb)

άντε! [andeh!] come on!
αντέχω [andekho] endure, tolerate
αντί [andi] instead of
ΑΝΤΙΒΙΟΤΙΚΟ αντιβιοτικό (το) [andiviotiko (to)] antibiotic
ΑΝΤΙ-ΙΣΤΑΜΙΝΙΚΟ ΦΑΡΜΑΚΟ αντι-ισταμινικό φάρμακο (το) [andi-istaminiko farmako (to)] antihistamine
αντίκα (η) [andika (i)] antique
ΑΝΤΙΚΕΣ αντίκες [andikes] antiques
αντίο [andio] goodbye
αντιπαθητικός [andipaTHitikos] obnoxious
ΑΝΤΙΠΡΟΣΩΠΕΙΑ ΑΥΤΟΚΙΝΗΤΩΝ αντιπροσωπεία αυτοκινήτων (η) [andiprosopia aftokiniton (i)] car dealer
ΑΝΤΙΠΡΟΣΩΠΟΣ αντιπρόσωπος (ο) [andiprosopos (o)] agent
αντιπυρετικό [andipiretiko] anti-fever
ΑΝΤΙΣΗΠΤΙΚΟ αντισηπτικό (το) [andisiptiko (to)] antiseptic
ΑΝΤΙΣΥΛΛΗΠΤΙΚΟ αντισυλληπτικό (το) [andisiliptiko (to)] contraceptive
ΑΝΤΙΣΥΛΛΗΠΤΙΚΟ ΧΑΠΙ αντισυλληπτικό χάπι (το) [andisiliptiko khapi (to)] contraceptive pill
ΑΝΤΙΤΙΜΟ (ΔΙΑΔΡΟΜΗΣ) αντίτιμο (διαδρομής) (το) [anditimo (thiathromis) (to)] fare
ΑΝΤΙΦΛΕΓΜΩΔΕΣ αντιφλεγμώδες anti-inflammation
αντλία (η) [andlia (i)] pump
ΑΝΤΛΙΑ ΒΕΝΖΙΝΗΣ αντλία βενζίνης petrol/gas pump
ΑΝΤΛΙΑ ΝΤΙΖΕΛ αντλία ντίζελ diesel pump
ΑΝΩ ανω [ano] up
ΑΞΕΣΟΥΑΡ ΑΥΤΟΚΙΝΗΤΩΝ αξεσουάρ αυτοκινήτων (τα) auto accessories
άξονας (ο) [axonas (o)] axle
ΑΠΑΓΟΡΕΥΕΤΑΙ απαγορεύεται it is prohibited
ΑΠΑΓΟΡΕΥΕΤΑΙ Η ΕΙΣΟΔΟΣ απαγορεύεται η είσοδος no entry, no admission
ΑΠΑΓΟΡΕΥΕΤΑΙ Η ΚΑΤΑΠΟΣΙΣ απαγορεύεται η κατάποσις do not swallow
ΑΠΑΓΟΡΕΥΕΤΑΙ Η ΚΑΤΑΣΚΗΝΩΣΗ απαγορεύεται η κατασκήνωση no camping
ΑΠΑΓΟΡΕΥΕΤΑΙ Η ΚΟΛΥΜΒΗΣΗ απαγορεύεται η κολύμβηση no swimming
ΑΠΑΓΟΡΕΥΕΤΑΙ Η ΛΗΨΙΣ ΔΙΑ ΤΟΥ ΣΤΟΜΑΤΟΣ απαγορεύεται η λήψις διά του στόματος not to be taken orally
ΑΠΑΓΟΡΕΥΕΤΑΙ Η ΣΤΑΘΜΕΥΣΗ απαγορεύεται η στάθμευση no parking
ΑΠΑΓΟΡΕΥΕΤΑΙ Η ΣΤΑΣΗ απαγορεύεται η στάση no waiting, no stopping

ΑΠΑΓΟΡΕΥΕΤΑΙ Η ΧΟΡΗΓΗΣΗ ΑΝΕΥ ΣΥΝΤΑΓΗΣ ΙΑΤΡΟΥ **απαγορεύεται η χορήγηση άνευ συνταγής ιατρού** available on prescription only

ΑΠΑΓΟΡΕΥΕΤΑΙ Ο ΓΥΜΝΙΣΜΟΣ **απαγορεύεται ο γυμνισμός** nudism prohibited

ΑΠΑΓΟΡΕΥΟΝΤΑΙ ΟΙ ΚΑΤΑΔΥΣΕΙΣ **απαγορεύονται οι καταδύσεις** no diving

ΑΠΑΓΟΡΕΥΕΤΑΙ ΤΟ ΚΑΜΠΙΝΓΚ **απαγορεύεται το κάμπινγκ** no camping

ΑΠΑΓΟΡΕΥΕΤΑΙ ΤΟ ΚΑΠΝΙΖΕΙΝ **απαγορεύεται το καπνίζειν** no smoking

ΑΠΑΓΟΡΕΥΕΤΑΙ ΤΟ ΚΑΠΝΙΣΜΑ **απαγορεύεται το κάπνισμα** no smoking

ΑΠΑΓΟΡΕΥΕΤΑΙ ΤΟ ΚΥΝΗΓΙ **απαγορεύεται το κυνήγι** no hunting

ΑΠΑΓΟΡΕΥΕΤΑΙ ΤΟ ΠΡΟΣΠΕΡΑΣΜΑ **απαγορεύεται το προσπέρασμα** no overtaking, no passing

ΑΠΑΓΟΡΕΥΕΤΑΙ ΤΟ ΨΑΡΕΜΑ **απαγορεύεται το ψάρεμα** no fishing

ΑΠΑΓΟΡΕΥΜΕΝΗ ΠΕΡΙΟΧΗ **απαγορευμένη περιοχή** restricted area

απαγορευμένος [apagorevmenos] forbidden

απαίσιος [apesios] appalling

απαιτώ [apeto] demand (verb)

απαλός [apalos] soft

απαντάω [apandao] answer (verb)

απάντηση (η) [apandisi (i)] answer

απένταρος [apendaros] broke

απίθανος [apiTHanos] incredible

ΑΠΛΗ ΒΕΝΖΙΝΗ **απλή βενζίνη (η)** [apli venzini (i)] two-star petrol/gas

ΑΠΛΗ ΔΙΑΔΡΟΜΗ **απλή διαδρομή (η)** [apli thiathromi (i)] single/one-way fare

ΑΠΛΟ ΕΙΣΙΤΗΡΙΟ **απλό εισιτήριο (το)** [aplo isitirio (to)] single/one-way ticket

απλός [aplos] simple

απλώνω [aplono] stretch (verb)

από [apo] from; since; than

από το ... στο ... [apo to ... sto ...] from ... to ...

από κάτω [apo kato] below, under

από πάνω [apo pano] over, above

αποβιβάζομαι [apovivazomeh] land (verb)

απογειώνομαι [apoyionomeh] take off (verb)

απόγευμα (το) [apoyevma (to)] afternoon

το απόγευμα [to apoyevma] in the afternoon

ΑΠΟΓΕΥΜΑΤΙΝΗ ΠΑΡΑΣΤΑΣΗ **απογευματινή παράσταση (η)** [apoyevmatini parastasi (i)] matinee

απογοητευμένος [apogo-itevmenos] disappointed

ΑΠΟΔΕΙΞΗ **απόδειξη (η)** [apothixi (i)] receipt, evidence

ΑΠΟ ΔΕΥΤΕΡΟ ΧΕΡΙ *από δεύτερο χέρι* [apo theftero kheri] second-hand

ΑΠΟΛΥΜΑΝΤΙΚΟ *απολυμαντικό (το)* [apolimandiko (to)] disinfectant

ΑΠΟΣΚΕΥΕΣ *αποσκευές (οι)* [aposkeves (i)] luggage, baggage

ΑΠΟΣΜΗΤΙΚΟ *αποσμητικό (το)* [aposmitiko (to)] deodorant

ΑΠΟΣΤΟΛΕΑΣ *αποστολέας* [apostoleas] sender

απότομος [apotomos] steep

απότομος βράχος (ο) [apotomos vrakhos (o)] cliff

αποφασίζω [apofasizo] decide

απόψε [apopseh] tonight

ΑΠΡΙΛΙΟΣ *Απρίλιος (ο)* [Aprilios (o)] April

Α΄ ΠΡΟΒΟΛΗΣ *α΄ προβολής* major cinema/movie theater

απρόσμενος [aprosmenos] surprising

ΑΠΩΛΕΣΘΕΝΤΑ ΑΝΤΙΚΕΙΜΕΝΑ *απωλεσθέντα αντικείμενα* [apolesTHenda adikimena] lost property

αράχνη (η) [arakhni (i)] spider

αργά [arga] late; slowly

αργίες (οι) [aryies (i)] public holidays

αργός [argos] slow

αργότερα [argotera] later

αργώ [argo] arrive late; go slowly

ΑΡΙΘΜΟΣ *αριθμός (ο)* [ariTHmos (o)] number

ΑΡΙΘΜΟΣ ΘΕΣΕΩΣ *αριθμός θέσεως* [ariTHmos THeseos] seat number

αριστερά [aristera] left

αριστερόχειρας [aristerokhiras] left-handed

αρκετά [arketa] enough; quite

αρκετοί [arketi] several

αρνητικό (το) [arnitiko (to)] negative

αρουραίος (ο) [arooreos (o)] rat

αρραβωνιασμένος [aravoniasmenos] engaged (to be married)

αρραβωνιαστικιά (η) [aravoniastikia (i)] fiancée

αρραβωνιαστικός (ο) [aravoniastikos (o)] fiancé

αρρενωπός [arenopos] manly; macho

αρρώστια (η) [arostia (i)] disease

άρρωστος [arostos] ill, sick

ΑΡΤΟΠΟΙΕΙΟ *αρτοποιείο (το)* [artopi-io (to)] bakery

αρχαιολογία (η) [arkheoloyia (i)] archaeology

αρχαίος [arkheos] ancient

αρχαιότητες (οι) [arkheotites (i)] ruins

αρχάρια (η) [arkharia (i)] beginner

αρχάριος (ο) [arkharios (o)] beginner

αρχή (η) [arkhi (i)] beginning

αρχίζω [arkhizo] begin

αρχιτέκτων (ο/η) [arkhitekton (o/i)] architect

άρωμα (το) [aroma (to)] perfume

ΑΣΑΝΣΕΡ *ασανσέρ (το)* [asanser

(to)] lift, elevator
ασετόν (το) [aseton (to)] nail varnish remover
ΑΣΗΜΕΝΙΟΣ ασημένιος [asimenios] silver
ΑΣΗΜΙΚΑ ασημικά (τα) [asimika (ta)] silver(ware)
ΑΣΘΕΝΟΦΟΡΟ ασθενοφόρο (το) [asTHenoforo (to)] ambulance
ΑΣΘΜΑ άσθμα (το) [asTHma (to)] asthma
ΑΣΠΙΡΙΝΗ ασπιρίνη (η) [aspirini (i)] aspirin
άσπρος [aspros] white
άστατος [astatos] changeable
αστείο (το) [astio (to)] joke
αστείος [astios] funny, amusing
αστέρι (το) [asteri (to)] star
αστράγαλος (ο) [astragalos (o)] ankle
ΑΣΤΥΝΟΜΙΑ αστυνομία (η) [astinomia (i)] police
ΑΣΤΥΝΟΜΙΚΟ ΤΜΗΜΑ αστυνομικό τμήμα (το) [astinomiko tmima (to)] police station
αστυφύλακας (ο) [astifilakas (o)] policeman
αστυνομικός (η) [astinomikos (i)] policewoman
ΑΣΦΑΛΕΙΑ ασφάλεια (η) [asfalia (i)] fuse; insurance
ΑΣΦΑΛΕΙΑΙ ασφάλειαι [asfalieh] insurance
ασφαλής [asfalis] safe
άσχημα [askhima] badly
άσχημος [askhimos] ugly
ατζέντα (η) [atzenda (i)] address book
ατμόπλοιο (το) [atmoplio (to)] steamer
άτομο (το) [atomo (to)] person
ΑΥΓΟΥΣΤΟΣ Αύγουστος (ο) [Avgoostos (o)] August
αυθεντικός [afTHendikos] genuine
αύριο [avrio] tomorrow
Αυστραλέζα (η) [Afstraleza (i)] Australian (woman)
Αυστραλέζικος [Afstralezikos] Australian (adj)
ΑΥΣΤΡΑΛΙΑ Αυστραλία (η) [Afstralia (i)] Australia
Αυστραλός (ο) [Afstralos (o)] Australian (man)
αυτά, αυτές [afta, aftes] these; they; them
αυτή [afti] she; this (one)
αυτής [aftis] of her
αυτί (το) [afti (to)] ear
αυτό [afto] it; this
αυτό εδώ [afto etho] this one
αυτοί [afti] these; they
ΑΥΤΟΚΙΝΗΤΟ αυτοκίνητο (το) [aftokinito (to)] car
αυτόματος [aftomatos] automatic (adj)
αυτό που [afto poo] what
αυτός [aftos] he; this (one)
αυτός ο ίδιος [aftos o ithios] himself
αυτού [aftoo] of him, of it
αυτούς [aftoos] them
ΑΥΤ/ΤΟ αυτ/το car
αυτών [afton] of them
αφεντικό (το) [afendiko (to)] boss
ΑΦΕΤΗΡΙΑ αφετηρία (η) [afetiria (i)] terminus

αφήνω [afino] leave (verb)
ΑΦΙΞΕΙΣ αφίξεις arrivals
ΑΦΙΞΗ άφιξη (η) [afixi (i)] arrival
αφίσα (η) [afisa (i)] poster
ΑΦΟΙ. αφοί. bros.
ΑΦΟΡΟΛΟΓΗΤΑ αφορολόγητα (τα) [aforoloyita (ta)] duty-free
αφροδίσιο νόσημα (το) [afrothisio nosima (to)] VD
ΑΦΡΟΣ ΞΥΡΙΣΜΑΤΟΣ αφρός ξυρίσματος (ο) [afros xirismatos (o)] shaving foam
αφρός (ο) [afros (o)] surf
αχθοφόρος (ο) [akhTHoforos (o)] doorman
αχινός (ο) [akhinos (o)] sea urchin

Β

ΒΑΓΟΝΙ βαγόνι (το) [vagoni (to)] coach, car (train)
ΒΑΓΚΟΝ-ΛΙ βαγκόν-λι [vagon-li] sleeper, sleeping car
βάζο (το) [vazo (to)] vase
βάζω [vazo] put
ΒΑΘΙΑ ΝΕΡΑ βαθιά νερά deep water
βάθος: στο βάθος [sto vaTHos] in the background; at the bottom
βαθύς [vaTHis] deep
βαλβίδα (η) [valvitha (i)] valve
βαλίτσα (η) [valitsa (i)] bag, suitcase
ΒΑΜΒΑΚΕΡΟ βαμβακερό (το) [vamvakero (to)] cotton
βαρετός [varetos] boring
ΒΑΡΚΑ βάρκα (η) [varka (i)] small boat; dinghy
βάρκα με κουπιά [varka meh koopia] rowing boat
βάρκα με μηχανή [varka meh mikhani] motorboat
ΒΑΡΟΣ βάρος (το) [varos (to)] weight
βαρύς [varis] heavy; rich (food)
βασιλιάς (ο) [vasilias (o)] king
βασίλισσα (η) [vasilisa (i)] queen
ΒΑΦΗ βαφή (η) [vafi (i)] hair dye
βάφω [vafo] paint; tint (verb)
βγάζω φωτογραφία [vgazo fotografia] photograph (verb)
βγαίνω [vgeno] go out
ΒΓΑΛΤΕ ΤΗΝ ΚΑΡΤΑ βγάλτε την κάρτα remove the card
βέβαια [veveh-a] of course
βελόνα (η) [velona (i)] needle
βελτιώνω [veltiono] improve
ΒΕΝΖΙΝΑΔΙΚΟ βενζινάδικο (το) [venzinathiko (to)] petrol station, gas station
ΒΕΝΖΙΝΗ βενζίνη (η) [venzini (i)] petrol, gas(oline)
βεντιλατέρ (το) [vendilater (to)] fan belt
ΒΕΡΝΙΚΙ ΠΑΠΟΥΤΣΙΩΝ βερνίκι παπουτσιών (το) [verniki papootsion (to)] shoe polish
ΒΗΧΑΣ βήχας (ο) [vikhas (o)] cough
βήχω [vikho] cough (verb)
βιάζομαι [viazomeh] hurry (verb)
βιάσου! [viasoo!] hurry up!
βιασμός (ο) [viasmos (o)] rape
βιβλίο (το) [vivlio (to)] book

βιβλίο διαλόγων [vivlio thialogon] phrase book
ΒΙΒΛΙΟΘΗΚΗ βιβλιοθήκη (η) [vivlioTHiki (i)] library
ΒΙΒΛΙΟΠΩΛΕΙΟ βιβλιοπωλείο (το) [vivliopolio (to)] bookshop, bookstore
ΒΙΔΑ βίδα (η) [vitha (i)] screw
ΒΙΖΑ βίζα (η) [viza (i)] visa
βίλλα (η) [vila (i)] villa
βίντεο (το) [video (to)] video
ΒΙΤΑΜΙΝΕΣ βιταμίνες (οι) [vitamines (i)] vitamins
Β΄ ΚΑΤΗΓΟΡΙΑΣ Β΄ κατηγορίας second class
βλάβη (η) [vlavi (i)] breakdown (car)
βλάκας (ο) [vlakas (o)] idiot; stupid
βλέπω [vlepo] see
βοήθεια (η) [voiTHia (i)] help
βοηθώ [vo-iTHo] help (verb)
βόμβα (η) [vomva (i)] bomb
Βόρειος Ιρλανδία (η) [vorios Irlanthia (i)] Northern Ireland
ΒΟΥΛΓΑΡΙΑ Βουλγαρία (η) [voolgaria (i)] Bulgaria
Βουλγαρικός [voolgarikos] Bulgarian (adj)
βουλιάζω [vooliazo] sink (verb)
ΒΟΥΛΚΑΝΙΖΑΤΕΡ βουλκανιζατέρ [voolkanizater] tyre repairs
βουνό (το) [voono (to)] mountain
βούρτσα (η) [voortsa (i)] brush
βουτάω [vootao] dive (verb)
Β΄ ΠΡΟΒΟΛΗΣ β΄ προβολής local cinema/movie theater
βράδυ (το) [vrathi (to)] evening
το βράδυ [to vrathi] in the evening
βραδυά (η) [vrathia (i)] evening
ΒΡΑΔΥΝΗ ΠΑΡΑΣΤΑΣΗ βραδυνή παράσταση evening performance
βράζω [vrazo] boil (verb)
βράχια (τα) [vrakhia (ta)] rocks; cliffs
βραχιόλι (το) [vrakhioli (to)] bracelet
βράχος (ο) [vrakhos (o)] rock
ΒΡΕΤΑΝΝΙΑ Βρετανία (η) [vretania (i)] Britain
Βρεταννίδα (η) [vretanitha (i)] Briton (woman)
Βρεταννικός [vretanikos] British
Βρεταννός (ο) [vretanos (o)] Briton (man)
βρέχει [vrekhi] it's raining
βρίσκω [vrisko] find (verb)
βροντή (η) [vrondi (i)] thunder
βροχή (η) [vrokhi (i)] rain
βρύση (η) [vrisi (i)] tap, faucet
βρώμικος [vromikos] dirty
βυζαίνω [vizeno] breastfeed
βυθός (ο) [viTHos (o)] bottom (of sea)

Γ

γάιδαρος (ο) [gaitharos (o)] donkey
ΓΑΛΑΚΤΟΠΩΛΕΙΟ γαλακτοπωλείο (το) [galaktopolio (to)] shop/take-away café selling dairy products
ΓΑΛΑΚΤΩΜΑ ΚΑΘΑΡΙΣΜΟΥ

γαλάκτωμα καθαρισμού (το) [galaktoma kaTHarismoo (to)] cleansing lotion

ΓΑΛΛΙΑ Γαλλία (η) [galia (i)] France

Γαλλικός [galikos] French (adj)

γάμος (ο) [gamos (o)] wedding

γαμπρός (ο) [gambros (o)] bridegroom; son-in-law; brother-in-law

γάντια (τα) [gandia (ta)] gloves

γάτα (η) [gata (i)] cat

γειά σου! [yia soo!] hello!; bless you!; cheers!

γείτονας (ο) [yitonas (o)] neighbour

γελοίο [yelio] ridiculous

γελώ [yelo] laugh (verb)

γεμάτος [yematos] full

γεμίζω [yemizo] fill (verb)

γενέθλια (τα) [yeneTHlia (ta)] birthday

γένια (τα) [yenia (ta)] beard

γενναίος [yeneos] brave

ΓΕΡΜΑΝΙΑ Γερμανία (η) [Yermania (i)] Germany

Γερμανικός [Yermanikos] German (adj)

γέρος [yeros] old (person)

ΓΕΥΜΑ γεύμα (το) [yevma (to)] meal

γεύση (η) [yefsi (i)] flavour; taste

ΓΕΦΥΡΑ γέφυρα (η) [yefira (i)] bridge

ΓΗΠΕΔΟ γήπεδο (το) [yipetho (to)] football pitch

ΓΗΠΕΔΟ ΤΕΝΝΙΣ γήπεδο τέννις [yipetho tenis] tennis court

για [ya] for

για μένα [ya mena] for me

γιαγιά (η) [yaya (i)] grandmother

ΓΙΑ ΕΞΩΤΕΡΙΚΗ ΧΡΗΣΗ ΜΟΝΟΝ για εξωτερική χρήση μόνον for external use only

ΓΙΑ ΕΣΩΤΕΡΙΚΗ ΧΡΗΣΗ ΜΟΝΟΝ για εσωτερική χρήση μόνον for internal use only

γιακάς (ο) [yakas (o)] collar

γιατί; [yati?] why?

ΓΙΑ ΤΟ ΣΠΙΤΙ για το σπίτι [ya to spiti] to take away, to go (food)

ΓΙΑΤΡΟΣ γιατρός (ο/η) [yatros (o/i)] doctor

γίνομαι [yinomeh] become; happen

τι γίνεται; [ti yineteh?] what's happening?

ΓΙΟΡΤΗ ΚΡΑΣΙΟΥ γιορτή κρασιού (η) [yorti krasioo (i)] wine festival

γιός (ο) [yos (o)] son

γιώτ (το) [yot (to)] yacht

γκάζι (το) [gazi (to)] gas; accelerator

ΓΚΑΛΕΡΙ γκαλερί (η) [galeri (i)] art gallery

ΓΚΑΡΑΖ γκαράζ (το) [garaz (to)] garage (for parking/repairs)

ΓΚΑΡΝΤΑΡΟΜΠΑ γκαρνταρόμπα (η) [gardaroba (i)] cloakroom (for coats)

Γ΄ ΚΑΤΗΓΟΡΙΑΣ Γ΄ κατηγορίας third class

γκολφ (το) [golf (to)] golf

γκρίζος [grizos] grey

γκρουπ (το) [groop (to)] group

γλάρος (ο) [glaros (o)] seagull

Α Β Γ Δ Ε Ζ Η Θ Ι Κ Λ Μ Ν Ξ Ο Π Ρ Σ Τ Υ Φ Χ Ψ Ω

ΓΛΙΦΙΤΖΟΥΡΙ γλιφιτζούρι (το) [glifidzoori (to)] lollipop
ΓΛΥΚΟ γλυκό (το) [gliko (to)] sweet, candy
γλυκός [glikos] sweet (adj)
γλυστερός [glisteros] slippery
γλυστράω [glistrao] skid (verb)
γλώσσα (η) [glosa (i)] language; tongue
γνωρίζω [gnorizo] know
δεν γνωρίζω [then gnorizo] I don't know
γόνατο (το) [gonato (to)] knee
γονείς (οι) [gonis (i)] parents
γουίντσερφ (το) [gooindserf (to)] sailboard
ΓΟΥΝΑΡΙΚΑ γουναρικά (τα) [goonarika (ta)] furrier
ΓΟΥΝΕΣ γούνες [goones] furs
γουόκμαν (το) [goo-okman (to)] personal stereo
γουρούνι (το) [goorooni (to)] pig
γοφός (ο) [gofos (o)] hip
γραβάτα (η) [gravata (i)] tie, necktie
γράμμα (το) [grama (to)] letter
γράμματα (τα) [gramata (ta)] post, mail
γραμματική (η) [gramatiki (i)] grammar
ΓΡΑΜΜΑΤΟΚΙΒΩΤΙΟ γραμματοκιβώτιο (το) [gramatokivotio (to)] letterbox, mailbox
γραμματόσημο (το) [gramatosimo (to)] stamp
ΓΡΑΜΜΕΣ ΤΡΑΙΝΟΥ γραμμές τραίνου railway crosses road
ΓΡΑΜΜΗ γραμμή (η) [grami (i)] route, line
γρασίδι (το) [grasithi (to)] lawn
γραφείο (το) [grafio (to)] office
ΓΡΑΦΕΙΟ ΤΑΞΙΔΙΩΝ γραφείο ταξιδίων [grafio taxithion] travel agency
γραφομηχανή (η) [grafomikhani (i)] typewriter
γράφω [grafo] write
γρήγορα [grigora] quick; quickly
γρήγορος [grigoros] fast
ΓΡΙΠΠΗ γρίππη (η) [gripi (i)] flu
γρύλλος (ο) [grilos (o)] jack
γυαλί (το) [yali (to)] glass (material)
ΓΥΑΛΙΑ γυαλιά (τα) [yalia (ta)] glasses, eyeglasses
ΓΥΑΛΙΑ ΗΛΙΟΥ γυαλιά ηλίου [yalia ilioo] sunglasses
ΓΥΜΝΑΣΙΟ γυμνάσιο (το) [yimnasio (to)] secondary school
γυμνασμένος [yimnasmenos] fit (healthy)
ΓΥΜΝΑΣΤΗΡΙΟ γυμναστήριο (το) [yimnastirio (to)] gym
γυμνός [yimnos] naked
γυναίκα (η) [yineka (i)] woman; wife
ΓΥΝΑΙΚΕΙΑ γυναικεία (τα) [yinekia (ta)] ladies' wear
ΓΥΝΑΙΚΕΙΑΙ ΚΟΜΜΩΣΕΙΣ γυναικείαι κομμώσεις (οι) [yinekieh komosis (i)] ladies' salon
ΓΥΝΑΙΚΕΙΑ ΦΟΡΕΜΑΤΑ γυναικεία φορέματα [yinekia foremata] ladies' dresses
ΓΥΝΑΙΚΕΙΕΣ ΚΑΛΤΣΕΣ - ΚΑΛΣΟΝ γυναικείες κάλτσες -

καλσόν [yinekies kaltses - kalson] ladies' socks - stockings
ΓΥΝΑΙΚΩΝ γυναικών ladies' (toilet), ladies' room
γυρνώ [yirno] turn (verb)
γυρνώ πίσω [yirno piso] arrive back, return; take back
γυρνώ σπίτι [yirno spiti] return home

Δ

δακτυλίδι (το) [thaktilithi (to)] ring (on finger)
δανείζομαι [thanizomeh] borrow
δανείζω [thanizo] lend
δασκάλα (η) [thaskala (i)] instructor; teacher
δάσκαλος (ο) [thaskalos (o)] instructor; teacher
δάσος (το) [thasos (to)] forest
δάχτυλο (το) [thakhtilo (to)] finger
δάχτυλο του ποδιού [thakhtilo too pothioo] toe
δε [theh] **ξου**
Δ.Ε.Η. public electricity company
δείκτης (ο) [thiktis (o)] gauge; index finger
ΔΕΙΠΝΟ δείπνο (το) [thipno (to)] evening meal
δείχνω [thikhno] show (verb)
δέκα [theka] ten
δεκαεννιά [theka-enia] nineteen
δεκαέξι [theka-exi] sixteen
δεκαεπτά [theka-epta] seventeen
δεκαοχτώ [theka-okhto] eighteen
δεκαπενθήμερο [thekapenTHimero] fortnight
δεκαπέντε [thekapendeh] fifteen
ΔΕΚΑΡΙΚΟ δεκάρικο (το) [thekariko (to)] 10-drachma coin
δεκατέσσερα [thekatesera] fourteen
δέκατος [thekatos] tenth
δεκατρία [thekatria] thirteen
ΔΕΚΕΜΒΡΙΟΣ Δεκέμβριος (ο) [thekemvrios (o)] December
δέμα (το) [thema (to)] parcel
ΔΕΜΑΤΑ δέματα parcels, packages
δεν [then] not
δένδρο (το) [thenthro (to)] tree
ΔΕΝ ΛΕΙΤΟΥΡΓΕΙ δεν λειτουργεί [then litooryi] out of order
ΔΕΝ ΣΙΔΕΡΩΝΕΤΑΙ δεν σιδερώνεται do not iron
δεξιός, δεξιά [thexios, thexia] right (side)
δεξίωση (η) [thexiosi (i)] reception (party)
ΔΕΡΜΑ δέρμα (το) [therma (to)] skin; leather
ΔΕΡΜΑΤΑ δέρματα (τα) [thermata (ta)] leather goods
ΔΕΣΠΟΙΝΙΔΑ δεσποινίδα (η) [thespinitha (i)] young woman; Miss; Ms
ΔΕΣΠΟΙΝΙΣ δεσποινίς [thespinis] Miss; Ms
ΔΕΥΤΕΡΑ Δευτέρα (η) [theftera (i)] Monday
ΔΕΥΤΕΡΗ ΘΕΣΗ δεύτερη θέση second class
δευτερόλεπτο (το) [thefterolepto

(to)] second
δεύτερος [thefteros] second (adj)
ΔΕΥΤΕΡΟ ΧΕΡΙ δεύτερο χέρι [theftero kheri] second-hand
δέχομαι [thekhomeh] accept; receive
δηλητηρίαση (η) [thilitiriasi (i)] poisoning
δηλητήριο (το) [thilitirio (to)] poison
ΔΗΜΑΡΧΕΙΟ δημαρχείο (το) [thimarkhio (to)] town hall
ΔΗΜΟΣΙΑ ΛΟΥΤΡΑ δημόσια λουτρά (τα) [thimosia lootra (ta)] public baths
δημόσιος [thimosios] public
δημοσιογράφος (ο/η) [thimosiografos (o/i)] reporter
δημοτική μουσική (η) [thimotiki moosiki (i)] folk music
διαβάζω [thiavazo] read
ΔΙΑΒΑΣΗ ΠΕΖΩΝ διάβαση πεζών (η) pedestrian crossing
ΔΙΑΒΑΤΗΡΙΟ διαβατήριο (το) [thiavatirio (to)] passport
διαβητικός (ο) [thiavitikos (o)] diabetic
διαβητική (η) [thiavitiki (i)] diabetic
ΔΙΑΔΡΟΜΗ ΜΕΤ' ΕΠΙΣΤΡΟΦΗΣ διαδρομή μετ' επιστροφής (η) [thiathromi met' epistrofis (i)] return/round trip fare
διάδρομος (ο) [thiathromos (o)] corridor
διάθεση (η) [thiaTHesi (i)] mood
δίαιτα (η) [thieta (i)] diet
διακοπές (οι) [thiakopes (i)] holiday, vacation
διακοπή (η) [thiakopi (i)] interruption; power cut
διακόπτης (ο) [thiakoptis (o)] switch
διακόπτω [thiakopto] interrupt
διακόσια [thiakosia] two hundred
διαλέγω [thialego] choose
ΔΙΑΛΕΙΜΜΑ διάλειμμα (το) [thialima (to)] interval, intermission
διάλεκτος (η) [thialektos (i)] dialect
ΔΙΑΛΥΜΑ διάλυμα (το) [thialima (to)] solution
διαμάντι (το) [thiamandi (to)] diamond
Διαμαρτυρόμενος (ο) [thiamartiromenos (o)] Protestant
ΔΙΑΜΕΡΙΣΜΑ διαμέρισμα (το) [thiamerisma (to)] apartment, flat
διά μέσου [thia mesoo] through
διαμονή (η) [thiamoni (i)] accommodation; stay
ΔΙΑΝΥΚΤΕΡΕΥΟΝ διανυκτερεύον open all night
διάρκεια (η) [thiarkia (i)] duration
ΔΙΑΡΚΕΙΑ ΠΤΗΣΕΩΣ διάρκεια πτήσεως [thiarkia ptiseos] flight time
διαρροή (η) [thiaroi (i)] leak
ΔΙΑΡΡΟΙΑ διάρροια (η) [thiaria (i)] diarrhoea
διάσημος [thiasimos] famous
ΔΙΑΣΤΑΥΡΩΣΗ διασταύρωση (η) [thiastavrosi (i)] junction,

crossroads, intersection
διασχίζω [thiaskhizo] go through
ΔΙΑΤΗΡΕΙΤΑΙ ΣΕ ΨΥΓΕΙΟ διατηρείται σε ψυγείο keep refrigerated
διαφημιστικό (το) [thiafimistiko (to)] leaflet; advertisements (on TV); trailer (cinema)
διαφορετικά [thiaforetika] otherwise
διαφορετικός [thiaforetikos] different
διάφραγμα (το) [thiafragma (to)] shutter (in camera)
διαχειριστής (ο) [thiakhiristis (o)] manager
διαχειρίστρια (η) [thiakhiristria (i)] manageress
διδάσκω [thithasko] teach
δίδυμοι (οι) [thithimi (i)] twins
ΔΙΕΥΘΥΝΣΗ διεύθυνση (η) [thiefTHinsi (i)] address
δίκαιος [thikeos] fair, just
δικά μας [thika mas] ours
δικά μου [thika moo] mine
δικά σας, δικά σου [thika sas, thika soo] yours
ΔΙΚΑΣΤΗΡΙΟ δικαστήριο (το) [thikastirio (to)] law court
δικά της [thika tis] hers
δικά του [thika too] his, its
δικά τους [thika toos] theirs
δικηγόρος (ο/η) [thikigoros (o/i)] lawyer
δική μας [thiki mas] ours
δική μου [thiki moo] mine
δική σας, δική σου [thiki sas, thiki soo] yours
δική του [thiki too] his
δική τους [thiki toos] theirs
ΔΙΚΛΙΝΟ ΔΩΜΑΤΙΟ δίκλινο δωμάτιο (το) [thiklino thomatio (to)] double room
δικό μας [thiko mas] ours
δικό μου [thiko moo] mine
δικό σας, δικό σου [thiko sas, thiko soo] yours
δικό τους [thiko toos] theirs
δικό της [thiko tis] hers
δικό του [thiko too] his; its
δικός μας [thikos mas] ours
δικός μου [thikos moo] mine
δικός σας, δικός σου [thikos sas, thikos soo] yours
δικός του [thikos too] his
δικός τους [thikos toos] theirs
δίνω [thino] give
ΔΙΟΔΙΑ διόδια (τα) [thiothia (ta)] toll
διορθώνω [thiorTHono] mend, correct
ΔΙΠΛΗ ΤΑΡΙΦΑ διπλή ταρίφα (η) double tariff
διπλό [thiplo] double
ΔΙΠΛΟ ΔΩΜΑΤΙΟ διπλό δωμάτιο (το) [thiplo thomatio (to)] double room
διπλό κρεβάτι (το) [thiplo krevati (to)] double bed
ΔΙΣ. δις. Miss
ΔΙΣΚΑΔΙΚΟ δισκάδικο (το) [thiskathiko (to)] record shop
ΔΙΣΚΟΙ - ΚΑΣΕΤΕΣ δίσκοι - κασέτες [thiski - kasetes] records - cassettes
δίσκος (ο) [thiskos (o)] record; tray
Δ΄ ΚΑΤΗΓΟΡΙΑΣ

Α Β Γ Δ Ε Ζ Η Θ Ι Κ Λ Μ Ν Ξ Ο Π Ρ Σ Τ Υ Φ Χ Ψ Ω

Δ΄ κατηγορίας fourth class
δοκιμάζω [thokimazo] taste (verb); try (on)
ΔΟΛΛΑΡΙΟ δολλάριο (το) [tholario (to)] dollar
δόντι (το) [thondi (to)] tooth
ΔΟΣΟΛΟΓΙΑ ΕΝΗΛΙΚΩΝ δοσολογία ενηλίκων adult dosage
ΔΟΣΟΛΟΓΙΑ ΠΑΙΔΩΝ δοσολογία παίδων children's dosage
δουλειά (η) [thoolia (i)] job; work
δουλειές (οι) [thoolies (i)] business
δουλεύω [thoolevo] work (verb)
δεν δουλεύει [then thoolevi] it's not working
ΔΡΑΧΜΗ δραχμή (η) [thrakhmi (i)] drachma
ΔΡΟΜΟΛΟΓΙΑ δρομολόγια (τα) [thromoloyia (ta)] timetable, (US) schedule
δρόμος (ο) [thromos (o)] road; street
δροσερός [throseros] cool
ΔΡΧ. δρχ. drachma
δυνατός [thinatos] loud; possible; strong
δύο [thio] two
ΔΥΟ ΠΑΡΑΣΤΑΣΕΙΣ δύο παραστάσεις two shows
δυσάρεστος [thisarestos] unpleasant
δύση του ήλιου (η) [thisi too ilioo (i)] sunset
ΔΥΣΚΟΙΛΙΑ δυσκοίλια (η) [thiskilia (i)] constipation
δύσκολος [thiskolos] difficult
ΔΥΣΠΕΨΙΑ δυσπεψία (η) [thispepsia (i)] indigestion
δυστύχημα (το) [thistikhima (to)] accident
δυστυχώς [thistikhos] unfortunately
δώδεκα [thotheka] twelve
ΔΩΔΕΚΑΔΑ δωδεκάδα (η) [thothekatha (i)] dozen
ΔΩΜΑΤΙΟ δωμάτιο (το) [thomatio (to)] room
ΔΩΡΑ δώρα gifts
ΔΩΡΕΑΝ δωρεάν [thorean] free (of charge)
δώρο (το) [thoro (to)] gift
ΔΩΡΟ ΠΑΣΧΑ Δώρο Πάσχα [thoro Paskha] Easter supplement paid to taxi drivers
ΔΩΡΟ ΧΡΙΣΤΟΥΓΕΝΝΩΝ Δώρο Χριστουγέννων [thoro khristooyenon] Christmas supplement paid to taxi drivers

E

Ε.Α.Σ. Athens Public Transport Corporation
εβδομάδα (η) [evthomatha (i)] week
εβδομήντα [evthominda] seventy
έβδομος [evthomos] seventh
Εβραίος [Evreos] Jewish
έγγραφο (το) [engrafo (to)] document
εγγύηση (η) [egi-isi (i)] guarantee
έγινε! [eyineh!] OK, coming up!
εγκαίρως [engeros] on time

έγκαυμα από τον ήλιο (το) [engavma apo ton ilio (to)] sunburn
έγκυος [engios] pregnant
έγκυρος [engiros] valid
έγχρωμο φιλμ (το) [enkhromo film (to)] colour film
εγώ [ego] I
εγώ ο ίδιος [ego o ithios] myself
εδώ [etho] here
έθιμο (το) [eTHimo (to)] custom
ΕΘΝΙΚΗ ΟΔΟΣ εθνική οδός (η) [eTHniki othos (i)] motorway, highway, freeway
ΕΘΝΙΚΗ ΠΙΝΑΚΟΘΗΚΗ Εθνική Πινακοθήκη [ETHniki PinakoTHiki] National Art Gallery
ΕΘΝΙΚΟΤΗΤΑ εθνικότητα (η) [eTHnikotita (i)] nationality
ΕΙΔΗ είδη (τα) [ithi (ta)] goods
ΕΙΔΗ ΑΥΤΟΚΙΝΗΤΟΥ είδη αυτοκινήτου auto accessories
ΕΙΔΗ ΔΩΡΩΝ είδη δώρων gifts
ΕΙΔΗ ΜΠΕΜΠΕ είδη μπεμπέ [ithi bebeh] babywear
ΕΙΔΗ ΡΟΥΧΙΣΜΟΥ είδη ρουχισμού [ithi roukhismoo] clothes
ΕΙΔΗ ΣΠΟΡ είδη σπορ [ithi spor] sports equipment, sportswear
ΕΙΔΗ ΧΑΡΤΟΠΩΛΕΙΟΥ είδη χαρτοπωλείου [ithi khartopolioo] stationery
ΕΙΔΙΚΗ ΠΡΟΣΦΟΡΑ ειδική προσφορά special price, special offer
ειδικώς [ithikos] especially
είχες [ikhes] you had
ΕΙΚΟΣΑΡΙΚΟ εικοσάρικο [ikosariko] 20-drachma coin
είκοσι [ikosi] twenty
ειλικρινής [ilikrinis] sincere
είμαι [imeh] I am
είμαστε [imasteh] we are
είναι [ineh] he/she/it is; they are
είστε [isteh] you are
ΕΙΣΑΓΩΓΗΣ εισαγωγής imported
είσαι [iseh] you are
ΕΙΣΙΤΗΡΙΟ εισιτήριο (το) [isitirio (to)] ticket
ΕΙΣΙΤΗΡΙΟ ΜΕ ΕΠΙΣΤΡΟΦΗ εισιτήριο με επιστροφή [isitirio meh epistrofi] return/round trip ticket
ΕΙΣΟΔΟΣ είσοδος (η) [isothos (i)] entrance, way in
ΕΙΣΟΔΟΣ ΕΛΕΥΘΕΡΑ είσοδος ελευθέρα admission free
ΕΙΣΟΔΟΣ ΠΡΑΤΗΡΙΟΥ είσοδος πρατηρίου entrance to petrol/gas station
ΕΙΣΠΡΑΚΤΩΡ εισπράκτωρ (ο) ticket collector
είχα [ikha] I had
είχαμε [ikhameh] we had
είχαν [ikhan] they had
είχατε [ikhateh] you had
είχε [ikheh] he/she/it had
είχες [ikhes] you had
Ε΄ ΚΑΤΗΓΟΡΙΑΣ Ε΄ κατηγορίας fifth class
εκατό [ekato] hundred
εκατομμύριο: ένα εκατομμύριο [ena ekatomirio] one million
ΕΚΔΟΣΗ ΕΙΣΙΤΗΡΙΩΝ έκδοση

εισιτηρίων [ekthosi isitirion] ticket office
εκεί [eki] there, over there
εκεί κάτω [eki kato] down there
εκείνα, εκείνες [ekina, ekines] those
εκείνη, εκείνο [ekini, ekino] that
εκείνοι [ekini] those
εκείνος [ekinos] that
ΕΚΘΕΣΗ **έκθεση (η)** [ekTHesi (i)] exhibition, showroom
ΕΚΚΛΗΣΙΑ **εκκλησία (η)** [eklisia (i)] church
Ε.Κ.Ο. Greek state petrol company
εκπληκτικός [ekpliktikos] surprising
έκπληξη (η) [ekplixi (i)] surprise
ΕΚΠΤΩΣΕΙΣ **εκπτώσεις (οι)** sales
ΕΚΤΑΚΤΗ ΑΝΑΓΚΗ **έκτακτη ανάγκη (η)** [ektakti anangi (i)] emergency
εκτός [ektos] except
έκτος [ektos] sixth
έλα! [ela!] you don't say!; come on!, hurry up!
ΕΛ.ΑΣ. Greek police
ΕΛΑΣΤΙΚΑ **ελαστικά** tyres
ελαστικός [elastikos] elastic
ελατήριο (το) [elatirio (to)] spring (in seat etc)
ελαττωματικός [elatomatikos] faulty
ΕΛΑΤΤΩΣΑΤΕ ΤΑΧΥΤΗΤΑ **ελαττώσατε ταχύτητα** reduce speed
ελαφρός [elafros] light (not heavy)
ελάχιστος [elakhistos] smallest; few
ελεγκτής (ο) [elenktis (o)] inspector (bus)
ΕΛΕΓΧΟΣ **έλεγχος (ο)** [elenkhos (o)] check, inspection
ΕΛΕΓΧΟΣ ΑΠΟΣΚΕΥΩΝ **έλεγχος αποσκευών** baggage control
ΕΛΕΓΧΟΣ ΔΙΑΒΑΤΗΡΙΩΝ **έλεγχος διαβατηρίων** passport control
ΕΛΕΓΧΟΣ ΕΙΣΙΤΗΡΙΩΝ **έλεγχος εισιτηρίων** ticket inspection
ΕΛΕΓΧΟΣ ΕΠΙΒΑΤΩΝ **έλεγχος επιβατών** passenger control
ΕΛΕΥΘΕΡΑ ΕΙΣΟΔΟΣ **ελευθέρα είσοδος** [elefTHera isothos] admission free
ΕΛΕΥΘΕΡΟΝ **ελεύθερον** [elefTheron] free; for hire (taxi)
ελεύθερος [elefTheros] free; single (unmarried)
ελιά (η) [elia (i)] olive; spot (blemish)
ελικόπτερο (το) [elikoptero (to)] helicopter
ελκυστικός [elkistikos] attractive
ΕΛΛΑΔΑ **Ελλάδα (η)** [Elatha (i)] Greece
Έλληνας (ο) [Elinas (o)] Greek (man)
Ελληνίδα (η) [Elinitha (i)] Greek (woman)
ΕΛΛΗΝΙΚΑ **Ελληνικά (τα)** [Elinika (ta)] Greek (language)
ΕΛΛΗΝΙΚΗ ΑΣΤΥΝΟΜΙΑ **Ελληνική Αστυνομία (η)** Greek

police

ΕΛΛΗΝΙΚΗ ΡΑΔΙΟΦΩΝΙΑ **Ελληνική Ραδιοφωνία** Greek radio

ΕΛΛΗΝΙΚΗ ΤΗΛΕΟΡΑΣΗ **Ελληνική Τηλεόραση** Greek television

ΕΛΛΗΝΙΚΗΣ ΚΑΤΑΣΚΕΥΗΣ **Ελληνικής κατασκευής** made in Greece

ΕΛΛΗΝΙΚΟ ΠΡΟΙΟΝ **Ελληνικό προιόν** produce of Greece

ΕΛΛΗΝΙΚΟΣ **Ελληνικός** [Elinikos] Greek (adj)

Ε.Λ.Π.Α. [E.L.P.A.] Greek motoring organization

ελπίζω [elpizo] hope (verb)

ΕΛ.ΤΑ. Greek Post Office

εμάς [emas] us

εμβολιασμός (ο) [emvoliasmos (o)] vaccination

εμβόλιο (το) [emvolio (to)] vaccine

εμείς [emis] we

εμένα [emena] me

ΕΜΠΟΡΙΚΟ ΚΕΝΤΡΟ **εμπορικό κέντρο (το)** [emboriko kendro (to)] shopping centre

εμπρός [ebros] come in; hello (response on phone)

ένα(ν) [ena(n)] a; one

εναντίον [enandion] against

ένας [enas] a; one

ένατος [enatos] ninth

ενδιαφέρον [enthiaferon] interesting

ενενήντα [eneninda] ninety

ένεση (η) [enesi (i)] injection

ενήλικη (η) [eniliki (i)] adult

ΕΝΗΛΙΚΟΣ **ενήλικος (ο)** [enilikos (o)] adult

ΕΝΘΥΜΙΟ **ενθύμιο (το)** [enThimio (to)] souvenir

εννιά [enia] nine

εννοώ [enoo] mean (verb)

ΕΝΟΙΚΙΑΖΟΝΤΑΙ **ενοικιάζονται** [enikiazondeh] for hire, to rent

ΕΝΟΙΚΙΑΖΟΝΤΑΙ ΑΥΤΟΚΙΝΗΤΑ **ενοικιάζονται αυτοκίνητα** car rental

ΕΝΟΙΚΙΑΖΟΝΤΑΙ ΒΑΡΚΕΣ **ενοικιάζονται βάρκες** boats for hire

ΕΝΟΙΚΙΑΖΟΝΤΑΙ ΔΩΜΑΤΙΑ **ενοικιάζονται δωμάτια** rooms to let

ΕΝΟΙΚΙΑΣΗ ΑΥΤΟΚΙΝΗΤΩΝ **ενοικίαση αυτοκινήτων** car rental

ενοίκιο (το) [enikio (to)] rent

ενός [enos] of a

ενοχλητικός [enokhlitikos] annoying

ενοχλώ [enokhlo] disturb

εντάξει [endaxi] that's all right; OK

έντεκα [endeka] eleven

έντομο (το) [endomo (to)] insect

ΕΝΤΥΠΑ **έντυπα** printed matter

ενώ [eno] while

εξαιρετικός [exeretikos] terrific

εξ αιτίας [ex etias] because of

εξαρτάται [exartateh] it depends

ΕΞΑΤΜΙΣΗ **εξάτμιση (η)** [exatmisi (i)] exhaust

εξαφανίζομαι [exafanizomeh]

disappear
ΕΞΕΤΑΣΕΙΣ εξετάσεις (οι) [exetasis (i)] check-up; exams
εξηγώ [exigo] explain
εξήντα [exinda] sixty
έξι [exi] six
ΕΞΟΔΟΣ έξοδος (η) [exothos (i)] exit; gate (at airport); door
ΕΞΟΔΟΣ ΑΥΤ/ΤΩΝ έξοδος αυτ/των vehicle exit
ΕΞΟΔΟΣ ΚΙΝΔΥΝΟΥ έξοδος κινδύνου emergency exit
εξοχή (η) [exokhi (i)] countryside
έξοχος [exokhos] excellent
ΕΞΠΡΕΣ εξπρές [expres] special delivery; express
εξυπηρετώ [exipireto] serve (verb), assist
έξυπνος [exipnos] clever, intelligent
έξω! [exo!] get out!
ΕΞΩΣΤΗΣ εξώστης [exostis] circle (in cinema etc)
εξωτερικός [exoterikos] external
στο εξωτερικό [sto exoteriko] abroad
ΕΞΩΤΕΡΙΚΟΥ εξωτερικού postage abroad
εξωφρενικός [exofrenikos] shocking
Ε.Ο.Κ. [E.O.K.] EEC, EU
Ε.Ο.Τ. [E.O.T.] National Tourist Agency
επαληθεύω [epaliTHevo] check (verb), verify
επαναλαμβάνω [epanalamvano] repeat
επαφή: έρχομαι σε επαφή [erkhomeh seh epafi] contact (verb)
Ε.Π.Ε. Ltd
επείγον [epigon] urgent
επειδή [epithi] because
επέκταση (η) [epektasi (i)] extension lead
επέτειος (η) [epetios (i)] anniversary
ΕΠΙΒΑΤΗΣ επιβάτης (ο/η) [epivatis (o/i)] passenger
επιβεβαιώνω [epiveveono] confirm
επίδεσμος (ο) [epithesmos (o)] bandage
επίθεση (η) [epiTHesi (i)] attack (noun)
επιθετικός [epiTHetikos] aggressive
ΕΠΙΘΕΤΟ επίθετο (το) [epiTHeto (to)] surname
επικίνδυνος [epikinthinos] dangerous
ΕΠΙΛΕΞΑΤΕ ΤΟΝ ΑΡΙΘΜΟ επιλέξατε τον αριθμό dial the number
επίπεδος [epipethos] flat (even)
έπιπλα (τα) [epipla (ta)] furniture
ΕΠΙΠΛΩΜΕΝΑ ΔΩΜΑΤΙΑ επιπλωμένα δωμάτια furnished rooms
επίσης [episis] too, also
επισκέπτομαι [episkeptomeh] visit (verb)
ΕΠΙΣΚΕΥΑΖΟΝΤΑΙ ΥΠΟΔΗΜΑΤΑ επισκευάζονται υποδήματα shoe repairs
επισκευή (η) [episkevi (i)] repair
επίσκεψη (η) [episkepsi (i)] visit

επιστήμη (η) [epistimi (i)] science
ΕΠΙΣΤΟΛΕΣ επιστολές letters
επιστρέφω [epistrefo] give back; arrive back
ΕΠΙΣΤΡΕΦΩ ΣΕ 5΄ επιστρέφω σε 5΄ back in 5 minutes
ΕΠΙΤΑΓΗ επιταγή (η) [epitayi (i)] cheque, (US) check
επιτέλους [epiteloos] at last
επίτηδες [epitithes] deliberately
επιτρέπω [epitrepo] let (allow)
επιτρέπεται [epitrepeteh] it is permitted
επιτυχία (η) [epitikhia (i)] success
επόμενος (ο) [epomenos (o)] next
εποχή (η) [epokhi (i)] season
επτά [epta] seven
Ε.Ρ.Α. Greek radio
ΕΡΓΑ έργα roadworks
ΕΡΓΑ ΕΠΙ ΤΗΣ ΟΔΟΥ ΣΕ ΜΗΚΟΣ ... ΧΙΛ. έργα επί της οδού σε μήκος ... χιλ. roadworks for ... kms
εργάζομαι [ergazomeh] work (verb)
ΕΡΓΑΛΕΙΑ ΠΥΡΑΣΦΑΛΕΙΑΣ εργαλεία πυρασφάλειας fire-fighting equipment
εργαλείο (το) [ergalio (to)] tool
ΕΡΓΑΣΤΗΡΙΟ ΗΛΕΚΤΡΟΝΙΚΩΝ εργαστήριο ηλεκτρονικών electronics
εργένης (ο) [eryenis (o)] bachelor
εργοστάσιο (το) [ergostasio (to)] factory
ερυθρά (η) [eriTHra (i)] German measles
έρχομαι [erkhomeh] come
έρωτας (ο) [erotas (o)] love
κάνω έρωτα [kano erota] make love
ερώτηση (η) [erotisi (i)] question
εσύς, εσείς, εσένα [esas, esis, esena] you
ΕΣΤΙΑΤΟΡΙΟ εστιατόριο (το) [estiatorio (to)] restaurant
εσύ [esi] you
Ε.Σ.Υ. National Health Service
εσώρουχα (τα) [esorookha (ta)] underwear
ΕΣΩΡΟΥΧΑ ΓΥΝΑΙΚΕΙΑ εσώρουχα γυναικεία [esorookha yinekia] ladies' underwear
ΕΣΩΤΕΡΙΚΟΥ εσωτερικού inland postage
Ε.Τ. Greek television
εταιρεία (η) [eteria (i)] company
ετικέτα (η) [etiketa (i)] label
ΕΤΟΙΜΑ ΓΥΝΑΙΚΕΙΑ έτοιμα γυναικεία ladies' clothing
ετοιμάζω [etimazo] prepare
ΕΤΟΙΜΑ ΠΑΙΔΙΚΑ έτοιμα παιδικά children's clothing
έτοιμος [etimos] ready
έτσι [etsi] so; like this
έτσι κι έτσι [etsi ki etsi] so-so
ευαίσθητος [evesTHitos] sensitive
ευγενικός [evyenikos] kind; polite
ευγνώμων [evgnomon] grateful
ΕΥΚΑΙΡΙΑ ευκαιρία (η) [efkeria (i)] bargain
ΕΥΚΑΙΡΙΕΣ ευκαιρίες bargains
εύκολος [efkolos] easy
ΕΥΡΩΠΑΪΚΟΣ Ευρωπαϊκός [Evropa-ikos] European
ΕΥΡΩΠΗ Ευρώπη (η) [Evropi (i)] Europe

ευτυχισμένος [eftikhismenos] happy
ευτυχώς [eftikhos] fortunately
ευχαριστημένος [efkharistimenos] glad; pleased
ευχάριστος [efkharistos] pleasant
ευχαριστώ [efkharisto] thank you
ΕΦΗΜΕΡΙΔΑ εφημερίδα (η) [efimeritha (i)] newspaper
εφημεριδοπώλης (ο) [efimerithopolis (o)] newsagent
ΕΦΟΡΙΑ εφορία (η) tax office
έχει [ekhi] he/she/it has
έχεις [ekhis] you have
έχεις ...; [ekhis ...?] do you have ...?
έχετε [ekheteh] you have
έχετε ...; [ekheteh ...?] do you have ...?
έχουμε [ekhoomeh] we have
έχουν [ekhoon] they have
έχω [ekho] I have

Z

ζακέτα (η) [zaketa (i)] cardigan
ΖΑΧΑΡΟΠΛΑΣΤΕΙΟ ζαχαροπλαστείο (το) [zakharoplastio (to)] cake shop or café selling cakes and soft drinks
ζέστη (η) [zesti (i)] heat
κάνει ζέστη [kani zesti] it's warm
ΖΕΣΤΟ ζεστό [zesto] hot
ΖΕΣΤΟ ΝΕΡΟ ζεστό νερό [zesto nero] hot water
ζεστός [zestos] hot; warm
ζευγάρι (το) [zevgari (to)] pair
ζηλιάρης [ziliaris] jealous
ζημιά (η) [zimia (i)] damage
ζημιές: κάνω ζημιές [kano zimies] break (verb)
ζητάω συγγνώμη [zitao signomi] apologize
ζω [zo] live (verb)
ζωγραφίζω [zografizo] paint (verb: pictures)
ζωγραφική (η) [zografiki (i)] painting
ζωή (η) [zoi (i)] life
ζώνη (η) [zoni (i)] belt
ζώνη ασφαλείας (η) [zoni asfalias (i)] seat belt
ζωντανός [zondanos] alive
ζώο (το) [zo-o (to)] animal
ΖΩΟΛΟΓΙΚΟΣ ΚΗΠΟΣ ζωολογικός κήπος (ο) [zo-oloyikos kipos (o)] zoo

H

η [i] the
ή [i] or
ή ... ή ... [i ... i ...] either ... or ...
ήδη [ithi] already
ήθελα: θα ήθελα [THa iTHela] I would like
ηθοποιός (ο/η) [iTHopios (o/i)] actor, actress
ΗΛ/ΓΕΙΟ ηλ/γειο electrical goods
ΗΛΕΚΤΡΙΚΑ ΕΙΔΗ ηλεκτρικά

είδη [ilektrika ithi] electrical goods
ηλεκτρική σκούπα (το) [ilektriki skoopa (i)] vacuum cleaner
ηλεκτρικό ρεύμα (το) [ilektriko revma (to)] electricity
ΗΛΕΚΤΡΙΚΟΣ ηλεκτρικός (ο) [ilektrikos (o)] underground, (US) subway
ηλεκτρικό σίδερο (το) [ilektriko sithero (to)] iron (for ironing)
ηλεκτρικός [ilektrikos] electric
ΗΛΕΚΤΡΟΛΟΓΟΣ ηλεκτρολόγος (ο) [ilektrologos (o)] electrician
ηλίαση (η) [iliasi (i)] sunstroke
ηλικία (η) [ilikia (i)] age
ηλιοθεραπεία: κάνω ηλιοθεραπεία [kano ilioTHerapia] sunbathe
ηλιόλουστος [ilioloostos] sunny
ήλιος (ο) [ilios (o)] sun
ήμαστε [imasteh] we were
ημέρα (η) [imera (i)] day
ημερολόγιο (το) [imerologio (to)] calendar, diary
ημερομηνία (η) [imerominia (i)] date (time)
ΗΜΕΡΟΜΗΝΙΑ ΛΗΞΗΣ ημερομηνία λήξης best before
ΗΜΕΡΟΜΗΝΙΑ ΠΑΡΑΣΚΕΥΗΣ ημερομηνία παρασκευής date of manufacture
ΗΜΙΔΙΑΤΡΟΦΗ ημιδιατροφή (η) [imithiatrofi (i)] half board
ΗΜΙΣΚΛΗΡΟΙ ΦΑΚΟΙ ΕΠΑΦΗΣ ημίσκληροι φακοί επαφής (οι) [imiskliri faki epafis (i)] gas permeable lenses
ήμουν [imoon] I was
ΗΝΩΜΕΝΕΣ ΠΟΛΙΤΕΙΕΣ ΑΜΕΡΙΚΗΣ Ηνωμένες Πολιτείες Αμερικής (οι) [Inomenes Polities Amerikis (i)] United States of America
Η.Π.Α. (οι) [I.P.A. (i)] USA
ηρεμώ [iremo] calm down
ΗΡΩΟΝ ηρώον (το) [iro-on (to)] war memorial
ήσουν, ήστε [isoon, isteh] you were
ΗΣΥΧΙΑ ησυχία [isikhia] quiet
ήσυχος [isikhos] quiet
ήταν [itan] he/she/it was; they were

Θ

θάλασσα (η) [THalasa (i)] sea
ΘΑΛΑΣΣΙΑ ΣΠΟΡ θαλάσσια σπορ water sports
ΘΑΛΑΣΣΙΟ ΣΚΙ θαλάσσιο σκι (το) [THalasio ski (to)] waterskiing
θάνατος (ο) [THanatos (o)] death
θα σε δω! [THa seh tho!] see you!
θαυμάσιος [THavmasios] wonderful
θεά (η) [THea (i)] goddess
θέα (η) [THea (i)] view
ΘΕΑΤΡΙΚΟ ΕΡΓΟ θεατρικό έργο (το) [THeh-atriko ergo (to)] play (theatre)
ΘΕΑΤΡΟ θέατρο (το) [THeatro (to)] theatre

θεία (η) [THía (i)] aunt
θείος (ο) [THios (o)] uncle
θέλετε ...; [THeleteh ...?] do you want ...?
θέλω [THelo] want (verb)
θεός (ο) [THeos (o)] God
ΘΕΡΙΝΟΣ θερινός (ο) open-air cinema/movie theater
θέρμανση (η) [THermansi (i)] heating
θερμοκρασία (η) [THermokrasía (i)] temperature
θερμόμετρο (το) [THermometro (to)] thermometer
θερμός (το) [THermos (to)] Thermos® flask
ΘΕΣΕΙΣ θέσεις seats
ΘΕΣΕΙΣ ΚΑΘΗΜΕΝΩΝ θέσεις καθημένων seats
ΘΕΣΕΙΣ ΟΡΘΙΩΝ θέσεις ορθίων standing room
θέση (η) [THesi (i)] seat
κλείνω θέση [klíno THesi] book a seat
ΘΕΩΡΕΙΑ θεωρεία [THeoría] boxes (in theatre)
θλιμμένος [THlimenos] depressed; sad
θορυβώδης [THorivothis] noisy
θρησκεία (η) [THriskía (i)] religion
θύελλα (η) [THíela (i)] storm; thunderstorm
θυμάμαι [THimameh] remember
θυμωμένος [THimomenos] angry
θυρωρός (ο) [THiroros (o)] doorman; caretaker

Ι

ΙΑΜΑΤΙΚΕΣ ΠΗΓΕΣ ιαματικές πηγές [iamatikes piyes] spa
ΙΑΝΟΥΑΡΙΟΣ Ιανουάριος (ο) [Ianooarios (o)] January
ιδέα (η) [ithea (i)] idea
ιδιοκτήτης (ο) [ithioktítis (o)] owner
ιδιοκτήτρια (η) [ithioktítria (i)] owner
ΙΔΙΟΚΤΗΤΟ ΠΑΡΚΙΝΓΚ ιδιόκτητο πάρκινγκ private parking
ίδιος [ithios] same
ΙΔΙΩΤΙΚΗ/ΚΡΑΤΙΚΗ ΙΔΙΟΚΤΗΣΙΑ ιδιωτική/κρατική ιδιοκτησία private/state property
ΙΔΙΩΤΙΚΗ ΠΙΝΑΚΟΘΗΚΗ ιδιωτική πινακοθήκη private art gallery
ΙΔΙΩΤΙΚΟΣ ιδιωτικός [ithiotikos] private
ΙΔΙΩΤΙΚΟΣ ΔΡΟΜΟΣ ιδιωτικός δρόμος private road
ιδρώνω [ithrono] sweat (verb)
ιλαρά (η) [ilara (i)] measles
ΙΝΣΤΙΤΟΥΤΟ ΑΙΣΘΗΤΙΚΗΣ ινστιτούτο αισθητικής (το) [institooto esTHitikis (to)] beauty salon
ΙΟΥΛΙΟΣ Ιούλιος (ο) [loolios (o)] July
ΙΟΥΝΙΟΣ Ιούνιος (ο) [loonios (o)] June
ιππασία (η) [ipasía (i)] horse-riding

ΙΠΠΟΔΡΟΜΟΣ ιππόδρομος (ο) [ipothromos (o)] race course (for horses)
Ιρλανδέζα (η) [Irlantheza (i)] Irishwoman
ΙΡΛΑΝΔΙΑ Ιρλανδία (η) [Irlanthia (i)] Ireland
Ιρλανδικός [Irlanthikos] Irish
Ιρλανδός (ο) [Irlanthos (o)] Irishman
ίσια [isia] straight
ΙΣΟΓΕΙΟ ισόγειο (το) [isoyio (to)] ground floor, (US) first floor
ΙΣΟΠΕΔΟΣ ΔΙΑΒΑΣΙΣ ισόπεδος διάβασις level crossing
ΙΣΠΑΝΙΑ Ισπανία (η) [Ispania (i)] Spain
Ισπανικός [Ispanikos] Spanish (adj)
ιστιοπλοΐα (η) [istioploia (i)] sailing
ιστιοπλοϊκό σκάφος (το) [istioploiko skafos (to)] sailing boat
ΙΣΤΙΟΦΟΡΟ ιστιοφόρο (το) [istioforo (to)] sailing boat
ιστορία (η) [istoria (i)] story; history
ίσως [isos] maybe, perhaps
ΙΤΑΛΙΑ Ιταλία (η) [Italia (i)] Italy
Ιταλικός [Italikos] Italian (adj)
ΙΧΘΥΟΠΩΛΕΙΟ ιχθυοπωλείο (το) [ikhThiopolio (to)] fishmonger's

K

Κ. κ. Mr
ΚΑ. κα. Mrs
ΚΑΖΙΝΟ καζίνο (το) [kazino (to)] casino
καθαρίζω [kaTharizo] clean
ΚΑΘΑΡΙΣΤΗΡΙΟ καθαριστήριο (το) [kaTharistirio (to)] laundry and dry cleaner's
ΚΑΘΑΡΙΣΤΙΚΟ ΔΕΡΜΑΤΟΣ καθαριστικό δέρματος (το) [kaTharistiko thermatos (to)] skin cleanser
ΚΑΘΑΡΟ ΒΑΡΟΣ καθαρό βάρος net weight
καθαρός [kaTharos] clean (adj)
ΚΑΘΑΡΤΙΚΟ καθαρτικό (το) [kaThartiko (to)] laxative
κάθε [kaTheh] every
καθεμία, καθένα, καθένας [kaThemia, kaThena, kaThenas] each
κάθε τι [kaTheh ti] everything
καθηγητής (ο) [kaThiyitis (o)] teacher, professor
καθηγήτρια (η) [kaThiyitria (i)] teacher, professor
ΚΑΘΗΜΕΡΙΝΑ καθημερινά [kaThimerina] daily
καθήστε [kaThisteh] please sit down
ΚΑΘΟΔΟΣ κάθοδος [kaThothos] way down, descent
καθολικός [kaTholikos] Catholic (adj)
καθόλου [kaTholoo] not at all; none; any

κάθομαι [kaTHomeh] sit down
καθρέφτης (ο) [kaTHreftis (o)] mirror
καθρέφτης αυτοκινήτου (ο) [kaTHreftis aftokinitoo (o)] rearview mirror
ΚΑΘΥΣΤΕΡΗΣΗ καθυστέρηση (η) [kaTHisterisi (i)] delay
καθυστερώ [kaTHistero] delay (verb); be late
και [keh] and
και εγώ επίσης [k ego episis] me too
και οι δύο [k i thio] both of them
ΚΑΙ ΛΟΙΠΑ και λοιπά etc
καινούργιο [kenooryio] brand-new
ευτυχισμένος ο καινούργιος χρόνος! [eftikhismenos o kenooryios khronos!] happy New Year!
καιρός (ο) [keros (o)] weather
καίω [keo] burn (verb)
κακός [kakos] bad
καλά [kala] well
καλά! [kala!] good!
καλάθι (το) [kalaTHi (to)] basket
καλεί [kali] it's ringing
ΚΑΛΕΣΑΤΕ καλέσατε dial
ΚΑΛΕΣΤΕ ΤΟΝ ΑΡΙΘΜΟ καλέστε τον αριθμό dial number
καλή διασκέδαση [kali thiaskethasi] have fun
καλημέρα [kalimera] good morning
καληνύχτα [kalinikhta] good night
καλησπέρα [kalispera] good afternoon; good evening
καλλιτέχνηδα (η) [kalitekhnitha (i)] artist
καλλιτέχνης (ο) [kalitekhnis (o)] artist
ΚΑΛΛΥΝΤΙΚΑ καλλυντικά (τα) [kalindika (ta)] perfume and cosmetics
ΚΑΛΟΚΑΙΡΙ καλοκαίρι (το) [kalokeri (to)] summer
καλοκαιρινές διακοπές (οι) [kalokerines thiakopes (i)] summer holidays/vacation
καλοριφέρ (το) [kalorifer (to)] radiator (heater)
καλός [kalos] good; kind
καλοψημένος [kalopsimenos] well-done (meat)
καλσόν (το) [kalson (to)] tights, pantyhose
κάλτσες (οι) [kaltses (i)] socks
καλύτερος (ο) [kaliteros (o)] the best
καλύτερος [kaliteros] better
καλύτερος από [kaliteros apo] better than
καλώς ήλθατε! [kalos iITHateh!] welcome!
ΚΑΛΩΣ ΩΡΙΣΑΤΕ ΣΤΗΝ ... καλώς ωρίσατε στην ... welcome to ...
καμαριέρα (η) [kamariera (i)] chambermaid
καμμία [kamia] no-one
καμμιά φορά [kamia fora] sometimes
καμπάνα (η) [kabana (i)] bell
ΚΑΜΠΙΝΑ καμπίνα (η) [kabina

(i)] cabin (on ship)
ΚΑΜΠΙΝΓΚ κάμπινγκ (το) [camping (to)] campsite, caravan site, trailer park
ΚΑΜΠΙΝΕΣ καμπίνες [kabines] changing rooms
ΚΑΝΑΔΑΣ Καναδάς (ο) [Kanathas (o)] Canada
Καναδή (η) [Kanathi (i)] Canadian (woman)
Καναδικός [Kanathikos] Canadian (adj)
Καναδός (ο) [Kanathos (o)] Canadian (man)
κανάτα (η) [kanata (i)] jug
κάνει ... [kani ...] it is ..., it costs ...
κάνεις [kanis] you do
τι κάνεις; [ti kanis?] how are you?, how do you do?
κανένα [kanena] nothing
κανένας [kanenas] no-one, nobody
κάνετε [kaneteh] you do
τι κάνετε; [ti kaneteh?] how are you?, how do you do?
κανό (το) [kano (to)] canoe
κάνω [kano] do; make
καπάκι (το) [kapaki (to)] lid, cap (of bottle)
καπαρντίνα (η) [kapardina (i)] raincoat
καπέλο (το) [kapelo (to)] hat, cap
ΚΑΠΕΤΑΝΙΟΣ καπετάνιος (ο) [kapetanios (o)] captain (of ship)
ΚΑΠΝΙΖΟΝΤΕΣ καπνίζοντες [kapnizondes] smoking
καπνίζω [kapnizo] smoke (verb)
ΚΑΠΝΙΣΤΕΣ καπνιστές [kapnistes] smokers
ΚΑΠΝΙΣΤΗΡΙΟ καπνιστήριο (το) [kapnistirio (to)] smoking room
ΚΑΠΝΟΠΩΛΕΙΟ καπνοπωλείο (το) [kapnopolio (to)] tobacconist's
ΚΑΠΝΟΣ καπνός (ο) [kapnos (o)] smoke; tobacco
καπό (το) [kapo (to)] bonnet (car), (US) hood
κάποιος [kapios] somebody
κάπου [kapoo] somewhere
ΚΑΡΑΜΕΛΑ καραμέλα (η) [karamela (i)] caramel
καρδιά (η) [karthia (i)] heart
καρδιακή προσβολή (η) [karthiaki prosvoli (i)] heart attack
καρέκλα (η) [karekla (i)] chair
καρμπιρατέρ (το) [karbirater (to)] carburettor
καρνέ επιταγών (το) [karneh epitagon (to)] cheque book, (US) check book
καροτσάκι (το) [karotsaki (to)] pram; pushchair, buggy
καρπός (ο) [karpos (o)] wrist
ΚΑΡΤΑ κάρτα (η) [karta (i)] postcard; business card
κάρτα επιβιβάσεως (η) [karta epivivaseos (i)] boarding pass
κάρτα επιταγών (η) [karta epitagon (i)] cheque card, (US) check card
ΚΑΡΤΠΟΣΤΑΛ καρτποστάλ (η) [kartpostal (i)] postcard
καρφί (το) [karfi (to)] nail (in wall)
καρφίτσα (η) [karfitsa (i)] pin; brooch

κασκόλ (το) [kaskol (to)] scarf (for neck)

ΚΑΣΣΕΤΑ κασσέτα (η) [kaseta (i)] cassette, tape

κασσεττόφωνο (το) [kasetofono (to)] cassette player

καστόρι (το) [kastori (to)] suede

κάστρο (το) [kastro (to)] castle

κατά [kata] against; about

κάταγμα (το) [katagma (to)] fracture

καταδύσεις (οι) [katathisis (i)] skin-diving

ΚΑΤΑΘΕΣΗ κατάθεση (η) [kataTHesi (i)] deposit

καταλαβαίνω [katalaveno] understand

δεν καταλαβαίνω [then katalaveno] I don't understand

ΚΑΤΑΛΛΗΛΟ κατάλληλο suitable for all ages

κατάλογος (ο) [katalogos (o)] list; menu

ΚΑΤΑΝΑΛΩΣΗ ΠΡΙΝ ... κατανάλωση πριν ... consume before ...

καταπίνω [katapino] swallow (verb)

καταρράκτης (ο) [kataraktis (o)] waterfall

ΚΑΤΑΣΚΕΥΑΖΟΝΤΑΙ ΚΛΕΙΔΙΑ κατασκευάζονται κλειδιά keys cut here

κατασκήνωση (η) [kataskinosi (i)] camping

ΚΑΤΑΣΤΗΜΑ ΑΦΟΡΟΛΟΓΗΤΩΝ κατάστημα αφορολογήτων (το) [katastima aforoloyiton (to)] duty-free shop

καταστροφή (η) [katastrofi (i)] disaster

ΚΑΤΑΣΤΡΩΜΑ κατάστρωμα (το) [katastroma (to)] deck

κατά τη διάρκεια [kata ti thiarkia] while, during

καταψύκτης (ο) [katapsiktis (o)] freezer

κατάψυξη (η) [katapsixi (i)] freezer compartment

κατεβαίνω [kateveno] get off; go down

ΚΑΤΕΙΛΗΜΜΕΝΟΣ κατειλημμένος [katilimenos] engaged, occupied

ΚΑΤΕΠΕΙΓΟΝ κατεπείγον [katepigon] express

κατευθείαν [katefTHian] direct

ΚΑΤΕΨΥΓΜΕΝΑ κατεψυγμένα (τα) [katepsigmena (ta)] frozen food

ΚΑΤΕΨΥΓΜΕΝΟ κατεψυγμένο [katepsigmeno] frozen (food)

κάτι [kati] something

κάτι άλλο [kati alo] something else

ΚΑΤΟΛΙΣΘΗΣΕΙΣ κατολισθήσεις falling rocks

ΚΑΤΟΣΤΑΡΙΚΟ κατοστάρικο (το) [katostariko (to)] 100-drachma note/bill

κατσαβίδι (το) [katsavithi (to)] screwdriver

κατσαρόλα (η) [katsarola (i)] saucepan

κατσίκα (η) [katsika (i)] goat

ΚΑΤΩ κάτω [kato] down; downstairs

κάτω από [kato apo] under

καυτερός [kafteros] spicy, hot
καυτός [kaftos] hot (to taste)
καφέ [kafe] brown
ΚΑΦΕΚΟΠΤΕΙΟ καφεκοπτείο (το) [kafekoptio (to)] coffee shop
ΚΑΦΕΝΕΙΟ καφενείο (το) [kafenio (to)] coffee house, where Greek coffee is served with traditional sweets
ΚΑΦΕΤΕΡΙΑ καφετέρια (η) [kafeteria (i)] café, coffee shop
κάψιμο (το) [kapsimo (to)] burn
ΚΕΛΣΙΟΥ Κελσίου [Kelsioo] centigrade
κέλυφος (το) [kelifos (to)] shell
ΚΕΝΤΗΜΑΤΑ κεντήματα (τα) [kendimata (ta)] embroidery
κεντρική θέρμανση (η) [kendriki THermansi (i)] central heating
ΚΕΝΤΡΟ κέντρο (το) [kendro (to)] centre
κέντρο της πόλης [kendro tis polis] city centre
ΚΕΡΑΜΙΚΑ κεραμικά (τα) [keramika (ta)] ceramics
κερδίζω [kerthizo] earn; win (verb)
κερί (το) [keri (to)] candle
ΚΕΡΚΥΡΑ Κέρκυρα (η) [Kerkira (i)] Corfu
ΚΕΡΜΑ κέρμα (το) [kerma (to)] coin
ΚΕΡΜΑΤΑ κέρματα [kermata] coins
ΚΕΣ. κες. Mrs
κεφάλι (το) [kefali (to)] head
κηδεία (η) [kithia (i)] funeral
ΚΗΠΟΘΕΑΤΡΟ κηποθέατρο (το) open-air theatre
ΚΗΠΟΣ κήπος (ο) [kipos (o)] garden, park
κιβώτιο ταχυτήτων (το) [kivotio takhititon (to)] gearbox
κιθάρα (η) [kiTHara (i)] guitar
ΚΙΛΟ κιλό (το) [kilo (to)] kilo
ΚΙΝΔΥΝΟΣ κίνδυνος (ο) [kinthinos (o)] danger; caution
ΚΙΝΔΥΝΟΣ ΠΥΡΚΑΓΙΑΣ κίνδυνος πυρκαγιάς fire risk
κινηματογραφική μηχανή (η) [kinimatografiki mikhani (i)] camcorder
ΚΙΝΗΜΑΤΟΓΡΑΦΟΣ κινηματογράφος (ο) [kinimatografos (o)] cinema, movie theater
κίτρινος [kitrinos] yellow
ΚΚ. κκ. Messrs
κλαίω [kleo] cry (verb)
κλάξον (το) [klaxon (to)] horn (in car)
κλέβω [klevo] steal
κλειδαριά (η) [klitharia (i)] lock
κλειδί (το) [klithi (to)] key; spanner, wrench
ΚΛΕΙΔΙΑ κλειδιά keys cut here
κλειδώνω [klithono] lock (verb)
ΚΛΕΙΝΕΤΕ ΤΗΝ ΠΟΡΤΑ κλείνετε την πόρτα close the door
κλείνω [klino] close (verb); switch off
ΚΛΕΙΣΤΑ κλειστά [klista] closed
ΚΛΕΙΣΤΟ ΑΠΟ ... ΩΣ ... κλειστό από ... ως ... [klisto apo ... os ...] closed from ... to ...

ΚΛΕΙΣΤΟΝ κλειστόν [kliston] closed
κλειστός [klistos] closed; off (lights)
κλέφτης (ο) [kleftis (o)] thief
κλέφτρα (η) [kleftra (i)] thief
κλίμα (το) [klima (to)] climate
ΚΛΙΜΑΤΙΖΟΜΕΝΟΣ κλιματιζόμενος [klimatizomenos] air-conditioned
ΚΛΙΜΑΤΙΣΜΟΣ κλιματισμός (ο) [klimatismos (o)] air-conditioning
κλοπή (η) [klopi (i)] theft
Κ.Λ.Π. κλπ etc
ΚΛΩΣΤΗ κλωστή (η) [klosti (i)] thread
κόβω [kovo] cut (verb)
κοιλάδα (η) [kilatha (i)] valley
κοιμάμαι [kimameh] sleep (verb); be asleep
ΚΟΙΜΗΤΗΡΙΟ κοιμητήριο (το) [kimitirio (to)] cemetery
ΚΟΙΝΟΤΙΚΟ ΓΡΑΦΕΙΟ κοινοτικό γραφείο (το) local government office
κοκκαλιάρης [kokaliaris] skinny
κόκκαλο (το) [kokalo (to)] bone
κόκκινος [kokinos] red
κόλλα (η) [kola (i)] glue
κολλιέ (το) [kolie (to)] necklace
κόλπος (ο) [kolpos (o)] vagina; gulf
ΚΟΛΥΜΒΗΤΗΡΙΟ κολυμβητήριο (το) [kolimvitirio (to)] swimming pool
κολυμπάω [kolibao] swim (verb)
κολύμπι (το) [kolibi (to)] swimming
κολυμπώ [kolibo] swim (verb)
κολώνια (η) [kolonia (i)] eau de toilette
κολώνια μετά το ξύρισμα [kolonia meta to xirisma] aftershave
κομμάτι (το) [komati (to)] piece
ΚΟΜΜΩΣΕΙΣ κομμώσεις (οι) [komosis (i)] hairdresser's
ΚΟΜΜΩΤΗΡΙΟ κομμωτήριο (το) [komotirio (to)] hairdresser's
κομμώτρια (η) [komotria (i)] hairdresser
κομπιουτεράκι (το) [kombi-ooteraki (to)] calculator
κομπολόι (το) [kombolοi (to)] worry beads
κοντά [konda] near, close by
κοντέρ (το) [konder (to)] speedometer
ΚΟΝΤΙΣΙΟΝΕΡ κοντίσιονερ (το) [kondisioner (to)] conditioner
κοντός [kondos] short (person)
ΚΟΡΔΟΝΙΑ ΠΑΠΟΥΤΣΙΩΝ κορδόνια παπουτσιών (τα) [korthonia papootsion (ta)] shoelaces
κόρη (η) [kori (i)] daughter
κορίτσι (το) [koritsi (to)] girl
κόρνα (η) [korna (i)] horn (in car)
κορυφή (η) [korifi (i)] top
ΚΟΣΜΗΜΑΤΑ κοσμήματα (τα) [kosmimata (ta)] jewellery
ΚΟΣΜΗΜΑΤΟΠΩΛΕΙΟ κοσμηματοπωλείο (το) [kosmimatopolio (to)] jeweller's
κόσμος (ο) [kosmos (o)] world; people, crowd
κοστίζει [kostizi] it costs
κόστος (το) [kostos (to)] cost

κουβάς (ο) [koovas (o)] bucket
κουβέρτα (η) [kooverta (i)] blanket
κουδούνι (το) [koothooni (to)] bell (for door)
ΚΟΥΖΙΝΑ κουζίνα (η) [koozina (i)] cooker; kitchen
ΚΟΥΚΕΤΑ κουκέτα (η) [kooketa (i)] couchette
κουκέτες (οι) [kooketes (i)] bunk beds
κούκλα (η) [kookla (i)] doll
κουμπί (το) [koobi (to)] button
κουνέλι (το) [kooneli (to)] rabbit
κούνια (η) [koonia (i)] cot
κουνούπι (το) [koonoopi (to)] mosquito
κουπέ (το) [koopeh (to)] compartment
κουρασμένος [koorasmenos] tired
ΚΟΥΡΕΑΣ κουρέας (ο) [koureas (o)] barber
ΚΟΥΡΕΙΟ κουρείο (το) [kourio (to)] barber's shop
κούρεμα (το) [koorema (to)] haircut
κουρτίνα (η) [kourtina (i)] curtain
κουστούμι (το) [koostoomi (to)] suit
κουτάλι (το) [kootali (to)] spoon
ΚΟΥΤΑΛΙΕΣ ΓΛΥΚΟΥ κουταλιές γλυκού teaspoonfuls
ΚΟΥΤΑΛΙΕΣ ΣΟΥΠΑΣ κουταλιές σούπας tablespoonfuls
κουτί (το) [kooti (to)] box; can
κουφός [koofos] deaf
ΚΡΑΓΙΟΝ κραγιόν (το) [krayon (to)] lipstick
κράμπα (η) [kramba (i)] cramp
κρανίο (το) [kranio (to)] skull
κρατάω [kratao] hold; keep
ΚΡΑΤΗΣΕΙΣ ΘΕΣΕΩΝ κρατήσεις θέσεων reservations; seat reservations
κράτηση θέσης (η) [kratisi THesis (i)] reservation
κρεβάτι (το) [krevati (to)] bed
ΚΡΕΜΑ ΠΡΟΣΩΠΟΥ κρέμα προσώπου (η) [krema prosopoo (i)] moisturizer
κρεμάστρα (η) [kremastra (i)] coathanger; peg
ΚΡΕΟΠΩΛΕΙΟ κρεοπωλείο (το) [kreopolio (to)] butcher's
κρίμα: είναι κρίμα [ineh krima] it's a pity
κρουαζιέρα (η) [kroo-aziera (i)] cruise
κρύβομαι [krivomeh] hide (oneself)
κρύβω [krivo] hide (something)
κρύο (το) [krio (to)] cold
κάνει κρύο [kani krio] it's cold
ΚΡΥΟ ΝΕΡΟ κρύο νερό [krio nero] cold water
κρύος [krios] cold (adj)
κρύωμα (το) [krioma (to)] cold (illness)
Κ.Τ.Ε.Λ. long-distance bus station
κτηνίατρος (ο/η) [ktiniatros (o/i)] vet
κτίριο (το) [ktirio (to)] building
κυβέρνηση (η) [kivernisi (i)] government
κυκλοφορία (η) [kikloforia (i)] traffic

κυκλοφοριακή συμφόρηση (η) [kikloforiaki simforisi (i)] traffic jam

ΚΥΛΙΚΕΙΟ κυλικείο (το) [kilikio (to)] snackbar

ΚΥΛΟΤΕΣ κυλότες (οι) [kilotes (i)] panties; underpants

κύμα (το) [kima (to)] wave

κυνηγώ [kinigo] hunt (verb), chase

ΚΥΠΡΟΣ Κύπρος (η) [Kipros (i)] Cyprus

Κυρία (η) [Kiria (i)] Mrs; Ms

κυρία (η) [kiria (i)] lady; madam

ΚΥΡΙΑΚΕΣ ΚΑΙ ΕΟΡΤΕΣ Κυριακές και Εορτές Sundays and holidays

ΚΥΡΙΑΚΗ Κυριακή (η) [Kiriaki (i)] Sunday

ΚΥΡΙΑΚΗ ΤΟΥ ΠΑΣΧΑ Κυριακή του Πάσχα (η) [Kiriaki too Paskha (i)] Easter Sunday

κύριε [kiri-eh] sir

ΚΥΡΙΕΣ κυρίες [kiries] Mrs

ΚΥΡΙΟΙ κύριοι Messrs

ΚΥΡΙΟΣ Κύριος [Kirios] Mr

κύριος (ο) [kirios (o)] gentleman

κύριος [kirios] main

κύστη (η) [kisti (i)] bladder

κυττάζω [kitazo] look (verb)

ΚΩΔΙΚΟΣ κωδικός (ο) [kothikos (o)] code

ΚΩΔΙΚΟΣ ΑΡΙΘΜΟΣ κωδικός αριθμός [kothikos ariTHmos] dialling code

Λ

ΛΑΔΙ λάδι (το) [lathi (to)] oil

ΛΑΔΙΑ λάδια (τα) [lathia (ta)] engine oil

ΛΑΔΙ ΜΑΥΡΙΣΜΑΤΟΣ λάδι μαυρίσματος [lathi mavrismatos] suntan oil

λάθος (το) [laTHos (to)] mistake

λάθος [laTHos] wrong

λάθος νούμερο [laTHos noomero] wrong number

λαιμός (ο) [lemos (o)] neck; throat

λακ (η) [lak (i)] hairspray

λάμπα (η) [lamba (i)] light bulb; lamp

λαστιχάκι (το) [lastikhaki (to)] rubber band

λάστιχο (το) [lastikho (to)] rubber (material); tyre

λεβιές ταχυτήτων (ο) [levies takhititon (o)] gear lever

λείπω [lipo] be missing; be out; be away

λειτουργία (η) [litooryia (i)] mass (church)

λεκές (ο) [lekes (o)] stain

ΛΕΜΒΟΣ λέμβος (η) [lemvos (i)] lifeboat

λένε: λένε ότι [leneh oti] they say that

με λένε ... [meh leneh ...] my name is ...

πως σε λένε; [pos seh leneh?] what's your name?

λέξη (η) [lexi (i)] word

λεξικό (το) [lexiko (to)] dictionary

λεπτό (το) [lepto (to)] minute
λεπτός [leptos] slim
λέσχη (η) [leskhi (i)] club
λευκοπλάστ (το) [lefkoplast (to)] (sticking) plaster, Bandaid®
ΛΕΦΤΑ **λεφτά (τα)** [lefta (ta)] money
λέω [leo] say
ΛΕΩΦΟΡΕΙΟ **λεωφορείο (το)** [leoforio (to)] bus
ΛΕΩΦΟΡΕΙΟ ΥΠ' ΑΡΙΘΜ ... **λεωφορείο υπ' αριθμ ...** bus number ...
ΛΕΩΦΟΡΟΣ **λεωφόρος (η)** [leoforos (i)] avenue
ΛΗΓΕΙ ΤΗΝ ... **λήγει την ...** expires on ...
λιακάδα (η) [liakatha (i)] sunshine
λίγα [liga] a few
λίγο [ligo] a little bit
ΣΕ ΛΙΓΟ **σε λίγο** [seh ligo] in a little while
λίγος [ligos] little, short
λιγότερος [ligoteros] fewer
λιγότερο [ligotero] less
ΛΙΜΑΝΙ **λιμάνι (το)** [limani (to)] harbour
λίμα νυχιών (η) [lima nikhion (i)] nailfile
ΛΙΜΕΝΑΡΧΕΙΟ **λιμεναρχείο (το)** port authorities
ΛΙΜΕΝΑΡΧΗΣ **λιμενάρχης (ο)** harbour master
ΛΙΜΕΝΙΚΗ ΑΣΤΥΝΟΜΙΑ **Λιμενική Αστυνομία (η)** [limeniki Astinomia (i)] harbour police
ΛΙΜΗΝ **λιμήν (ο)** [limin (o)] port
λίμνη (η) [limni (i)] lake
λιμνούλα (η) [limnoola (i)] pond
λίμπρα (η) [libra (i)] pound (weight)
λιπαρός [liparos] greasy
λιποθυμώ [lipoTHimo] faint (verb)
ΛΙΡΑ ΑΓΓΛΙΑΣ **λίρα Αγγλίας (η)** [lira Anglias (i)] pound sterling
ΛΙΤΑΝΕΙΑ **λιτανεία (η)** litany
ΛΙΤΡΟ **λίτρο (το)** [litro (to)] litre
ΛΟΓΑΡΙΑΣΜΟΣ **λογαριασμός (ο)** [logariasmos (o)] bill, (US) check
λογικός [loyikos] sensible
ΛΟΓΙΣΤΗΡΙΟ **λογιστήριο (το)** [loyistirio (to)] purser's office
ΛΟΝΔΙΝΟ **Λονδίνο (το)** [Lonthino (to)] London
λόξυγγας (ο) [loxingas (o)] hiccups
λουλούδι (το) [looloothi (to)] flower
λούσιμο (το) [loosimo (to)] wash
ΛΟΥΤΡΟ **λουτρό (το)** [lootro (to)] bathroom
λόφος (ο) [lofos (o)] hill
λυπάμαι [lipameh] I'm sorry
λυπημένος [lipimenos] sad
ΛΥΡΙΚΗ ΣΚΗΝΗ **λυρική σκηνή (η)** [liriki skini (i)] opera house

M

μαγαζί (το) [magazi (to)] shop
μαγειρεύω [mayirevo] cook (verb)
μαγειρικά σκεύη (τα) [mayirika skevi (ta)] cooking utensils
μαγείρισσα (η) [mayirisa (i)] cook
μάγειρος (ο) [mayiros (o)] cook
μάγκας (ο) [mangas (o)]

streetwise/smart person
μαγιό (το) [mayo (to)] swimming trunks
μάγουλο (το) [magoolo (to)] chin
μαζί [mazi] together
μαζί με [mazi meh] with, together with
μαθαίνω [maTHeno] learn
μάθημα (το) [maTHima (to)] lesson
κάνω μάθημα [kano maTHima] teach; take a lesson
ΜΑΘΗΜΑΤΑ ΣΚΙ μαθήματα σκι [maTHimata ski] skiing lessons
ΜΑΙΟΣ Μάιος (ο) [Maios (o)] May
μακριά [makria] far, at a distance
μαλάκας (ο) [malakas (o)] arsehole, wanker
μακρύς [makris] long
ΜΑΛΑΚΟΙ ΦΑΚΟΙ μαλακοί φακοί (οι) [malaki faki (i)] soft lenses
μάλιστα [malista] yes, certainly
μάλιστα! [malista!] well!
ΜΑΛΛΙ μαλλί (το) [mali (to)] wool
μαλλιά (τα) [malia (ta)] hair
ΜΑΛΛΙΝΟ μάλλινο [malino] wool
μάλλον [malon] rather; probably
μαλώνω [malono] fight (verb)
μαμά (η) [mama (i)] mum
ΜΑΝΑΒΗΣ μανάβης (ο) [manavis (o)] greengrocer's
ΜΑΝΟ μανό (το) [mano (to)] nail polish
μανταλάκι (το) [mandalaki (to)] clothes peg
μαντήλι (το) [mandili (to)] handkerchief; headscarf
μαξιλάρι (το) [maxilari (to)] pillow
μαραγκός (ο) [marangos (o)] carpenter
ΜΑΡΙΝΑ μαρίνα (η) [marina (i)] marina
μαρκαδόρος (ο) [markathoros (o)] felt-tip pen
ΜΑΡΤΙΟΣ Μάρτιος (ο) [Martios (o)] March
μάρτυρας (ο) [martiras (o)] witness
μασέλα (η) [masela (i)] dentures
μας [mas] us; our
μάτι (το) [mati (to)] eye; ring (on cooker)
ματς (το) [mats (to)] match (sport)
μαυρίζω [mavrizo] tan (verb)
μαύρισμα (το) [mavrisma (to)] tan (colour)
μαύρισμα από τον ήλιο [mavrisma apo ton ilio] suntan
μαύρος [mavros] black
μαχαίρι (το) [makheri (to)] knife
μαχαιροπήρουνα (τα) [makheropiroona (ta)] cutlery
με [meh] with; by; me
με αυτοκίνητο [meh aftokinito] by car
ΜΕΓΑΛΗ ΒΡΕΤΑΝΝΙΑ Μεγάλη Βρεταννία (η) [Megali Vretania (i)] Great Britain
Μεγάλη Παρασκευή (η) [Megali Paraskevi (i)] Good Friday
μεγάλος [megalos] big
μεγαλύτερος [megaliteros] bigger

ΜΕΓΕΘΟΣ μέγεθος (το) [meyeTHos (to)] size
μεγέθυνση (η) [meyeTHinsi (i)] enlargement
ΜΕΓΙΣΤΟ ΒΑΡΟΣ μέγιστο βάρος maximum permitted weight
μέγιστος (ο) [meyistos (o)] biggest
μεζ (η) [mez (i)] highlights (in hair)
μεθαύριο [meTHavrio] the day after tomorrow
μεθυσμένος [meTHismenos] drunk
μέικ απ (το) [meik ap (to)] make-up
μελανιά (η) [melania (i)] bruise
μέλλον (το) [melon (to)] future
ΜΕ ΜΠΑΝΙΟ με μπάνιο [meh banio] with bathroom
ΜΕ ΝΤΟΥΣ με ντους [meh doos] with shower
μένω [meno] live (in town etc); stay (in hotel etc)
μέρα (η) [mera (i)] day
μερίδα (η) [meritha (i)] portion
μερικά, μερικές, μερικοί [merika, merikes, meriki] some
μέρος (το) [meros (to)] part, place; WC
μέσα [mesa] in; inside
μεσάνυχτα (τα) [mesanikhta (ta)] midnight
μέση (η) [mesi (i)] middle; waist
μεσημέρι (το) [mesimeri (to)] midday
Μεσόγειος (η) [Mesoyios (i)] Mediterranean
μετά [meta] after; afterwards
μετά από σας [meta apo sas] after you
μετά μεσημβρίας [meta mesimvrias] pm
μετακινούμαι [metakinoomeh] move (verb)
μέταλλο (το) [metalo (to)] metal
ΜΕΤΑΞΙ μετάξι (το) [metaxi (to)] silk
μεταξύ [metaxi] between
μεταφέρω [metafero] carry
μεταφράζω [metafrazo] translate
μετεωρολογικό δελτίο (το) [meteoroloyiko theltio (to)] weather forecast
ΜΕΤΡΗΤΑ μετρητά [metrita] cash
ΤΟΙΣ ΜΕΤΡΗΤΟΙΣ τοις μετρητοίς [tis metritis] in cash
μετρητής βενζίνης (ο) [metritis venzinis (o)] fuel gauge
μέτριο μέγεθος [metrio meyeTHos] medium-sized
ΜΕΤΡΙΟΣ μέτριος [metrios] medium; average
ΜΕΤΡΟ μέτρο (το) [metro (to)] metre
μέτωπο (το) [metopo (to)] forehead
μέχρι [mekhri] until
ΜΗ μη do not
ΜΗ ΒΓΑΖΕΤΕ ΤΗΝ ΚΑΡΤΑ μη βγάζετε την κάρτα do not remove the card yet
μηδέν [mithen] zero
ΜΗΝ ΚΑΠΝΙΖΕΤΕ μην καπνίζετε no smoking
ΜΗ ΚΑΠΝΙΖΟΝΤΕΣ μη καπνίζοντες [mi kapnizondes] non-smoking

ΜΗ ΚΑΠΝΙΣΤΕΣ μη καπνιστές [mi kapnistes] non-smokers
μήκος (το) [mikos (to)] length
μήνας (ο) [minas (o)] month
μήνας του μέλιτος [minas too melitos] honeymoon
ΜΗΝ ΕΝΟΧΛΕΙΤΕ μην ενοχλείτε do not disturb
ΜΗΝ ΟΜΙΛΕΙΤΕ ΣΤΟΝ ΟΔΗΓΟ μην ομιλείτε στον οδηγό do not speak to the driver
ΜΗΝ ΠΑΤΑΤΕ ΤΟ ΧΟΡΤΟ μην πατάτε το χόρτο keep off the grass
ΜΗ ΠΟΣΙΜΟ (ΝΕΡΟ) μη πόσιμο (νερό) not for drinking (water)
μητέρα (η) [mitera (i)] mother
ΜΗ ΤΟΞΙΚΟ μη τοξικό non-toxic
μητρόπολη (η) [mitropoli (i)] cathedral
μηχανάκι (το) [mikhanaki (to)] moped
μηχανή (η) [mikhani (i)] engine
μηχανικός (ο) [mikhanikos (o)] mechanic; engineer
μία [mia] a; one
μία φορά [mia fora] once
μιάς [mias] of a
μίζα (η) [miza (i)] ignition
ΜΙΚΡΟ ΟΝΟΜΑ μικρό όνομα (το) [mikro onoma (to)] Christian name
ΜΙΚΡΟΣ μικρός [mikros] little, small
ΜΙΚΤΟ ΒΑΡΟΣ μικτό βάρος gross weight
μικρότερος [mikroteros] smaller
ΜΙΛΑΕΙ μιλάει [milai] engaged, occupied
μιλάω [milao] speak
μιλάτε ...; [milateh ...?] do you speak ...?
μισός [misos] half
ΜΙΣΟΤΙΜΗΣ μισοτιμής half-price
μισώ [miso] hate (verb)
μ.μ. [m.m.] pm
μνημείο (το) [mnimio (to)] monument
μόδα (η) [motha (i)] fashion
της μόδας [tis mothas] fashionable
ΜΟΔΕΣ μόδες fashions
μοιάζει [miazi] it looks/seems
μοιράζομαι [mirazomeh] share (verb)
μοκέτα (η) [moketa (i)] carpet
μολύβι (το) [molivi (to)] pencil
μόλυνση (η) [molinsi (i)] infection
ΜΟΛΥΣΜΕΝΑ ΥΔΑΤΑ μολυσμένα ύδατα polluted water
μολυσμένος [molismenos] polluted
ΜΟΝΑΔΕΣ μονάδες units
ΜΟΝΑΔΙΚΗ ΕΥΚΑΙΡΙΑ μοναδική ευκαιρία (η) special offer
μονή [moni] monastery
μόνο [mono] only
ΜΟΝΟΔΡΟΜΟΣ μονόδρομος one-way street
ΜΟΝΟ ΔΩΜΑΤΙΟ μονό δωμάτιο (το) [mono thomatio (to)]

single room

ΜΟΝΟΚΛΙΝΟ ΔΩΜΑΤΙΟ
μονόκλινο δωμάτιο (το) [monoklino thomatio (to)] single room

μονό κρεβάτι [mono krevati] single bed

μονοπάτι (το) [monopati (to)] path

μόνος [monos] alone

μοντέρνος [mondernos] modern

μοτοσυκλέτα (η) [motosikleta (i)] motorbike

μου [moo] my

ΜΟΥΣΕΙΟ μουσείο (το) [moosio (to)] museum

ΜΟΥΣΙΚΑ ΟΡΓΑΝΑ μουσικά όργανα [moosika organa] musical instruments

μουσική (η) [moosiki (i)] music

μουσική ποπ (η) [moosiki pop (i)] pop music

μουστάκι (το) [moostaki (to)] moustache

μπαίνω [beno] go in, enter

ΜΠΑΚΑΛΙΚΟ μπακάλικο (το) [bakaliko (to)] grocer's

μπαλκόνι (το) [balkoni (to)] balcony

μπάλλα (η) [bala (i)] ball (large)

μπαλλάκι (το) [balaki (to)] ball (small)

μπαμπάς (ο) [babas (o)] dad

μπανιέρα (η) [baniera (i)] bathtub

ΜΠΑΝΙΟ μπάνιο (το) [banio (to)] bath

κάνω μπάνιο [kano banio] swim (verb); have a bath

πάω για μπάνιο [pao ya banio] go swimming

ΜΠΑΡ μπαρ (το) [bar (to)] bar

μπάρμαν (ο) [barman (o)] barman

μπάρ γούμαν (η) [bar woman (i)] barmaid

μπαταρία (η) [bataria (i)] battery

μπεζ [bez] beige

μπέιμπι-σίττερ (η) [baby-sitter (i)] babysitter

μπερδεμένος [berthemenos] complicated

μπικίνι (το) [bikini (to)] bikini

μπλε [bleh] blue

μπλούζα (η) [blooza (i)] blouse

μπλουζάκι (το) [bloozaki (to)] T-shirt

μπόρα (η) [bora (i)] shower (rain)

μπορείς [boris] you can

μπορείς να ...; [boris na ...?] can you ...?

μπορείτε [boriteh] you can

μπορείτε να ...; [boriteh na ...?] can you ...?

μπρος [bros] forwards; in front of

βάζω μπρος [vazo bros] switch on (engine)

μπορώ [boro] I can

μπότα (η) [bota (i)] boot (shoe)

μπουγάδα (η) [boogatha (i)] washing

βάζω μπουγάδα [vazo boogatha] do the washing

μπουζί (το) [boozi (to)] spark plug

ΜΠΟΥΖΟΥΚΙΑ μπουζούκια (τα) [boozookia (ta)] club with bouzouki music

μπουκάλι (το) [bookali (to)] bottle

μπουκιά (η) [bookia (i)] bite

μπούτι (το) [**boo**ti (to)] thigh
ΜΠΟΥΤΙΚ μπουτίκ (η) [bootik (i)] boutique
μπροστινό μέρος (το) [brostino meros (to)] front (part)
ΜΠΥΡΑ μπύρα [bira] beer, lager
μπωλ (το) [bol (to)] bowl
μύγα (η) [miga (i)] fly
μυθιστόρημα (το) [miTHistorima (to)] novel
μυρίζω [mirizo] smell (verb)
μυρμήγκι (το) [mirmingi (to)] ant
μυρωδιά (η) [mirothia (i)] smell
μυστικός [mistikos] secret
μυς (ο) [mis (o)] muscle
μύτη (η) [miti (i)] nose
μύωπας [miopas] shortsighted
μωβ [mov] purple
μωρό (το) [moro (to)] baby

N

να [na] here is/are
ναι [neh] yes
ναι, ναι! [neh neh!] oh yes I do!
νάιτκλαμπ (το) [nightclub (to)] nightclub
ΝΑ ΛΑΜΒΑΝΕΤΑΙ ΜΟΝΟΝ ΑΠΟ ΤΟ ΣΤΟΜΑ **να λαμβάνεται μόνον από το στόμα** to be taken orally only
ΝΑ ΛΑΜΒΑΝΕΤΑΙ ... ΦΟΡΕΣ ΗΜΕΡΗΣΙΩΣ **να λαμβάνεται ... φορές ημερησίως** to be taken ... times daily
ναρκωτικά (τα) [narkotika (ta)] drugs (narcotics)
ΝΑ ΦΥΛΑΣΣΕΤΑΙ ΜΑΚΡΙΑ ΑΠΟ ΠΑΙΔΙΑ **να φυλάσσεται μακριά από παιδιά** keep out of reach of children
νέα (η) [nea (i)] teenager
νέα (τα) [nea (ta)] news
ΝΕΑ ΖΗΛΑΝΔΙΑ **Νέα Ζηλανδία (η)** [Nea Zilanthia (i)] New Zealand
ΝΕΚΡΟΤΑΦΕΙΟ **νεκροταφείο (το)** [nekrotafio (to)] cemetery
Νέο Έτος (το) [Neo Etos (to)] New Year
ΝΕΟΖΗΛΑΝΔΕΖΑ **Νεοζηλανδέζα (η)** [Neozilantheza (i)] New Zealander
ΝΕΟΖΗΛΑΝΔΟΣ **Νεοζηλανδός (ο)** [Neozilanthos (o)] New Zealander
νέοι (οι) [nei (i)] young people
νέος (ο) [neos (o)] teenager
νέος [neos] new; young
ΝΕΡΟ **νερό (το)** [nero (to)] water
νεροχύτης (ο) [nerokhitis (o)] sink
νευρικός [nevrikos] nervous
νεφρά (τα) [nefra (ta)] kidneys
νησί (το) [nisi (to)] island
νιπτήρας (ο) [niptiras (o)] washbasin
νιώθω [nioTHo] feel
ΝΟΕΜΒΡΙΟΣ **Νοέμβριος (ο)** [Noemvrios (o)] November
νοικιάζω [nikiazo] rent (verb)
ΝΟΜΑΡΧΙΑ **νομαρχία (η)** local government office
νομίζω [nomizo] think
ΝΟΜΟΣ **νομός (ο)** county
νόμος (ο) [nomos (o)] law

ΝΟΣΟΚΟΜΕΙΟ νοσοκομείο (το) [nosokomio (to)] hospital
νόστιμο [nostimo] tasty
νοστιμώτατο [nostimotato] delicious
ΝΟΥΜΕΡΟ νούμερο (το) [noomero (to)] number
ΝΤΕΜΙ ΠΑΝΣΙΟΝ ντεμί πανσιόν (η) [demi pansion (i)] half board
ντεπόζιτο (το) [ndepozito (to)] tank
ΝΤΗΖΕΛ ντήζελ (το) [dizel (to)] diesel
ντισκοτέκ (η) [ndiskotek (i)] disco
ντιστριμπυτέρ (το) [ndistribiter (to)] distributor
ντουλάπι (το) [ndoolapi (to)] cupboard
ΝΤΟΥΣ ντους (το) [doos (to)] shower (in bathroom)
ΝΤΡΑΙΒ - ΙΝ ντραιβ - ιν drive-in
ντροπαλός [ndropalos] shy
ντύνομαι [ndinomeh] dress (oneself)
ντύνω [ndino] dress (verb: someone)
νύφη (η) [nifi (i)] daughter-in-law; sister-in-law; bride
νύχι (το) [nikhi (to)] fingernail
νυχοκόπτης (ο) [nikhokoptis (o)] nail clippers
νύχτα (η) [nikhta (i)] night
ΝΥΧΤΕΡΙΝΟ ΚΕΝΤΡΟ νυχτερινό κέντρο [nikhterino kendro] nightclub
νυχτικό (το) [nikhtiko (to)] nightdress
νωρίς [noris] early

Ξ

ξαδέλφη (η) [xathelfi (i)] cousin
ξάδελφος (ο) [xathelfos (o)] cousin
ξανά [xana] again
ξανθός [xanTHos] blond
ξαπλώνω [xaplono] lie down
ξαφνικά [xafnika] suddenly
ξεκουράζομαι [xekoorazomeh] relax
ξεναγός (ο/η) [xenagos (o/i)] guide
ΞΕΝΟΔΟΧΕΙΟ ξενοδοχείο (το) [xenothokhio (to)] hotel
ξένος [xenos] foreign
ΞΕΝΩΝΑΣ ξενώνας (ο) [xenonas (o)] guesthouse
ΞΕΝΩΝΑΣ ΝΕΟΤΗΤΑΣ ξενώνας νεότητας [xenonas neotitas] youth hostel
ΞΕΝΩΝΑΣ ΝΕΩΝ ξενώνας νέων [xenonas neon] youth hostel
ΞΕΠΟΥΛΗΜΑ ξεπούλημα closing-down sale
ξέρω [xero] know
δεν ξέρω [then xero] I don't know
ξεφωνίζω [xefonizo] scream (verb)
ξεχνώ [xekhno] leave (verb); forget
ξεχωριστά [xekhorista] separately
ξηρός [xiros] dry
ξοδεύω [xothevo] spend
ξύλο (το) [xilo (to)] wood
ξυνός [xinos] sour
ξυπνάω [xipnao] wake up

ξυπνητήρι (το) [xipnitiri (to)] alarm clock
ξύπνιος [xipnios] awake
ξυραφάκι (το) [xirafaki (to)] razor
ξυρίζομαι [xirizomeh] shave (verb)
ξύρισμα (το) [xirisma (to)] shave
ξυριστική μηχανή (η) [xiristiki mikhani (i)] electric shaver

O

ο [o] the
Ο.Α. Olympic Airways
Ο/Γ ferry
ογδόντα [ogthonda] eighty
όγδοος [ogthoos] eighth
οδηγάω [othigao] drive
οδηγός (ο/η) [othigos (o/i)] driver
ΟΔΙΚΑ ΕΡΓΑ **οδικά έργα** roadworks
ΟΔΟΝΤΙΑΤΡΟΣ **οδοντίατρος (ο/η)** [othondiatros (o/i)] dentist
οδοντόβουρτσα (η) [othondovoortsa (i)] toothbrush
ΟΔΟΝΤΟΓΙΑΤΡΟΣ **οδοντογιατρός (ο/η)** [othondoyatros (o/i)] dentist
ΟΔΟΝΤΙΑΤΡΕΙΟ **οδοντιατρείο (το)** [othondiatrio (to)] dentist's
ΟΔΟΝΤΟΚΡΕΜΑ **οδοντόκρεμα (η)** [othondokrema (i)] toothpaste
ΟΔΟΣ **οδός (η)** [othos (i)] road, street
ΟΔΟΣ ΑΝΕΥ ΣΗΜΑΝΣΕΩΣ ΣΕ ΜΗΚΟΣ ... ΧΙΛ. **οδός άνευ σημάνσεως σε μήκος ... χιλ** no road markings for ... kms
οδυνηρός [othiniros] painful
όζα (η) [oza (i)] nail polish
Ο.Η.Ε. UN
ΟΧΙ ΕΠΙΤΑΓΕΣ **όχι επιταγές** no cheques/checks
οι [i] the
οικογένεια (η) [ikoyenia (i)] family
ΟΚΤΩΒΡΙΟΣ **Οκτώβριος (ο)** [Oktovrios (o)] October
όλα [ola] all
όλα καλά [ola kala] that'll do nicely, everything's fine
όλα πληρωμένα [ola pliromena] all inclusive
όλες, όλη [oles, oli] all
ΟΛΙΣΘΗΡΟ ΟΔΟΣΤΡΩΜΑ **ολισθηρό οδόστρωμα** slippery road surface
όλο [olo] **αμμ**
όλοι [oli] everyone; all
ολόκληρος [olokliros] whole
όλος [olos] all
Ο.Λ.Π. Piraeus Port Authorities
ΟΛΥΜΠΙΑΚΗ ΑΕΡΟΠΟΡΙΑ **Ολυμπιακή Αεροπορία** Olympic Airways
ομάδα (η) [omatha (i)] group; team
ομάδα αίματος (η) [omatha ematos (i)] blood group
ομίχλη (η) [omikhli (i)] fog
όμοιος [omios] similar
όμορφος [omorfos] fine, beautiful
ομοφυλόφιλος (ο) [omofilofilos (o)] gay
ομπρέλλα (η) [ombrella (i)]

umbrella
όνειρο (το) [**o**niro (to)] dream
ΟΝΟΜΑ **όνομα (το)** [**o**noma (to)] name; first name
οπά! [**o**pa!] watch it!
ΟΠΕΡΑ **όπερα (η)** [**o**pera (i)] opera
όπισθεν (η) [**o**pisTHen (i)] reverse (gear)
όπλο (το) [**o**plo (to)] gun; rifle
ΟΠΤΙΚΑ **οπτικά (τα)** [**o**ptika (ta)] optician's
ΟΠΤΙΚΟΣ **οπτικός (ο)** [**o**ptikos (o)] optician
ΟΠΩΡΟΠΩΛΕΙΟ **οπωροπωλείο (το)** [**o**poropolio (to)] grocer's
όπως [**o**pos] like; as
όπως και νάναι [**o**pos keh naneh] anyway
ΟΡΓΑΝΙΣΜΟΣ ΗΝΩΜΕΝΩΝ ΕΘΝΩΝ **Οργανισμός Ηνωμένων Εθνών** United Nations Organization
οργανωμένη εκδρομή (η) [organomeni ekthromi (i)] package tour
οργανώνω [organono] organize
όρεξη (η) [**o**rexi (i)] appetite
καλή όρεξη! [kali **o**rexi!] enjoy your meal!, bon appetit!
ΟΡΘΙΩΝ **ορθίων** standing
ΟΡΙΟ ΤΑΧΥΤΗΤΑΣ **όριο ταχύτητας (το)** speed limit
ορίστε; [**o**risteh?] can I help you?
όροφος (ο) [**o**rofos (o)] floor, storey
ΟΡΥΚΤΕΛΑΙΟ **ορυκτέλαιο (το)** [**o**rikteleo (to)] engine oil
ορχήστρα (η) [**o**rkhistra (i)] orchestra
Ο.Σ.Ε. Greek Railways
όταν [**o**tan] when
Ο.Τ.Ε. Greek Telecommunications Company
ότι [**o**ti] that
οτιδήποτε [**o**tithipoteh] anything
Ο.Υ. water authorities
Ουαλλή (η) [**O**oali (i)] Welshwoman
ΟΥΑΛΛΙΑ **Ουαλλία (η)** [**O**oalia (i)] Wales
Ουαλλικός [**O**oalikos] Welsh (adj)
Ουαλλός (ο) [**O**oalos (o)] Welshman
ΟΥΖΕΡΙ **ουζερί (το)** [oozeri] bar serving ouzo and beer with snacks or full meals
ούλο (το) [**oo**lo (to)] gum (in mouth)
ΟΥΡΑ **ουρά (η)** [**oo**ra (i)] queue; tail; queue here
κάνω ουρά [kano **oo**ra] queue (verb)
ουρανός (ο) [**oo**ranos (o)] sky
ούτε ... ούτε ... [**oo**te ... **oo**te ...] neither ... nor ...
ΟΦΘΑΛΜΙΑΤΡΟΣ **οφθαλμίατρος (ο/η)** eye specialist
όχημα (το) [**o**khima (to)] vehicle
ΟΧΙ **όχι** [**o**khi] no; not
όχι άλλο [**o**khi allo] no more
ΟΧΙ ΥΠΕΡΑΣΤΙΚΑ **όχι υπεραστικά** no long-distance calls
οχτώ [**o**khto] eight

Π

ΠΑΓΟΣ πάγος (ο) [pagos (o)] ice
παγωτο παγωτό (το) [pagoto (to)] ice cream
παγωτο ξυλακι παγωτό ξυλάκι (το) [pagoto xilaki (to)] ice lolly
πάει: πώς πάει; [pos pai?] how are things?
ΠΑΖΑΡΙ παζάρι (το) [pazari (to)] bazaar
ΠΑΘΟΛΟΓΟΣ παθολόγος (ο/η) [paTHologos (o/i)] doctor, general practitioner
ΠΑΙΔΙ παιδί (το) [pethi (to)] child
ΠΑΙΔΙΑΤΡΟΣ παιδίατρος (ο/η) paediatrician
ΠΑΙΔΙΚΑ παιδικά (τα) [pethika (ta)] children's wear
ΠΑΙΔΙΚΑ ΕΙΔΗ παιδικά είδη (τα) [pethika ithi (ta)] children's department
ΠΑΙΔΙΚΑ ΕΣΩΡΟΥΧΑ παιδικά εσώρουχα [pethika esorookha] children's underwear
ΠΑΙΔΙΚΑ ΦΟΡΜΑΚΙΑ παιδικά φορμάκια [pethika formakia] babywear, toddlers' clothes
ΠΑΙΔΙΚΟ παιδικό [pethiko] children's (adj)
παίζω [pezo] play (verb)
παίρνω [perno] get; take
παίρνω τηλέφωνο [perno tilefono] phone (verb)
ΠΑΙΧΝΙΔΙ παιχνίδι (το) [pekhnithi (to)] game; toy
ΠΑΚΕΤΟ πακέτο (το) [paketo (to)] package; packet
ΠΑΛΑΙΟΠΩΛΕΙΟ παλαιοπωλείο (το) [paleopolio (to)] antique shop
παλαιός [paleos] old, ancient, antique
παλάτι (το) [palati (to)] palace
παλίρροια (η) [paliria (i)] tide
παλτό (το) [palto (to)] coat
πάνα (η) [pana (i)] nappy, diaper
ΠΑΝΕΠΙΣΤΗΜΙΟ πανεπιστήμιο (το) [panepistimio (to)] university
ΠΑΝΗΓΥΡΙ πανηγύρι (το) [paniyiri (to)] fair, funfair
πανί (το) [pani (to)] sail
ΠΑΝ/ΜΙΟ παν/μιο university
ΠΑΝΣΙΟΝ πανσιόν (η) [pansion (i)] guesthouse
πάντα [panda] always; still
πανταλόνι (το) [pandaloni (to)] trousers, (US) pants
παντζούρια (τα) [pandzooria (ta)] shutters
ΠΑΝΤΟΠΩΛΕΙΟ παντοπωλείο (το) [pandopolio (to)] grocery store
πάντοτε [pandoteh] always
παντού [pandoo] everywhere
παντόφλες (οι) [pandofles (i)] slippers
παντρεμένος [pandremenos] married
παντρεμένη [pandremeni] married
πάνω [pano] on; up; upstairs
πάνω από [pano apo] above
παξιμάδι (το) [paximathi (to)] nut (for bolt)

παπάς (ο) [papas (o)] priest
πάπια (η) [papia (i)] duck
πάπλωμα (το) [paploma (to)] quilt
παπούτσι (το) [papootsi (to)] shoe
παππούς (ο) [pappoos (o)] grandfather
παραγγελία (η) [parangelia (i)] message
παραγγέλνω [parageIno] order (verb: in restaurant)
παράδειγμα (το) [parathigma (to)] example
παραδείγματος χάρι [parathigmatos khari] for example
παράδοση (η) [parathosi (i)] tradition
παραδοσιακός [parathosiakos] traditional
παράθυρο (το) [paraTHiro (to)] window
παρακαλώ [parakalo] please; excuse me; don't mention it
παρακαλώ; [parakalo?] can I help you?
ΠΑΡΑΚΑΜΠΤΗΡΙΟΣ παρακαμπτήριος (η) diversion
ΠΑΡΑΛΑΒΗ ΑΠΟΣΚΕΥΩΝ παραλαβή αποσκευών (η) [paralavi aposkevon (i)] baggage claim
ΠΑΡΑΛΙΑ παραλία (η) [paralia (i)] beach
κοντά στην παραλία [konda stin paralia] at the seaside
παραμάνα (η) [paramana (i)] safety pin
παραμένω [parameno] stay (verb), remain
παράξενος [paraxenos] strange
παραπονούμαι [paraponoomeh] complain
ΠΑΡΑΣΚΕΥΗ Παρασκευή (η) [Paraskevi (i)] Friday
παρατηρώ [paratiro] watch (verb)
παρατσούκλι (το) [paratsookli (to)] nickname
παρεξήγηση (η) [parexiyisi (i)] misunderstanding
παρκάρω [parkaro] park (verb)
ΠΑΡΚΙΝΓΚ πάρκινγκ (το) [parking (to)] car park, parking lot
πάρκο (το) [parko (to)] park
ΠΑΡΟΔΟΣ πάροδος (η) [parothos (i)] side street
παρπρίζ (το) [parpriz (to)] windscreen
πάρτυ (το) [parti (to)] party, celebration
παστίλιες λαιμού (οι) [pastili-es lemoo (i)] throat pastilles
Πάσχα (το) [Paskha (to)] Easter
πατέρας (ο) [pateras (o)] father
πατερίτσες (οι) [pateritses (i)] crutches
πάτωμα (το) [patoma (to)] floor (of room)
ΠΑΥΣΙΠΟΝΟ παυσίπονο (το) [pafsipono (to)] painkiller
πάχος (το) [pakhos (to)] fat (on meat)
παχύς [pakhis] fat; thick
πάω [pao] go (verb)
πεζοδρόμιο (το) [pezothromio (to)] pavement, sidewalk
ΠΕΖΟΔΡΟΜΟΣ πεζόδρομος (ο) pedestrian precinct

ΠΕΖΟΙ **πεζοί** pedestrians
πεθαίνω [peTHeno] die
πεθαμένος [peTHamenos] dead
πεθερά (η) [peTHera (i)] mother-in-law
πεθερός (ο) [peTHeros (o)] father-in-law
πειράζει [pirazi] it matters
θα σε πείραζε αν ...; [THa seh pirazeh an ...?] do you mind if I ...?
δεν πειράζει [then pirazi] it doesn't matter
ΠΕΙΡΑΙΑΣ **Πειραιάς** [Pireas] Piraeus
ΠΕΜΠΤΗ **Πέμπτη (η)** [Pempti (i)] Thursday
πέμπτος [pemptos] fifth
πενήντα [peninda] fifty
ΠΕΝΗΝΤΑΡΙΚΟ
πενηντάρικο (το) [penindariko (to)] 50-drachma coin or note/bill
πενικιλλίνη (η) [penikilini (i)] penicillin
πέννα (η) [pena (i)] pen
πένσα (η) [pensa (i)] pliers
ΠΕΝΤΑΚΟΣΑΡΙΚΟ
πεντακοσάρικο (το) [pendakosariko (to)] 500-drachma note/bill
πέντε [pendeh] five
πέος (το) [peos (to)] penis
περάστε [perasteh] come in; come back
ΠΕΡΙΕΧΟΜΕΝΟ **περιεχόμενο** contains
περίμενε [perimeneh] wait
περιμένω [perimeno] wait (for); expect
ΠΕΡΙΟΔΙΚΟ **περιοδικό (το)** [periothiko (to)] magazine
περίοδος (η) [periothos (i)] period
περιοχή (η) [periokhi (i)] area
περίπατος (ο) [peripatos (o)] walk
πάω περίπατο [pao peripato] go for a walk
περίπου [peripoo] about, approximately
ΠΕΡΙΠΤΕΡΟ **περίπτερο** [periptero] newspaper kiosk
ΣΕ ΠΕΡΙΠΤΩΣΗ ΑΝΑΓΚΗΣ ΣΠΑΣΤΕ ΤΟ ΤΖΑΜΙ **σε περίπτωση ανάγκης σπάστε το τζάμι** [seh periptosi anangis spasteh to tzami] in emergency break glass
περισσότερο [perisotero] more, most (of)
περισσότερος [perisoteros] more, most (of)
ΠΕΡΜΑΝΑΝΤ **περμανάντ (η)** [permanand (i)] perm
περνάω [pernao] cross, go through
περπατάω [perpatao] walk (verb)
πέρσυ [persi] last year
πετάλι (το) [petali (to)] pedal
πετάω [petao] throw away (verb)
πέτρα (η) [petra (i)] stone
πετσέτα (η) [petseta (i)] napkin; towel
πετσέτα κουζίνας [petseta koozinas] tea towel
πετώ [peto] fly (verb)
πέφτω [pefto] fall (verb)
πηγή (η) [piyi (i)] fountain
πηγούνι (το) [pigooni (to)] chin

πηδάω [pithao] jump (verb)
πηρούνι (το) [pir**oo**ni (to)] fork
πιάνω [piano] catch (verb)
πιατάκι (το) [piataki (to)] saucer
πιατικά (τα) [piatika (ta)] crockery
πιάτο (το) [piato (to)] dish; plate
ΠΙΕΣΗ ΑΙΜΑΤΟΣ πίεση αίματος (η) blood pressure
πιθανώς [piTHan**os**] probably
πικάντικος [pikandikos] spicy
πικάπ (το) [pikap (to)] record player
πικνίκ (το) [piknik (to)] picnic
πικρός [pikr**os**] bitter
πιλότος (ο) [pil**o**tos (o)] pilot
πινακίδες (οι) [pinakithes (i)] number plates
ΠΙΝΑΚΟΘΗΚΗ πινακοθήκη (η) [pinakoTHiki (i)] art gallery
πινγκ-πονγκ (το) [ping-pong (to)] table tennis
πινέλο (το) [pinelo (to)] paintbrush
πινέλο γιά ξύρισμα [pinelo ya xirisma] shaving brush
πίνω [pino] drink (verb)
πίπα (η) [pipa (i)] pipe (for smoking)
ΠΙΣΙΝΑ πισίνα (η) [pisina (i)] swimming pool
πιστεύω [pistevo] believe
πιστολάκι (το) [pistolaki (to)] hairdryer
πιστόλι (το) [pist**o**li (to)] gun, pistol
πιστοποιητικό (το) [pistopi-itik**o** (to)] certificate
ΠΙΣΤΩΤΙΚΗ ΚΑΡΤΑ πιστωτική κάρτα (η) [pistotiki karta (i)] credit card
πίσω [piso] back; behind
πίσω φώτα (τα) [piso fota (ta)] rear lights
ΠΙΤΣΑΡΙΑ πιτσαρία (η) [pitsaria (i)] pizzeria
πλαστική σακούλα (η) [plastiki sak**oo**la (i)] plastic bag
πλαστικός [plastik**os**] plastic
ΠΛΑΤΕΙΑ πλατεία (η) [platia (i)] square (in town); stalls (in theatre)
πλάτη (η) [plati (i)] back (of person)
πλατύς [platis] wide
ΠΛΑΤΦΟΡΜΑ πλατφόρμα (η) [platforma (i)] platform, (US) track
πλέκω [pleko] knit
πλένομαι [plenomeh] wash (oneself)
πλένω [pleno] wash (verb: something)
πλευρά (η) [plevra (i)] side
πλευρό (το) [plevro (to)] rib
πληγή (η) [pliyi (i)] wound
πλήθος (το) [pliTHos (to)] crowd
ΠΛΗΡΕΣ πλήρες no vacancies, full
ΠΛΗΡΟΦΟΡΙΕΣ πληροφορίες (οι) [plirofories (i)] information; directory enquiries
ΠΛΗΡΩΜΑ πλήρωμα (το) crew
πληρώνω [pliro**no**] pay (verb)
πλοίο (το) [plio (to)] boat, ship
πλούσιος [pl**oo**sios] rich
πλυντήριο (το) [plindiri**o** (to)] washing machine
ΠΛΥΝΤΗΡΙΟ ΑΥΤΟΚΙΝΗΤΩΝ

πλυντήριο αυτοκινήτων car wash

ΠΛΥΝΤΗΡΙΟ ΡΟΥΧΩΝ

πλυντήριο ρούχων [plindirio rookhon] launderette, laundromat

ΠΛΥΣΙΜΟ ΜΕ ΤΟ ΧΕΡΙ

πλύσιμο με το χέρι handwash only

πλύσιμο των πιάτων (το) [plisimo ton piaton (to)] washing up

πνεύμονες (οι) [pnevmones (i)] lungs

ποδηλασία (η) [pothilasia (i)] cycling

ποδηλάτης (ο/η) [pothilatis (o/i)] cyclist

ΠΟΔΗΛΑΤΟ **ποδήλατο (το)** [pothilato (to)] bicycle

πόδι (το) [pothi (to)] foot; leg

με τα πόδια [meh ta pothia] on foot

ποδόσφαιρο (το) [pothosfero (to)] football

ποιά; [pia?] who?

ποιανού; [pianoo?] whose?

ποιό; [pio?] which?

ποιός; [pios?] who?

ποιός είναι; [pios ineh?] who is it?

πόλεμος (ο) [polemos (o)] war

πόλη (η) [poli (i)] city, town

πολιτεία (η) [politia (i)] state

πολιτικά (τα) [politika (ta)] politics

πολιτικός [politikos] political; politician

πολλά, πολλές, πολλή, πολλοί [pola, poles, poli, poli] many, a lot (of)

πολύ [poli] a lot of; very; too much

πάρα πολύ [para poli] too much; very much

πολυσύχναστος [polisikhnastos] busy (place)

πολύς [polis] a lot (of)

ΠΟΛΥΤΕΛΕΙΑΣ **πολυτελείας** luxury class, four-star (hotel)

πονάει [ponai] hurt

πονόδοντος (ο) [ponothondos (o)] toothache

πονοκέφαλος (ο) [ponokefalos (o)] headache

πόνος (ο) [ponos (o)] ache, pain

ποντίκι (το) [pondiki (to)] mouse

πόνυ (το) [poni (to)] pony

πορεία (η) [poria (i)] route

πόρτα (η) [porta (i)] door

πορτ-μπαγκάζ (το) [port-bangaz (to)] boot (car), (US) trunk

πορτ-μπε-μπέ (το) [port-be-be (to)] carrycot

πορτοκαλί [portokali] orange (colour)

πορτοφολάς (ο) [portofolas (o)] pickpocket

πορτοφόλι (το) [portofoli (to)] wallet

πόσα;, πόσες;, [posa?, poses?] how many?

ΠΟΣΙΜΟ ΝΕΡΟ **πόσιμο νερό (το)** [posimo nero (to)] drinking water

πόσο; [poso?] how much?

πόσοι; [posi?] how many?

πόστερ (το) [poster (to)] poster

ΠΟΣΤ ΡΕΣΤΑΝΤ **ποστ ρεστάντ**

[post restant] poste restante
ποτάμι (το) [potami (to)] river
ποτέ [poteh] never
πότε; [poteh?] when?
έχετε ποτέ ...; [ekheteh poteh ...?] have you ever ...?
ποτήρι (το) [potiri (to)] glass
ΠΟΤΟΠΩΛΕΙΟ ποτοπωλείο (το) [potopolio (to)] off-licence, liquor store
που [poo] who, which, that
πού; [poo?] where?
πούδρα τάλκ (η) [poothra talk (i)] talcum powder
πουθενά [pooTHena] nowhere
πουκάμισο (το) [pookamiso (to)] shirt
πουλί (το) [pooli (to)] bird
ΠΟΥΛΜΑΝ πούλμαν (το) [poolman (to)] bus, coach
πουλόβερ (το) [poolover (to)] jumper
πουλώ [poolo] sell
πούρο (το) [pooro (to)] cigar
πράγμα (το) [pragma (to)] thing
πραγματικά [pragmatika] really
πρακτικός [praktikos] practical
πρακτορείο (το) [praktorio (to)] agency
ΠΡΑΚΤΟΡΕΙΟ ΕΦΗΜΕΡΙΔΩΝ πρακτορείο εφημερίδων newsagent, news vendor
ΠΡΑΚΤΟΡΕΙΟ ΛΕΩΦΟΡΕΙΩΝ πρακτορείο λεωφορείων [praktorio leoforion] bus station
πράσινος [prasinos] green
ΠΡΑΤΗΡΙΟ ΒΕΝΖΙΝΗΣ πρατήριο βενζίνης (το) [pratirio venzinis (to)] petrol station, gas station
πρέπει να ... [prepi na ...] I must ...
ΠΡΕΣΒΕΙΑ πρεσβεία (η) [presvia (i)] embassy
πρησμένος [prismenos] swollen
πρίγκηπας (ο) [pringipas (o)] prince
πριγκίπισσα (η) [pringipisa (i)] princess
πρίζα (η) [priza (i)] socket; plug
πρίζα ταυ (η) [priza taf (i)] adaptor
πριν [prin] before; ago
πριν τρεις μέρες [prin tris meres] three days ago
προάστια (τα) [proastia (ta)] suburbs
πρόβατο (το) [provato (to)] sheep
πρόβλημα (το) [provlima (to)] problem
ΠΡΟΒΛΗΤΑ προβλήτα (η) [provlita (i)] quay
προβολείς (οι) [provolis (i)] headlights
ΠΡΟΓΕΥΜΑ πρόγευμα (το) [proyevma (to)] breakfast
πρόγονος (ο/η) [progonos (o/i)] ancestor
ΠΡΟΓΡΑΜΜΑ πρόγραμμα (το) [programa (to)] timetable, (US) schedule; programme
προκαταβάλλω [prokatavalo] advance (verb)
προκαταβολικά [prokatavolika] in advance
ΠΡΟΞΕΝΕΙΟ προξενείο (το) [proxenio (to)] consulate
ΠΡΟΟΡΙΣΜΟΣ προορισμός

[pro-orismos] destination
προσβάλλω [prosvalo] offend
ΠΡΟΣ ΓΚΑΡΑΖ **προς γκαράζ** to car deck
ΠΡΟΣΔΕΘΗΤΕ **προσδεθήτε** fasten your seat belt
προσεκτικός [prosektikos] careful
πρόσεξε! [prosexeh!] look out!
ΠΡΟΣΕΧΕ! **πρόσεχε!** [prosekheh!] look out!
προσέχω [prosekho] take care of
ΠΡΟΣΕΧΩΣ **προσεχώς** coming soon
πρόσθετο (το) [prosTHeto (to)] supplementary
προσκαλώ [proskalo] invite
πρόσκληση (η) [prosklisi (i)] invitation
ΠΡΟΣ ΟΡΟΦΟΥΣ **προς ορόφους** to all floors
ΠΡΟΣΟΧΗ! **προσοχή!** caution!
ΠΡΟΣΟΧΗ ΑΡΓΑ **προσοχή αργά** caution: slow
ΠΡΟΣΟΧΗ ΕΞΟΔΟΣ ΟΧΗΜΑΤΩΝ **προσοχή έξοδος οχημάτων** caution: vehicle exit
ΠΡΟΣΟΧΗ ΕΥΦΛΕΚΤΟΝ **προσοχή εύφλεκτον** caution: highly inflammable
ΠΡΟΣΟΧΗ ΚΙΝΔΥΝΟΣ **προσοχή κίνδυνος** caution: danger
προσοχή παρακαλώ [prosokhi parakalo] attention please
ΠΡΟΣΟΧΗ ΣΚΥΛΟΣ **προσοχή σκύλος** beware of the dog
ΠΡΟΣ ΠΑΡΑΣΚΗΝΙΑ **προς παρασκήνια** to dressing rooms
προσπέκτους (το) [prospektoos (to)] brochure
προσπερνώ [prosperno] overtake
προστατεύω [prostatevo] protect
ΠΡΟΣΤΙΜΟ **πρόστιμο (το)** [prostimo (to)] fine
προσφέρω [prosfero] offer (verb); give
ΠΡΟΣΦΟΡΑ **προσφορά** special bargain
πρόσωπο (το) [prosopo (to)] face
προς [pros] towards
προτείνω [protino] recommend
ΠΡΟΤΕΡΑΙΟΤΗΤΑ **προτεραιότητα (η)** right of way
προτιμώ [protimo] prefer
προφανής [profanis] obvious
προφέρω [profero] pronounce
προφορά (η) [profora (i)] accent
προφυλακτήρας (ο) [profilaktiras (o)] bumper, fender
ΠΡΟΦΥΛΑΚΤΙΚΑ **προφυλακτικά** contraceptives
ΠΡΟΦΥΛΑΚΤΙΚΟ **προφυλακτικό (το)** [profilaktiko (to)] condom
προχτές [prokhtes] the day before yesterday
πρωί (το) [proi (to)] morning
το πρωί [to proi] in the morning
ΠΡΩΙΝΟ **πρωινό (το)** [pro-ino (to)] breakfast
πρώτα [prota] first, firstly
ΠΡΩΤΕΣ ΒΟΗΘΕΙΕΣ **πρώτες βοήθειες (οι)** [protes voiThi-es (i)] first aid
ΠΡΩΤΗ ΘΕΣΗ **πρώτη θέση** first class

πρώτο! [proto!] great!
ΠΡΩΤΟ ΠΑΤΩΜΑ πρώτο πάτωμα (το) [proto patoma (to)] first floor, (US) second floor
πρώτος [protos] first
ΠΡΩΤΟΣ ΟΡΟΦΟΣ πρώτος όροφος [protos orofos] first floor, (US) second floor
Πρωτοχρονιά (η) [Protokhronia (i)] New Year's Day
ΠΤΗΣΕΙΣ ΕΞΩΤΕΡΙΚΟΥ πτήσεις εξωτερικού international flights
ΠΤΗΣΕΙΣ ΕΣΩΤΕΡΙΚΟΥ πτήσεις εσωτερικού domestic flights
ΠΤΗΣΗ πτήση (η) [ptisi (i)] flight
ΠΤΗΣΗ ΤΣΑΡΤΕΡ πτήση τσάρτερ charter flight
πυζάμες (οι) [pizames (i)] pyjamas
πυξίδα (η) [pixitha (i)] compass
πύργος (ο) [pirgos (o)] tower
πυρετός (ο) [piretos (o)] fever
πυρκαγιά (η) [pirkaya (i)] fire
ΠΥΡΟΣΒΕΣΤΗΡ πυροσβεστήρ (ο) fire extinguisher
ΠΥΡΟΣΒΕΣΤΗΡΑΣ πυροσβεστήρας (ο) fire extinguisher
ΠΥΡΟΣΒΕΣΤΙΚΗ ΣΩΛΗΝΑ πυροσβεστική σωλήνα (η) fire hose
ΠΥΡΟΣΒΕΣΤΙΚΗ (ΥΠΗΡΕΣΙΑ) πυροσβεστική (υπηρεσία) (η) [pirosvestiki ipiresia (i)] fire brigade
πυροτεχνήματα (τα) [pirotekhnimata (ta)] fireworks
πυτζάμες (οι) [pitzames (i)] pyjamas
ΠΩΛΕΙΤΑΙ πωλείται for sale
ΠΩΛΗΣΗ πώληση (η) sale
πώς; [pos?] how?; what?

Ρ

ράβω [ravo] sew
ραδιόφωνο (το) [rathiofono (to)] radio
ραντεβού (το) [randevoo (to)] appointment
ράντζο (το) [randzo (to)] campbed
ΡΑΦΕΙΟ ραφείο (το) [rafio (to)] tailor's
ρεζέρβα (η) [rezerva (i)] spare tyre
ΡΕΣΕΨΙΟΝ ρεσεψιόν (η) [resepsion (i)] reception
ρεσεψιονίστ (ο/η) [resepsionist (o/i)] receptionist
ρε συ! [reh si!] you there!, oy you!
ρεύμα (το) [revma (to)] current; draught
ρευματισμοί (οι) [revmatismi (i)] rheumatism
ρίχνω [rikhno] throw (verb)
ρόδα (η) [rotha (i)] wheel
ροζ [roz] pink
ρόκ (η) [rok (i)] rock music
ρολόι (το) [roloi (to)] clock; watch
ρόμπα (η) [roba (i)] dressing gown
ΡΟΥΦ - ΓΚΑΡΝΤΕΝ Ρουφ - Γκάρντεν [Roof - garden] roof

garden
ρούχα (τα) [**roo**kha (ta)] clothes
ροχαλίζω [rokhalizo] snore
ρυμούλκα (η) [rim**oo**lka (i)] trailer (for car)
ρυμουλκό [rimoolk**o**] trailer (for car etc)
ρωτώ [roto] ask

Σ

ΣΑΒΒΑΤΟ Σάββατο (το) [**Sa**vato (to)] Saturday
σαββατοκύριακο (το) [savatok**i**riako (to)] weekend
ΣΑΓΙΟΝΑΡΕΣ σαγιονάρες [sayon**a**res] beach sandals, flip-flops
σαγόνι (το) [sag**o**ni (to)] jaw
σακάκι (το) [sak**a**ki (to)] jacket
σακβουαγιάζ (το) [sakvooay**a**z (to)] hand luggage, hand baggage
σακίδιο (το) [sak**i**thio (to)] rucksack
σάκος (ο) [**sa**kos (o)] backpack, rucksack
ΣΑΛΟΝΙ σαλόνι (το) [sal**o**ni (to)] lounge
ΣΑΜΠΟΥΑΝ σαμπουάν (το) [sampo**o**an (to)] shampoo
σαμπρέλα (η) [sab**re**la (i)] inner tube
σαν [san] like, as
σανδάλια (τα) [santh**a**lia (ta)] sandals
σάουνα (η) [sa**oo**na (i)] sauna
σάπιος [sa**pi**os] rotten
ΣΑΠΟΥΝΙ ΠΙΑΤΩΝ σαπούνι πιάτων (το) [sap**oo**ni pi**a**ton (to)] washing-up liquid
ΣΑΠΟΥΝΙ σαπούνι (το) [sap**oo**ni (to)] soap
σαράντα [sar**a**nda] forty
σας [sas] you; your
σβήνω [sv**i**no] switch off (engine); put out (fire)
ΣΒΗΣΤΕ ΤΗΝ ΜΗΧΑΝΗ σβήστε την μηχανή switch off engine
σβήστρα (η) [sv**i**stra (i)] rubber, eraser
σγουρά [sgoor**a**] curly
σε [seh] you; to; at; in
σεζ λόνγκ (η) [sez l**o**ng (i)] deckchair
ΣΕΙΡΑ σειρά (η) [s**i**ra (i)] row (of seats)
σελίδα (η) [sel**i**tha (i)] page
ΣΕΛΛΟΤΕΗΠ σέλλοτέηπ (το) [sell**o**teip (to)] Sellotape®, Scotch tape®
ΣΕΛΦ ΣΕΡΒΙΣ σελφ σέρβις [self s**e**rvis] self-service
σεντόνι (το) [send**o**ni (to)] sheet
σέξυ [s**e**xi] sexy
ΣΕ ΠΕΡΙΠΤΩΣΗ ΑΝΑΓΚΗΣ ΣΠΑΣΤΕ ΤΟ ΤΖΑΜΙ σε περίπτωση ανάγκης σπάστε το τζάμι in emergency break glass
ΣΕΠΤΕΜΒΡΙΟΣ Σεπτέμβριος (ο) [Sept**e**mvrios (o)] September
ΣΕΡΒΙΕΤΕΣ σερβιέτες (οι) [serv**i**etes (i)] sanitary towels/napkins
σερβιτόρα (η) [servit**o**ra (i)] barmaid; waitress

σερβιτόρος (ο) [servitoros (o)] waiter

ΣΗΚΩΣΤΕ ΤΟ ΑΚΟΥΣΤΙΚΟ σηκώστε το ακουστικό lift receiver

σημαδούρα (η) [simathoora (i)] buoy

σημαία (η) [simea (i)] flag

σημειωματάριο (το) [simiomatario (to)] notebook

ΣΗΜΕΡΑ σήμερα [simera] today

ΣΗΜΕΡΟΝ σήμερον showing today

σήραγγα (η) [siranga (i)] tunnel

σιγά-σιγά [siga-siga] slowly; slow down

σίγουρος [sigooros] sure

σίδερο (το) [sithero (to)] iron

σιδερώνω [sitherono] iron (verb)

ΣΙΔΗΡΟΔΡΟΜΙΚΟΣ ΣΤΑΘΜΟΣ σιδηροδρομικός σταθμός (ο) [sithirothromikos staTHmos (o)] railway station

σιδηρόδρομος (ο) [sithirothromos (o)] railway

ΣΙΔΗΡΟΥΡΓΕΙΟ σιδηρουργείο (το) [sithirooryio (to)] hardware store

ΣΙΝΕΜΑ σινεμά (το) [sinema (to)] cinema, movie theater

σιωπή (η) [siopi (i)] silence

σκάλα (η) [skala (i)] ladder

ΣΚΑΛΕΣ σκάλες (οι) [skales (i)] stairs

σκέπτομαι [skeptomeh] think

ΣΚΗΝΗ σκηνή (η) [skini (i)] tent

σκιά (η) [skia (i)] shade, shadow

στη σκιά [sti skia] in the shade

ΣΚΙΑ ΜΑΤΙΩΝ σκιά ματιών (η) [skia matiōn (i)] eye shadow

ΣΚΛΗΡΟΙ ΦΑΚΟΙ σκληροί φακοί (οι) [skliri faki (i)] hard lenses

σκληρός [skliros] hard

ΣΚΟΝΗ ΠΛΥΝΤΗΡΙΟΥ σκόνη πλυντηρίου (η) [skoni plindirioo (i)] washing powder

σκοτεινός [skotinos] dark

σκοτώνω [skotono] kill (verb)

σκουλαρίκια (τα) [skoolarikia (ta)] earrings

σκούπα [skoopa] broom

σκουπίδια (τα) [skoopithia (ta)] rubbish, garbage

σκουπιδοντενεκές (ο) [skoopithondenekes (o)] dustbin, trashcan

σκύλος (ο) [skilos (o)] dog

σκωληκοειδίτις (η) [skoliko-ithitis (i)] appendicitis

ΣΚΩΤΙΑ Σκωτία (η) [Skotia (i)] Scotland

Σκωτσέζικος [Skotsezikos] Scottish

σλάιντ (το) [slaid (to)] slide

σλίπ (το) [slip (to)] underpants; panties

ΣΛΙΠΙΝΓΚ ΜΠΑΓΚ σλίπινγκ μπαγκ (το) [sliping bag (to)] sleeping bag

σοβαρός [sovaros] serious

σοκ (το) [sok (to)] shock

ΣΟΚΟΛΑΤΑ σοκολάτα (η) [sokolata (i)] chocolate

ΣΟΚΟΛΑΤΑ ΓΑΛΑΚΤΟΣ σοκολάτα γάλακτος (η) [sokolata galaktos (i)] milk chocolate

ΣΟΚΟΛΑΤΑΚΙΑ σοκολατάκια (τα) [sokolatakia (ta)] chocolates
σόλα (η) [sola (i)] sole (of shoe)
σόμπα (η) [soba (i)] oil heater
σορτς (το) [sorts (to)] shorts
σου [soo] you; your
σουγιάς (ο) [sooyas (o)] penknife
ΣΟΥΠΕΡ ΒΕΝΖΙΝΗ σούπερ βενζίνη (η) [sooper venzini (i)] four-star petrol, premium
ΣΟΥΠΕΡΜΑΡΚΕΤ σούπερμάρκετ (το) [soopermarket (to)] supermarket
σουτιέν (το) [sootien (to)] bra
ΣΠΑΓΓΟΣ σπάγγος (ο) [spangos (o)] string
σπασμένος [spasmenos] broken
σπάω [spao] break (verb)
σπηλιά (το) [spilia (to)] cave
σπιράλ (το) [spiral (to)] spiral; IUD; incense coil (mosquito repellent)
σπίρτα (τα) [spirta (ta)] matches
σπίτι (το) [spiti (to)] house
στο σπίτι [sto spiti] at home
σπορ (το) [spor (to)] sport
σπουδαίος [spootheos] important
σπρώχνω [sprokhno] push (verb)
σταγόνα (η) [stagona (i)] drop
ΣΤΑΓΟΝΕΣ σταγόνες drops
ΣΤΑΔΙΟ στάδιο (το) [stathio (to)] stadium
ΣΤΑΘΜΟΣ σταθμός (ο) [staTHmos (o)] station
ΣΤΑΘΜΟΣ ΑΝΕΦΟΔΙΑΣΜΟΥ ΘΑΛΑΜΗΓΩΝ σταθμός ανεφοδιασμού θαλαμηγών yacht refuelling station
ΣΤΑΘΜΟΣ ΛΕΩΦΟΡΕΙΩΝ σταθμός λεωφορείων [staTHmos leoforion] bus station
ΣΤΑΘΜΟΣ ΠΡΩΤΩΝ ΒΟΗΘΕΙΩΝ σταθμός πρώτων βοηθειών [staTHmos proton voiTHion] first aid post
ΣΤΑΘΜΟΣ ΤΑΞΙ σταθμός ταξί [staTHmos taxi] taxi stand
ΣΤΑΘΜΟΣ ΥΠΕΡΑΣΤΙΚΩΝ ΛΕΩΦΟΡΕΙΩΝ σταθμός υπεραστικών λεωφορείων [staTHmos iperastikon leoforion] bus station (long distance)
ΣΤΑΘΜΟΣ ΧΩΡΟΦΥΛΑΚΗΣ σταθμός χωροφυλακής [staTHmos khorofilakis] police station
σταματάω [stamatao] stop (verb)
ΣΤΑΣΗ στάση (η) [stasi (i)] stop (for bus, train)
ΣΤΑΣΗ ΑΣΤΙΚΩΝ ΣΥΓΚΟΙΝΩΝΙΩΝ στάση αστικών συγκοινωνιών city bus stop
ΣΤΑΣΗ ΛΕΩΦΟΡΕΙΟΥ στάση λεωφορείου bus stop
ΣΤΑΣΗ ΤΑΞΙ στάση ταξί [stasi taxi] taxi stand
ΣΤΑΣΙΣ στάσις (η) [stasis (i)] bus stop
στέγη (η) [steyi (i)] roof
ΣΤΕΓΝΟ ΚΑΘΑΡΙΣΜΑ ΜΟΝΟΝ στεγνό καθάρισμα μόνον dryclean only
ΣΤΕΓΝΟΚΑΘΑΡΙΣΤΗΡΙΟ στεγνοκαθαριστήριο (το) [stegnokaTHaristirio (to)] dry cleaner's
στεγνός [stegnos] dry

στεγνώνω [stegnono] dry (verb)
στέλνω [stelno] send
στενός [stenos] narrow; tight
στενοχώρια (η) [stenokhoria (i)] worry (verb)
στήθος (το) [stiTHos (to)] breast; chest
στην [stin] at; in; to; on
ΣΤΙΒΟΣ στίβος (ο) athletics stadium
στο [sto] at; in; to
στόμα (το) [stoma (to)] mouth
στομάχι (το) [stomakhi (to)] stomach
στον [ston] at; in; to;
ΣΤΟΠ! στοπ! stop!
στριφτό (το) [strifto (to)] hand-rolled cigarette
στρογγυλός [strongilos] round
στρόφαλος (ο) [strofalos (o)] crankshaft
στροφή (η) [strofi (i)] bend
στρώμα (το) [stroma (to)] mattress
στυλό (το) [stilo (to)] biro®
συγγενείς (οι) [singenis (i)] relatives
συγγνώμη [signomi] sorry; excuse me
συγγνώμη; [signomi?] pardon (me)?, sorry?
σύγκρουση (η) [singroosi (i)] crash
συγχαρητήρια! [sinkharitiria!] congratulations!
συγχωρείτε: με συγχωρείτε [meh sinkhoriteh] excuse me
σύζυγος (ο) [sizigos (o)] husband
συκότι (το) [sikoti (to)] liver
συλλαμβάνω [silamvano] arrest
συλλογή (η) [siloyi (i)] collection
συμβαίνω [simveno] happen
συμβουλεύω [simvoolevo] advise
ΣΥΜΠΕΡΙΛΑΜΒΑΝΕΤΑΙ συμπεριλαμβάνεται included
συμπλέκτης (ο) [siblektis (o)] clutch
συμφωνώ [simfono] agree
ΣΥΝΑΓΕΡΜΟΣ συναγερμός (ο) [sinayermos (o)] alarm
συναίσθημα (το) [sinesTHima (to)] feeling
ΣΥΝΑΛΛΑΓΜΑ συνάλλαγμα (το) [sinalagma (to)] foreign exchange
ΣΥΝΑΛΛΑΓΜΑΤΙΚΗ ΙΣΟΤΙΜΙΑ συναλλαγματική ισοτιμία (η) [sinalagmatiki isotimia (i)] exchange rate
συνάντηση (η) [sinandisi (i)] meeting
συναντώ [sinando] meet
συναρπαστικός [sinarpastikos] exciting
συναυλία (η) [sinavlia (i)] concert
ΣΥΝ/ΓΕΙΟ συν/γειο auto repairs
σύνδεση (η) [sinthesi (i)] connection (electrical)
ΣΥΝΕΡΓΕΙΟ (ΑΥΤΟΚΙΝΗΤΩΝ) συνεργείο (αυτοκινήτων) (το) auto repairs
συνήθεια (η) [siniTHia (i)] habit
συνηθισμένος [siniTHismenos] usual
συνήθως [siniTHos] usually
ΣΥΝΘΕΤΙΚΟ συνθετικό synthetic
συννεφιασμένος [sinefiasmenos]

Α Β Γ Δ Ε Ζ Η Θ Ι Κ Λ Μ Ν Ξ Ο Π Ρ Σ Τ Υ Φ Χ Ψ Ω

cloudy
σύννεφο (το) [sinefo (to)] cloud
συνοδεύω [sinothevo] accompany
ΣΥΝΟΙΚΙΑ συνοικία (η) [sinikia (i)] district
συνολικά [sinolika] altogether
σύνορα (τα) [sinora (ta)] border
συνταγή (η) [sindayi (i)] prescription; recipe
συνταξιούχος (ο/η) [sindaxiookhos (o/i)] old-age pensioner
ΣΥΝΤΗΡΗΤΙΚΟ ΔΙΑΛΥΜΑ συντηρητικό διάλυμα (το) [sindiritiko thialima (to)] soaking solution
σύντομα [sindoma] soon
ΣΥΡΑΤΕ σύρατε pull
σύρμα (το) [sirma (to)] wire
ΣΥΣΤΑΤΙΚΑ συστατικά ingredients
ΣΥΣΤΗΜΕΝΑ συστημένα [sistimena] registered mail
συστήνω [sistino] introduce; recommend
συχνά [sikhna] often
σφήγγα (η) [sfinga (i)] wasp
σφράγισμα (το) [sfrayisma (to)] filling (in tooth)
σφυρί (το) [sfiri (to)] hammer
σχάρα αυτοκινήτου (η) [skhara aftokinitoo (i)] roof rack
σχέδιο (το) [skhethio (to)] plan
σχεδόν [skhethon] almost
σχοινί (το) [skhini (to)] rope
ΣΧΟΛΕΙΟ σχολείο (το) [skholio (to)] school
σωλήνας (ο) [solinas (o)] pipe (water)
σώμα (το) [soma (to)] body
ΣΩΣΙΒΙΑ σωσίβια lifejackets
σωστός [sostos] correct

Τ

τα [ta] the; them
ταβάνι (το) [tavani (to)] ceiling
ΤΑΒΕΡΝΑ ταβέρνα (η) [taverna (i)] restaurant
τακούνι (το) [takooni (to)] heel (of shoe)
ΤΑΛΗΡΟ τάληρο (το) [taliro (to)] 5-drachma coin
ΤΑΜΕΙΟ ταμείο (το) [tamio (to)] box office; cash desk, till, cashier
ΤΑΜΙΕΥΤΗΡΙΟ ταμιευτήριο (το) [tami-eftirio (to)] savings bank
ΤΑΜΠΛΕΤΑ ταμπλέτα (η) [tableta (i)] tablet
ΤΑΜΠΟΝ ταμπόν (τα) [tampon (ta)] tampons
τάξη (η) [taxi (i)] class
ΤΑΞΙ ταξί (το) [taxi (to)] taxi
ταξιδεύω [taxithevo] travel (verb)
ταξίδι (το) [taxithi (to)] journey, trip
καλό ταξίδι! [kalo taxithi!] have a good journey!, bon voyage!
ταξίδι για δουλειές [taxithi ya thoolies] business trip
ΤΑΞΙΔΙΩΤΙΚΗ ΕΠΙΤΑΓΗ ταξιδιωτική επιταγή (η) [taxithiotiki epitayi (i)] traveller's cheque/traveler's check
ΤΑΞΙΔΙΩΤΙΚΟ ΓΡΑΦΕΙΟ

ταξιδιωτικό γραφείο (το) [taxithiotik**o** grafi**o** (to)] travel agent's
τάπα (η) [tapa (i)] plug (in sink)
ΤΑ ΡΕΣΤΑ ΣΑΣ **τα ρέστα σας** your change
ΤΑΡΙΦΑ **ταρίφα** [tarifa] taxi tariff
τασάκι (το) [tasaki (to)] ashtray
ταύρος (ο) [tavros (o)] bull
ΤΑΥΤΟΤΗΤΑ **ταυτότητα (η)** [taft**o**tita (i)] pass, identity card
ΤΑΧΥΔΡΟΜΕΙΟ **ταχυδρομείο (το)** [takhithrom**i**o (to)] post office
ΤΑΧΥΔΡΟΜΙΚΟΣ ΤΟΜΕΥΣ **ταχυδρομικός τομεύς (ο)** [takhithromik**o**s tom**e**fs (o)] postcode, zipcode
ταχυδρόμος (ο) [takhithr**o**mos (o)] postman
ταχυδρομώ [takhithrom**o**] post, mail (verb)
ταχύτητα (η) [takh**i**tita (i)] gear (in car)
ταχύτητα (η) [takh**i**tita (i)] speed
τέλειος [tel**i**os] perfect
τελειώνω [teli**o**no] finish (verb)
ΤΕΛΕΥΤΑΙΑ ΠΑΡΑΣΤΑΣΗ **τελευταία παράσταση** last performance
τελευταίος [telef**e**os] last
τελεφερίκ (το) [teleferik (to)] cable car
ΤΕΛΟΣ **τέλος (το)** [tel**o**s (to)] end
ΤΕΛΩΝΕΙΟ **Τελωνείο (το)** [Telon**i**o (to)] Customs
τεμπέλης [teb**e**lis] lazy
τέννις (το) [t**e**nis (to)] tennis
τέντα (η) [t**e**nda (i)] tent, marquee
τέσσερα [t**e**sera] four
ΤΕΤΑΡΤΗ **Τετάρτη (η)** [Tet**a**rti (i)] Wednesday
τέταρτο (το) [t**e**tarto (to)] quarter
τέταρτος [t**e**tartos] fourth
τέχνη (η) [t**e**khni (i)] art
τεχνητός [t**e**khnit**o**s] artificial
ΤΕΧΝΗΤΟ ΧΡΩΜΑ **τεχνητό χρώμα** artificial colouring
τζαζ (η) [tzaz (i)] jazz
τζηνς (τα) [tzins (ta)] jeans
τζόγγιγκ (το) [tz**o**ging (to)] jogging
τη [ti] the
τηγάνι (το) [tig**a**ni (to)] frying pan
τηγανίζω [tiganizo] fry
ΤΗΛΕΓΡΑΦΗΜΑ **τηλεγράφημα (το)** [tilegr**a**fima (to)] telegram
ΤΗΛΕΓΡΑΦΗΜΑΤΑ **τηλεγραφήματα** telegrams
ΤΗΛΕΓΡΑΦΙΚΗ ΕΝΤΟΛΗ **τηλεγραφική εντολή** [tilegrafik**i** endol**i**] telegram
ΤΗΛΕΚΑΡΤΑ **τηλεκάρτα (η)** [tilek**a**rta (i)] phonecard
ΤΗΛΕΟΡΑΣΗ **τηλεόραση (η)** [tile**o**rasi (i)] television
ΤΗΛΕΦΩΝΗΜΑ **τηλεφώνημα** [tilef**o**nima] call
ΤΗΛΕΦΩΝΗΜΑ ΚΟΛΛΕΚΤ **τηλεφώνημα κολλέκτ (το)** [tilef**o**nima kollekt (to)] reverse charge call
ΤΗΛΕΦΩΝΙΚΗ ΕΝΤΟΛΗ **τηλεφωνική εντολή** operator-

Α Β Γ Δ Ε Ζ Η Θ Ι Κ Λ Μ Ν Ξ Ο Π Ρ Σ Τ Υ Φ Χ Ψ Ω

controlled phone call

ΤΗΛΕΦΩΝΙΚΟΣ ΘΑΛΑΜΟΣ **τηλεφωνικός θάλαμος (ο)** [tilefonikos THalamos (o)] phone box

ΤΗΛΕΦΩΝΙΚΟΣ ΚΑΤΑΛΟΓΟΣ **τηλεφωνικός κατάλογος (ο)** [tilefonikos katalogos (o)] phone book

ΤΗΛΕΦΩΝΟ **τηλέφωνο (το)** [tilefono (to)] phone

ΤΗΛΕΦΩΝΩ **τηλεφωνώ** [tilefono] ring, phone (verb)

την [tin] her; on; per; the

την εβδομάδα [tin evthomatha] per week

της [tis] her; to her; of her

τι; [ti?] what?

ΤΙΜΗ **τιμή (η)** [timi (i)] price

ΤΙΜΗ ΑΓΟΡΑΣ **τιμή αγοράς** buying rate

ΤΙΜΗ ΑΝΕΥ ΠΟΣΟΣΤΩΝ **τιμή άνευ ποσοστών** price exclusive of extras

ΤΙΜΗ ΔΩΜΑΤΙΟΥ **τιμή δωματίου** room price

ΤΙΜΗ ΚΑΤ' ΑΤΟΜΟ **τιμή κατ' άτομο** price per person

ΤΙΜΗ ΚΛΙΝΗΣ **τιμή κλίνης** price per bed

ΤΙΜΗ ΜΕΤΑ ΠΟΣΟΣΤΩΝ **τιμή μετά ποσοστών** price inclusive of extras

ΤΙΜΗ ΠΩΛΗΣΗΣ **τιμή πώλησης** selling rate

τίμιος [timios] honest

τιμόνι (το) [timoni (to)] steering wheel

τίνος; [tinos?] whose

τίποτε [tipoteh] nothing

ΤΙΠΟΤΕ ΠΡΟΣ ΔΗΛΩΣΗ **τίποτε προς δήλωση** nothing to declare

τις [tis] them

ΤΜΗΜΑ **τμήμα (το)** [tmima (to)] department

το [to] in; it; the; per

τοις εκατό [tis ekato] per cent

ΤΟΙΣ ΜΕΤΡΗΤΟΙΣ **τοις μετρητοίς** cash only, no credit cards

τοίχος (ο) [tikhos (o)] wall

ΤΟ ΚΑΤΑΣΤΗΜΑ ΜΕΤΑΦΕΡΘΗΚΕ ΕΙΣ ... **το κατάστημα μεταφέρθηκε εις ...** we have moved to ...

ΤΟ ΚΟΜΜΑΤΙ **το κομμάτι** per item

ΤΟΚΟΣ **τόκος (ο)** [tokos (o)] interest

τολμάω [tolmao] dare (verb)

τον [ton] him; the

ΤΟΞΙΚΟ **τοξικό** toxic

ΤΟΠΙΚΗ ΩΡΑ **τοπική ώρα** local time

ΤΟΠΙΚΟ (ΤΗΛΕΦΩΝΗΜΑ) **τοπικό (τηλεφώνημα) (το)** [topiko tilefonima (to)] local call

τοπίο (το) [topio (to)] landscape

τόσο [toso] so (much); that much

τότε [toteh] then

του [too] his; its; to him

ΤΟΥΑΛΕΤΑ **τουαλέτα (η)** [tooaleta (i)] toilet, rest room

ΤΟΥΑΛΕΤΑ ΤΩΝ ΓΥΝΑΙΚΩΝ **τουαλέτα των γυναικών (η)** [tooaleta ton yinekon (i)] ladies'

toilet, ladies' room

ΤΟΥΑΛΕΤΕΣ **τουαλέτες** [tooaletes] toilets, rest room

τουλάχιστον [toolakhiston] at least

του οποίου [too opioo] whose

τουρίστας (ο) [tooristas (o)] tourist

ΤΟΥΡΙΣΤΙΚΗ ΑΣΤΥΝΟΜΙΑ **Τουριστική Αστυνομία (η)** [Tooristiki Astinomia (i)] Tourist Police

τουριστικός οδηγός (ο) [tooristikos othigos (o)] guidebook

τουρίστρια (η) [tooristria (i)] tourist

ΤΟΥΡΚΑΛΑ **τουρκάλα (η)** [toorkala (i)] Turk

ΤΟΥΡΚΙΑ **Τουρκία (η)** [Toorkia (i)] Turkey

Τούρκος (ο) [Toorkos (o)] Turk

ΤΟΥΡΚΙΚΟΣ **Τουρκικός** [Toorkikos] Turkish (adj)

τους [toos] them; to them

τραβάω [travao] pull (verb)

τραγούδι (το) [tragoothi (to)] song

τραγουδώ [tragootho] sing

ΤΡΑΠΕΖΑΡΙΑ **τραπεζαρία (η)** [trapezaria (i)] dining room

ΤΡΑΠΕΖΑ **τράπεζα (η)** [trapeza (i)] bank

τραπέζι (το) [trapezi (to)] table

τραπεζομάντηλο (το) [trapezomandilo (to)] tablecloth

τραυματίζομαι [travmatizomeh] hurt, injure

τραυματισμένος [travmatismenos] injured

τρελλός [trelos] mad

ΤΡΕΝΟ **τρένο (το)** [treno (to)] train

τρέχω [trekho] run (verb)

τρία [tria] three

τριακόσια [triakosia] three hundred

τριάντα [trianda] thirty

τριαντάφυλλο (το) [triandafilo (to)] rose

ΤΡΙΚΛΙΝΟ ΔΩΜΑΤΙΟ **τρίκλινο δωμάτιο (το)** [triklino thomatio (to)] triple room

ΤΡΙΤΗ **Τρίτη (η)** [Triti (i)] Tuesday

ΤΡΙΤΗ ΘΕΣΗ **τρίτη θέση** third class

τρίτος [tritos] third

τρόλλεϋ (το) [troleh-i (to)] trolley, trolleybus

τρομερός [tromeros] tremendous

ΤΡΟΦΗ ΓΙΑ ΔΙΑΒΗΤΙΚΟΥΣ **τροφή γιά διαβητικούς** [trofi ya thiavitikoos] diabetic foods

τροφική δηλητηρίαση (η) [trofiki thilitiriasi (i)] food poisoning

ΤΡΟΧΑΙΑ **τροχαία (η)** traffic police

τροχονόμος (ο) [trokhonomos (o)] traffic warden

τροχόσπιτο (το) [trokhospito (to)] caravan, (US) trailer

ΤΡΟΧΟΣΠΙΤΑ **τροχόσπιτα (το)** caravans, (US) trailers

τρύπα (η) [tripa (i)] hole

τρώω [troo] eat; have dinner

τσαγιέρα (η) [tsayera (i)] teapot

ΤΣΑΓΚΑΡΗΣ **τσαγκάρης (ο)** [tsangaris (o)] shoe repairer's

τσάντα (η) [tsanda (i)] bag; handbag, (US) purse

ΤΣΑΝΤΕΣ ΜΠΑΝΙΟΥ τσάντες μπάνιου beach bags
τσέπη (η) [tsepi (i)] pocket
ΤΣΙΓΑΡΟ τσιγάρο (το) [tsigaro (to)] cigarette
τσίμπημα (το) [tsibima (to)] bite (insect)
τσιμπιδάκι (το) [tsibithaki (to)] tweezers
τσιμπώ [tsibo] sting (verb)
ΤΣΙΠΣ τσιπς (τα) [tsips (ta)] crisps, (US) potato chips
ΤΣΙΧΛΑ τσίχλα (η) [tsikhla (i)] chewing gum
τσόκ (το) [tsok (to)] choke (on car)
τσούχτρα (η) [tsookhtra (i)] jellyfish
τυλίγω [tiligo] wrap (verb)
τυφλός [tiflos] blind
τύχη (η) [tikhi (i)] luck
καλή τύχη! [kali tikhi!] good luck!
των [ton] of them
τώρα [tora] now

Υ

υαλοκαθαριστήρας (ο) [ialokaTHaristiras (o)] windscreen wiper
υγεία: στην υγειά σας/σου! [stin iya sas/soo!] your health!, cheers!
υγιής [iyi-is] healthy
ΥΓΡΑΕΡΙΟ υγραέριο (το) [igraerio (to)] camping gas
υγρός [igros] damp, wet
ΥΔΡΑΥΛΙΚΑ υδραυλικά (τα) [ithravlika (ta)] plumber
ΥΔΡΑΥΛΙΚΟΣ υδραυλικός (ο) [ithravlikos (o)] plumber
υπάρχει [iparkhi] there is
υπάρχουν [iparkhoon] there are
ΥΠΕΡΑΣΤΙΚΟ (ΤΗΛΕΦΩΝΗΜΑ) υπεραστικό (τηλεφώνημα) (το) [iperastiko tilefonima (to)] long-distance call, international call
υπερβάλλω [ipervallo] exaggerate
υπέρβαρο (το) [ipervaro (to)] excess baggage
υπερβολικά [ipervolika] too
υπερήφανος [iperifanos] proud
ΥΠΕΡΠΟΛΥΤΕΛΕΙΑΣ υπερπολυτελειας five-star (hotel)
υπεύθυνος [ipefThinos] responsible
ΥΠΗΡΕΣΙΑ υπηρεσία (η) [ipiresia (i)] service
ύπνο: πάω για ύπνο [pao ya ipno] go to bed
υπνοδωμάτιο (το) [ipnothomatio (to)] bedroom
ύπνος (ο) [ipnos (o)] sleep
ΥΠΝΩΤΙΚΟ ΧΑΠΙ υπνωτικό χάπι (το) [ipnotiko khapi (to)] sleeping pill
ΥΠΟΓΕΙΑ ΔΙΑΒΑΣΗ ΠΕΖΩΝ υπόγεια διάβαση πεζών (η) pedestrian subway
ΥΠΟΓΕΙΟ υπόγειο (το) [ipoyio (to)] basement
ΥΠΟΓΕΙΟΣ υπόγειος (ο) [ipoyios (o)] underground, (US) subway
υπογράφω [ipografo] sign (verb)
ΥΠΟΔΗΜΑΤΑ υποδήματα (τα) [ipothimata (ta)] shoes

ΥΠΟΔΗΜΑΤΑ ΓΥΝΑΙΚΕΙΑ **υποδήματα γυναικεία** [ipothimata yinekia] ladies' shoes
ΥΠΟΔΗΜΑΤΟΠΟΙΕΙΟ **υποδηματοποιείο (το)** [ipothimatopi-io (to)] shoe shop
υπολογιστής (ο) [ipoloyistis (o)] computer
υπόλοιπο (το) [ipolipo (to)] rest, remainder
υπόσχομαι [iposkhomeh] promise (verb)
ΥΠΟΥΡΓΕΙΟ **υπουργείο (το)** ministry
ύφασμα (το) [ifasma (to)] material
ΥΦΑΣΜΑΤΑ **υφάσματα** [ifasmata] clothing; cloth, material

Φ

ΦΑΓΗΤΟ **φαγητό (το)** [fayito (to)] food; meal; lunch
φαγούρα (η) [fagoora (i)] itch
φάκελος (ο) [fakelos (o)] envelope
ΦΑΚΟΙ ΕΠΑΦΗΣ **φακοί επαφής (οι)** [faki epafis (i)] contact lenses
φακός (ο) [fakos (o)] lens; torch
φαλακρός [falakros] bald
φαλλοκράτης (ο) [falokratis (o)] male chauvinist
φανάρια τροχαίας (τα) [fanaria trokheas (ta)] traffic lights
φανταστικός [fandastikos] fantastic
ΦΑΡΜΑΚΕΙΟ **φαρμακείο (το)** [farmakio (to)] chemist's, pharmacy
φάρμακο (το) [farmako (to)] medicine
φαρμακοποιός (ο) [farmakopios (o)] chemist, pharmacist
φασαρία (η) [fasaria (i)] noise
ΦΕΒΡΟΥΑΡΙΟΣ **Φεβρουάριος (ο)** [Fevrooarios (o)] February
φεγγάρι (το) [fengari (to)] moon
φεμινίστρια (η) [feministria (i)] feminist
φερμουάρ (το) [fermooar (to)] zip
φέρνω [ferno] bring
ΦΕΡΡΥ ΜΠΩΤ **φέρρυ μπωτ (το)** [feri bot (to)] ferry
φέτα (η) [feta (i)] slice
φεύγω [fevgo] go away
φθινόπωρο (το) [fTHinoporo (to)] autumn, (US) fall
φίδι (το) [fithi (to)] snake
φιλενάδα (η) [filenatha (i)] girlfriend; friend
φιλί (το) [fili (to)] kiss
ΦΙΛΜ **φιλμ (το)** [film (to)] film, movie
ΦΙΛΟΔΩΡΗΜΑ **φιλοδώρημα (το)** [filothorima (to)] service charge; tip
φιλοξενία (η) [filoxenia (i)] hospitality
φιλοξενούμενη (η) [filoxenoomeni (i)] guest
φιλοξενούμενος (ο) [filoxenoomenos (o)] guest
φίλος (ο) [filos (o)] boyfriend; friend
φιλοφρόνηση (η) [filofronisi (i)] compliment
φίλτρο (το) [filtro (to)] filter

φιλώ [filo] kiss (verb)
φλας (το) [flas (to)] flash; indicator
φλέβα (η) [fleva (i)] vein
φλυτζάνι (το) [flitzani (to)] cup
φοβάμαι [fovameh] be afraid
φοβερός [foveros] terrible
φόβος (ο) [fovos (o)] fear
φοιτητής (ο) [fititis (o)] student
ΦΟΙΤΗΤΙΚΑ ΕΙΣΙΤΗΡΙΑ φοιτητικά εισιτήρια [fititika isitiria] student tickets
φοιτήτρια (η) [fititria (i)] student
φορά (η) [fora (i)] time, occasion
φόρεμα (το) [forema (to)] dress
φορτηγό (το) [fortigo (to)] lorry
ΦΟΥΑΓΙΕ φουαγιέ (το) [fooaye (to)] foyer
ΦΟΥΛ ΠΑΝΣΙΟΝ φουλ πανσιόν (η) [fool pansion (i)] full board
ΦΟΥΛ-ΣΑΙΖΟΝ φουλ-σαιζόν high season
ΦΟΥΡΝΟΣ φούρνος (ο) [foornos (o)] baker's; oven
φουσκάλα (η) [fooskala (i)] blister
φούστα (η) [foosta (i)] skirt
φρακαρισμένος [frakarismenos] blocked; stuck
φράκτης (ο) [fraktis (o)] fence
φρενάρω [frenaro] brake (verb)
φρένο (το) [freno (to)] brake
ΦΡΕΣΚΟΣ φρέσκος [freskos] fresh
φρικτός [friktos] horrible
φρύδι (το) [frithi (to)] eyebrow
φτάνει [ftani] that's enough
φτάνω [ftano] arrive
φτέρνα (η) [fterna (i)] heel (of foot)
φτερνίζομαι [fternizomeh] sneeze (verb)
φτερό (το) [ftero (to)] wing
ΦΤΗΝΟΣ φτηνός [ftinos] cheap, inexpensive
φτιάχνω τις βαλίτσες [ftiakhno tis valitses] pack (verb)
φτυάρι (το) [ftiari (to)] spade
φτωχός [ftokhos] poor
φύγε! [fiyeh!] go away!
φύκια (τα) [fikia (ta)] seaweed
ΦΥΛΑΚΗ φυλακή (η) [filaki (i)] prison
ΦΥΛΑΞΗ ΑΠΟΣΚΕΥΩΝ φύλαξη αποσκευών [filaxi aposkevon] left luggage, baggage check
φύλλο (το) [filo (to)] leaf
φύλο (το) [filo (to)] gender
φύση (η) [fisi (i)] nature
ΦΥΣΙΚΟ ΠΡΟΪΟΝ φυσικό προϊόν natural product
ΦΥΣΙΚΟΣ φυσικός [fisikos] natural
ΦΥΣΙΚΟ ΧΡΩΜΑ φυσικό χρώμα natural colouring
φυσιολογικός [fisioloyikos] normal
ΦΥΤΟ φυτό (το) [fito (to)] plant
φωνάζω [fonazo] call; shout (verb)
φωνή (η) [foni (i)] voice
ΦΩΣ φως (το) [fos (to)] light
φώτα (τα) [fota (ta)] lights (on car)
ΦΩΤΙΑ φωτιά (η) [fotia (i)] fire
έχεις φωτιά; [ekhis fotia?] have you got a light?
φωτογραφία (η) [fotografia (i)] photograph
ΦΩΤΟΓΡΑΦΙΚΑ φωτογραφικά

cameras
φωτογραφική μηχανή (η) [fotografiki mikhani (i)] camera
φωτόμετρο (το) [fotometro (to)] light meter

X

χαίρετε [khereteh] hello
χαλάκι (το) [khalaki (to)] rug
χαλί (το) [khali (to)] carpet
χάλια [khalia] awful
χαμηλά φώτα (τα) [khamila fota (ta)] sidelights
χαμηλός [khamilos] low
χαμόγελο (το) [khamoyelo (to)] smile
χαμογελώ [khamoyelo] smile (verb)
χάνω [khano] lose; miss
ΧΑΠΙ **χάπι (το)** [khapi (to)] pill
χάρηκα! [kharika!] pleased to meet you!
ΧΑΡΠΙΚ **χάρπικ (το)** [kharpik (to)] bleach (for toilet)
ΧΑΡΤΗΣ **χάρτης (ο)** [khartis (o)] map
ΧΑΡΤΙ **χαρτί (το)** [kharti (to)] paper
χαρτιά (τα) [khartia (ta)] playing cards
ΧΑΡΤΙ ΑΛΛΗΛΟΓΡΑΦΙΑΣ **χαρτί αλληλογραφίας (το)** [kharti alilografias (to)] writing paper
ΧΑΡΤΙΚΑ **χαρτικά (τα)** [khartika (ta)] stationery
ΧΑΡΤΙ ΠΕΡΙΤΥΛΙΓΜΑΤΟΣ **χαρτί περιτυλίγματος** [kharti peritiligmatos] wrapping paper
ΧΑΡΤΙ ΥΓΕΙΑΣ **χαρτί υγείας** [kharti iyias] toilet paper
ΧΑΡΤΟΜΑΝΤΗΛΑ **χαρτομάντηλα (τα)** [khartomandila (ta)] tissues, Kleenex®
χαρτόνι (το) [khartoni (to)] cardboard
χαρτονόμισμα [khartonomisma] banknote, (US) bill
ΧΑΡΤΟΠΩΛΕΙΟ **χαρτοπωλείο (το)** [khartopolio (to)] stationer's
χαρτοφύλακας (ο) [khartofilakas (o)] briefcase
ΧΑΣΑΠΗΣ **χασάπης (ο)** [khasapis (o)] butcher's
χείλι (το) [khili (to)] lip
ΧΕΙΜΕΡΙΝΟΣ **χειμερινός** [khimerinos] (winter) cinema/movie theater
χειμώνας (ο) [khimonas (o)] winter
ΧΕΙΡΟΠΟΙΗΤΟ **χειροποίητο** [khiropi-ito] handmade
χειρότερος [khiroteros] worse
χειρότερος (ο) [khiroteros (o)] worst
ΧΕΙΡΟΤΕΧΝΙΑ **χειροτεχνία (η)** crafts
χειρόφρενο (το) [khirofreno (to)] handbrake
χέρι (το) [kheri (to)] arm; hand
χερούλι (το) [kherooli (to)] handle
χήρα (η) [khira (i)] widow
χήρος (ο) [khiros (o)] widower
χθες [khThes] yesterday
ΧΙΛ. **χιλ.** thousand, thousands
ΧΙΛΙΑ **χίλια** [khilia] thousand,

thousands

ΧΙΛΙΑΔΕΣ χιλιάδες [khiliathes] thousand, thousands

ΧΙΛΙΑΡΙΚΟ χιλιάρικο (το) [khiliariko (to)] 1,000-drachma note/bill

χιλιόμετρο (το) [khiliometro (to)] kilometre

χιούμορ (το) [khioomor (to)] humour

χλιαρός [khliaros] lukewarm; cool

ΧΛΩΡΙΝΗ χλωρίνη (η) [khlorini (i)] bleach

χόμπυ (το) [khobi (to)] hobby

ΧΟΝΔΡΙΚΗΣ χονδρικής wholesale

χορεύω [khorevo] dance (verb)

χορός (ο) [khoros (o)] dance

χορτάρι (το) [khortari (to)] grass

χορτοφαγικός [khortofayikos] vegetarian

χορτοφάγος (ο/η) [khortofagos (o/i)] vegetarian

χρειάζομαι [khriazomeh] need (verb)

ΧΡΗΜΑΤΙΣΤΗΡΙΟ

χρηματιστήριο (το) [khrimatistirio (to)] currency exchange; stock exchange

χρήση (η) [khrisi (i)] use

χρησιμοποιώ [khrisimopio] use (verb)

χρήσιμος [khrisimos] useful

Χριστούγεννα (τα) [KHristooyena (ta)] Christmas

Καλά Χριστούγεννα! [Kala KHristooyena!] Happy Christmas!

χρονιά (η) [khronia (i)] year

Χρόνια Πολλά! [khronia pola!] Happy Birthday!

του χρόνου [too khronoo] next year

πόσο χρονών είσαι; [poso khronon iseh?] how old are you?

χρόνος (ο) [khronos (o)] time; year

ΧΡΥΣΟΣ χρυσός (ο) [khrisos (o)] gold

ΧΡΥΣΟΣ ΟΔΗΓΟΣ χρυσός οδηγός (ο) [khrisos othigos (o)] yellow pages

ΧΡΥΣΟΧΟΕΙΟ χρυσοχοείο (το) [khrisokhoio (to)] jeweller's

χρώμα (το) [khroma (to)] colour

ΧΡΩΜΑΤΑ - ΣΙΔΕΡΙΚΑ

χρώματα - σιδερικά paint and hardware store

χτένα (η) [khtena (i)] comb

χτυπώ [khtipo] hit (verb)

χώμα (το) [khoma (to)] earth

χώρα (η) [khora (i)] country

χωράφι (το) [khorafi (to)] field

ΧΩΡΗΤΙΚΟΤΗΤΟΣ ... ΑΤΟΜΩΝ χωρητικότητος ... ατόμων max load ... persons

χωριό (το) [khorio (to)] village

χωρίς [khoris] without

ΧΩΡΙΣ ΕΙΣΠΡΑΚΤΟΡΑ

χωρίς εισπράκτορα no ticket collector

χωρισμένος [khorismenos] divorced

ΧΩΡΙΣ ΜΠΑΝΙΟ χωρίς μπάνιο [khoris banio] without bathroom

ΧΩΡΙΣ ΝΤΟΥΣ χωρίς ντους

[khoris doos] without shower
ΧΩΡΙΣ ΣΥΝΤΗΡΗΤΙΚΑ
χωρίς συντηρητικά no preservatives
χωριστός [khoristos] separate
ΧΩΡΟΣ ΔΙΑ ΠΟΔΗΛΑΤΕΣ
χώρος διά ποδηλάτες cycle path
χώρος φύλαξης αποσκευών (ο) [khoros filaxis aposkevon (o)] left luggage, baggage check

Ψ

ψαλίδι (το) [psalithi (to)] scissors
ΨΑΡΑΔΙΚΟ ψαράδικο (το) [psarathiko (to)] fishmonger's
ψάρεμα (το) [psarema (to)] fishing
ΨΑΡΟΤΑΒΕΡΝΑ ψαροταβέρνα (η) [psarotaverna (i)] restaurant specializing in seafood
ψάχνω [psakhno] look for
ψέματα: λέω ψέματα [leo psemata] lie (say untruth)
ψεύτικος [pseftikos] false
ψήνω [psino] bake
ΨΗΣΤΑΡΙΑ ψησταριά (η) [psistaria (i)] restaurant specializing in charcoal-grilled food
ψιλά (τα) [psila (ta)] small change
ΨΙΛΙΚΑ ψιλικά (τα) [psilika (ta)] small shop
ψυγείο (το) [psiyio (to)] fridge
ψυγείο αυτοκινήτου (το) [psiyio aftokinitoo (to)] radiator (car)
ΨΩΜΑΔΙΚΟ ψωμάδικο [psomathiko] baker's
ψωμάς (ο) [psomas (o)] baker
ψηλός [psilos] high; tall
ψώνια (τα) [psonia (ta)] shopping
πάω για ψώνια [pao ya psonia] go shopping

Ω

ΩΘΗΣΑΤΕ ωθήσατε push
ώμος (ο) [omos (o)] shoulder
ώρα (η) [ora (i)] hour
τι ώρα είναι; [ti ora ineh?] what time is it?
σε λίγη ώρα [seh liyi ora] soon
στην ώρα του [stin ora too] on time
ωραίος [oreos] beautiful; handsome; lovely
ΩΡΕΣ ΕΠΙΣΚΕΨΕΩΣ ώρες επισκέψεως visiting hours
ΩΡΕΣ ΛΕΙΤΟΥΡΓΕΙΑΣ ώρες λειτουργείας opening hours
ως [os] as, since
ΩΤΟΡΙΝΟΛΑΡΥΓΓΟΛΟΓΟΣ ωτορινολαρυγγολόγος (ο/η) ear, nose and throat specialist
ωτοστόπ (το) [otostop (to)] hitchhiking
ωτοστόπ: κάνω ωτοστόπ [kano otostop] hitchhike

Menu Reader: Food

Essential Terms

bread to psomi
butter to vootiro
cup to flidzani
dessert to glikisma
fish to psari
fork to pirooni
glass to potiri
knife to makheri
main course to kirio piato
meat to kreas
menu to menoo
pepper to piperi
plate to piato
salad i salata
salt to alati
set menu to tabl-dot
soup i soopa
spoon to kootali
starter to proto piato
table to trapezi

another ..., please ali mia ..., parakalo
excuse me! parakalo
could I have the bill, please? boro na ekho ton logariasmo, parakalo?

ΑΓΓΙΝΑΡΕΣ ΑΥΓΟΛΕΜΟΝΟ **αγγινάρες αυγολέμονο** [aginares avgolemono] artichokes in egg and lemon sauce

ΑΓΓΟΥΡΑΚΙΑ **αγγουράκια** [agoorakia] cucumbers

ΑΓΓΟΥΡΙ **αγγούρι** [agoori] cucumber

ΑΓΓΟΥΡΙΑ ΚΑΙ ΝΤΟΜΑΤΕΣ ΣΑΛΑΤΑ **αγγούρια και ντομάτες σαλάτα** [agooria keh domates salata] cucumber and tomato salad

ΑΚΤΙΝΙΔΙΟ **ακτινίδιο** [aktinithio] kiwi fruit

ΑΛΑΤΙ **αλάτι** [alati] salt

ΑΛΕΥΡΙ **αλεύρι** [alevri] flour

ΑΛΕΥΡΙ ΚΑΛΑΜΠΟΚΙΟΥ **αλεύρι καλαμποκιού** [alevri kalabokioo] cornflour

ΑΛΕΥΡΙ ΣΤΑΡΙΟΥ **αλεύρι σταριού** [alevri starioo] wheat flour

ΑΛΛΑΝΤΙΚΑ **αλλαντικά** [alandika] sausages, salami, ham etc

ΑΜΥΓΔΑΛΑ **αμύγδαλα** [amigthala] almonds

ΑΜΥΓΔΑΛΩΤΑ **αμυγδαλωτά** [amigthalota] macaroons; almond pastries

ΑΝΑΝΑΣ **ανανάς** [ananas] pineapple

ΑΝΘΟΤΥΡΟ **ανθότυρο** [anTHotiro] type of cottage cheese

ΑΝΤΖΟΥΓΙΑ ΣΤΟ ΛΑΔΙ **αντζούγια στο λάδι** [andsoo-yia sto lathi] anchovies in oil

ΑΡΑΚΑΣ **αρακάς** [arakas] peas

ΑΡΑΚΑΣ ΛΑΔΕΡΟΣ **αρακάς λαδερός** [arakas latheros] peas cooked with tomato and oil

ΑΡΑΚΑΣ ΣΩΤΕ **αρακάς σωτέ** [arakas soteh] peas fried in butter

ΑΡΝΑΚΙ **αρνάκι** [arnaki] lamb

ΑΡΝΑΚΙ ΕΞΟΧΙΚΟ **αρνάκι εξοχικό** [arnaki exokhiko] leg of lamb baked in greaseproof paper

ΑΡΝΑΚΙ ΜΕ ΜΠΑΜΙΕΣ **αρνάκι με μπάμιες** [arnaki meh bami-es] lamb and okra stew

ΑΡΝΑΚΙ ΜΕ ΠΑΤΑΤΕΣ ΣΤΟ ΦΟΥΡΝΟ **αρνάκι με πατάτες στο φούρνο** [arnaki meh patates sto foorno] roast lamb and potatoes

ΑΡΝΑΚΙ ΤΑΣ ΚΕΜΠΑΠ **αρνάκι τας κεμπάπ** [arnaki tas kebap] lamb in tomato sauce

ΑΡΝΑΚΙ ΤΗΣ ΣΟΥΒΛΑΣ **αρνάκι της σούβλας** [arnaki tis soovlas] spit-roast lamb

ΑΡΝΑΚΙ ΦΡΙΚΑΣΕ **αρνάκι φρικασέ με μαρούλια** [arnaki frikaseh meh maroolia] lamb and lettuce in egg and lemon sauce

ΑΡΝΙ **αρνί** [arni] mutton, lamb

ΑΡΝΙ ΓΕΜΙΣΤΟ ΣΤΟ ΦΟΥΡΝΟ **αρνί γεμιστό στο φούρνο** [arni yemisto sto foorno] oven-cooked stuffed lamb

ΑΡΝΙ ΕΞΟΧΙΚΟ **αρνί εξοχικό** [arni exokhiko] lamb cooked in greased foil with cheese and spices

ΑΡΝΙ ΚΟΚΚΙΝΙΣΤΟ **αρνί κοκκινιστό** [arni kokinisto] lamb in tomato sauce

ΑΡΝΙ ΛΑΔΟΡΙΓΑΝΗ ΣΤΟ ΦΟΥΡΝΟ **αρνί λαδορίγανη στο φούρνο** [arni lathorigani sto foorno] oven-cooked lamb with oil and oregano

ΑΡΝΙ ΜΕ ΑΡΑΚΑ **αρνί με αρακά** [arni meh araka] lamb with peas

ΑΡΝΙ ΜΕ ΚΟΛΟΚΥΘΑΚΙΑ ΑΥΓΟΛΕΜΟΝΟ **αρνί με κολοκυθάκια αυγολέμονο** [arni meh kolokiTHakia avgolemono] lamb with courgettes/zucchini in egg and lemon sauce

ΑΡΝΙ ΜΕ ΚΡΙΘΑΡΑΚΙ **αρνί με κριθαράκι** [arni meh kriTHaraki] lamb with pasta

ΑΡΝΙ ΜΕ ΜΑΚΑΡΟΝΙΑ **αρνί με μακαρόνια** [arni meh makaronia] lamb with spaghetti

ΑΡΝΙ ΜΕ ΜΕΛΙΤΖΑΝΕΣ **αρνί με μελιτζάνες** [arni meh melitzanes] lamb with aubergines/eggplants

ΑΡΝΙ ΜΕ ΜΠΑΜΙΕΣ **αρνί με μπάμιες** [arni meh bami-es] lamb with okra

ΑΡΝΙ ΜΕ ΠΑΤΑΤΕΣ ΡΑΓΟΥ **αρνί με πατάτες ραγού** [arni meh patates ragoo] lamb with potatoes cooked in tomato sauce

ΑΡΝΙ ΜΕ ΦΑΣΟΛΑΚΙΑ ΦΡΕΣΚΑ **αρνί με φασολάκια φρέσκα** [arni meh fasolakia freska] lamb with runner beans

ΑΡΝΙ ΜΕ ΧΥΛΟΠΙΤΕΣ **αρνί με χυλοπίτες** [arni meh khilopites] lamb with a type of lasagne

ΑΡΝΙ ΜΠΟΥΤΙ ΣΤΟ ΦΟΥΡΝΟ **αρνί μπούτι στο φούρνο** [arni booti sto foorno] oven-cooked leg of lamb

ΑΡΝΙ ΜΠΡΙΖΟΛΕΣ **αρνί μπριζόλες** [arni brizoles] lamb chops

ΑΡΝΙ ΠΑΪΔΑΚΙΑ **αρνί παϊδάκια** [arni paithakia] grilled lamb chops

ΑΡΝΙ ΤΑΣ ΚΕΜΠΑΠ **αρνί τας κεμπάπ** [arni tas kebab] chopped lamb kebab with tomato sauce

ΑΡΝΙ ΤΗΣ ΚΑΤΣΑΡΟΛΑΣ ΜΕ ΠΑΤΑΤΕΣ **αρνί της κατσαρόλας με πατάτες** [arni tis katsarolas meh patates] casseroled lamb cooked with potatoes

ΑΡΝΙ ΤΗΣ ΣΟΥΒΛΑΣ **αρνί της σούβλας** [arni tis soovlas] spit-roast lamb

ΑΡΝΙ ΦΡΙΚΑΣΕ **αρνί φρικασέ** [arni frikaseh] lamb fricassee

ΑΣΤΑΚΟΣ **αστακός** [astakos] lobster

ΑΣΤΑΚΟΣ ΜΕ ΛΑΔΟΛΕΜΟΝΟ **αστακός με λαδολέμονο** [astakos meh latholemono] lobster cooked in lemon and oil sauce

ΑΣΤΑΚΟΣ ΜΕ ΜΑΓΙΟΝΕΖΑ **αστακός με μαγιονέζα** [astakos meh mayoneza] lobster with mayonnaise

ΑΤΖΕΜ ΠΙΛΑΦΙ **ατζέμ πιλάφι** [atzem pilafi] rice pilaf

ΑΥΓΑ **αυγά** [avga] eggs

ΑΥΓΑ ΒΡΑΣΤΑ **αυγά βραστά** [avga vrasta] boiled eggs

ΑΥΓΑ ΒΡΑΣΤΑ ΣΦΙΧΤΑ **αυγά βραστά σφιχτά** [avga vrasta sfikhta] hard-boiled eggs

ΑΥΓΑ ΓΕΜΙΣΤΑ **αυγά γεμιστά** [avga yemista] stuffed eggs

ΑΥΓΑ ΓΕΜΙΣΤΑ ΜΕ ΜΑΓΙΟΝΕΖΑ **αυγά γεμιστά με μαγιονέζα** [avga yemista meh mayoneza] stuffed eggs with mayonnaise

ΑΥΓΑ ΜΑΤΙΑ **αυγά μάτια** [avga matia] fried eggs

ΑΥΓΑ ΜΕΛΑΤΑ **αυγά μελάτα** [avga melata] soft-boiled eggs

ΑΥΓΑ ΜΕ ΜΑΝΙΤΑΡΙΑ **αυγά με μανιτάρια** [avga meh manitaria] mushroom omelette

ΑΥΓΑ ΜΕ ΜΠΕΙΚΟΝ **αυγά με μπέικον** [avga meh bacon] bacon and eggs

ΑΥΓΑ ΜΕ ΝΤΟΜΑΤΕΣ **αυγά με ντομάτες** [avga meh domates] eggs cooked in tomato sauce

ΑΥΓΑ ΜΕ ΤΥΡΙ **αυγά με τυρί** [avga meh tiri] cheese omelette

ΑΥΓΑ ΟΜΕΛΕΤΑ **αυγά ομελέτα** [avga omeleta] plain omelette

ΑΥΓΑ ΟΜΕΛΕΤΑ ΜΕ ΠΑΤΑΤΕΣ **αυγά ομελέτα με πατάτες** [avga omeleta meh patates] omelette with chips/fries

ΑΥΓΑ ΠΟΣΕ **αυγά ποσέ** [avga poseh] poached eggs

ΑΥΓΑ ΣΦΙΧΤΑ **αυγά σφιχτά** [avga sfikhta] hard-boiled eggs

ΑΥΓΑ ΤΗΓΑΝΗΤΑ **αυγά τηγανητά** [avga tiganita] fried eggs

ΑΥΓΑ Ω ΓΚΡΑΤΕΝ **αυγά ω γκρατέν** [avga o graten] eggs au gratin

ΑΥΓΟ **αυγό** [avgo] egg

ΑΥΓΟΛΕΜΟΝΟ **αυγολέμονο** [avgolemono] egg and lemon sauce

ΑΥΓΟΛΕΜΟΝΟ ΣΟΥΠΑ **αυγολέμονο σούπα** [avgolemono soopa] chicken broth with egg and lemon

ΑΥΓΟΤΑΡΑΧΟ **αυγοτάραχο** [avgotarakho] roe

ΑΧΛΑΔΙ **αχλάδι** [akhlathi] pear

ΒΑΝΙΛΙΑ **βανίλια** [vanilia] vanilla

ΒΑΤΟΜΟΥΡΟ **βατόμουρο** [vatomooro] blackberry

ΒΕΡΙΚΟΚΟ **βερίκοκο** [verikoko] apricot

ΒΟΔΙΝΟ **βοδινό** [vothino] beef

ΒΟΔΙΝΟ ΒΡΑΣΤΟ **βοδινό βραστό** [vothino vrasto] boiled beef

ΒΟΔΙΝΟ ΡΟΣΜΠΙΦ **βοδινό ροσμπίφ** [vothino rosbif] roast beef

ΒΟΤΑΝΑ βότανα [votana] herbs
ΒΟΥΤΥΡΟ βούτυρο [**oo**tiro] butter
ΒΡΑΣΤΟ βραστό [vrast**o**] boiled
ΒΥΣΣΙΝΟ βύσσινο [visino] sour cherries

ΓΑΛΑΚΤΟΜΠΟΥΡΕΚΟ γαλακτομπούρεκο [galaktob**oo**reko] cream-filled sweet filo pastry with honey
ΓΑΛΟΠΟΥΛΑ γαλοπούλα [galop**oo**la] turkey
ΓΑΛΟΠΟΥΛΑ ΓΕΜΙΣΤΗ γαλοπούλα γεμιστή [galop**oo**la yemisti] stuffed turkey
ΓΑΛΟΠΟΥΛΑ ΚΟΚΚΙΝΙΣΤΗ γαλοπούλα κοκκινιστή [galop**oo**la kokinisti] turkey cooked with tomatoes
ΓΑΛΟΠΟΥΛΑ ΨΗΤΗ ΣΤΟ ΦΟΥΡΝΟ γαλοπούλα ψητή στο φούρνο [galop**oo**la psiti sto f**oo**rno] roast turkey
ΓΑΡΔΟΥΜΠΑ γαρδούμπα [garth**oo**mba] spit-roast rolled lamb offal
ΓΑΡΙΔΕΣ γαρίδες [garithes] prawns
ΓΑΡΙΔΕΣ ΒΡΑΣΤΕΣ γαρίδες βραστές [garithes vrastes] boiled shrimps
ΓΑΡΙΔΕΣ ΚΟΚΤΑΙΗΛ γαρίδες κοκταίηλ [garithes cocktail] shrimp cocktail
ΓΑΡΙΔΕΣ ΠΙΛΑΦΙ γαρίδες πιλάφι [garithes pilafi] shrimp pilaf
ΓΑΡΙΔΟΠΙΛΑΦΟ γαριδοπίλαφο [garithopilafo] prawns with rice cooked in butter
ΓΑΡΝΙΤΟΥΡΑ γαρνιτούρα [garnit**oo**ra] vegetables
ΓΑΡΝΙΤΟΥΡΑ ΚΑΡΟΤΑ ΣΩΤΕ γαρνιτούρα καρότα σωτέ [garnit**oo**ra karota sot**eh**] sautéed carrots
ΓΑΡΝΙΤΟΥΡΑ ΚΟΥΝΟΥΠΙΔΙ ΣΩΤΕ γαρνιτούρα κουνουπίδι σωτέ [garnit**oo**ra koonoopithi sot**eh**] sautéed cauliflower
ΓΑΡΝΙΤΟΥΡΑ ΠΑΤΑΤΕΣ γαρνιτούρα πατάτες [garnit**oo**ra patates] potatoes
ΓΑΡΝΙΤΟΥΡΑ ΣΠΑΝΑΚΙ ΣΩΤΕ γαρνιτούρα σπανάκι σωτέ [garnit**oo**ra spanaki sot**eh**] sautéed spinach
ΓΑΡΝΙΤΟΥΡΑ ΦΑΣΟΛΙΑ ΠΡΑΣΙΝΑ ΣΩΤΕ γαρνιτούρα φασόλια πράσινα σωτέ [garnit**oo**ra fasolia prasina sot**eh**] sautéed runner beans
ΓΕΜΙΣΤΑ γεμιστά [yemista] stuffed, usually with rice and/or minced meat
ΓΕΜΙΣΤΕΣ γεμιστές [yemistes] stuffed vegetables
ΓΙΑΛΑΝΤΖΗ ΝΤΟΛΜΑΔΕΣ γιαλαντζή ντολμάδες [yalantzi dolmathes] vine leaves stuffed with rice
ΓΙΑΟΥΡΤΙ γιαούρτι [ya-**oo**rti] yoghurt
ΓΙΓΑΝΤΕΣ γίγαντες [yigandes] white haricot beans; butter

beans

ΓΙΟΥΒΑΡΛΑΚΙΑ γιουβαρλάκια [yoovarlakia] meatballs, rice and seasoning in a sauce

ΓΙΟΥΒΑΡΛΑΚΙΑ ΑΥΓΟΛΕΜΟΝΟ γιουβαρλάκια αυγολέμονο [yoovarlakia avgolemono] meatballs with egg and lemon sauce

ΓΙΟΥΒΑΡΛΑΚΙΑ ΜΕ ΣΑΛΤΣΑ ΝΤΟΜΑΤΑΣ γιουβαρλάκια με σάλτσα ντομάτας [yoovarlakia meh saltsa domatas] meatballs with rice cooked with tomatoes

ΓΙΟΥΒΕΤΣΙ γιουβέτσι [yoovetsi] oven-roasted lamb with pasta

ΓΚΡΕΙΠΦΡΟΥΤ γκρέιπφρουτ [grapefruit] grapefruit

ΓΛΥΚΑ γλυκά [glika] cakes, desserts

ΓΛΥΚΙΣΜΑ γλύκισμα [glikisma] dessert

ΓΛΥΚΟ γλυκό [gliko] sweet, dessert

ΓΛΥΚΟ ΒΥΣΣΙΝΟ γλυκό βύσσινο [gliko visino] candied cherries in syrup

ΓΛΥΚΟ ΚΑΡΥΔΑΚΙ ΦΡΕΣΚΟ γλυκό καρυδάκι φρέσκο [gliko karithaki fresko] dried fresh green walnuts in syrup

ΓΛΥΚΟ ΜΑΣΤΙΧΑ γλυκό μαστίχα [gliko mastikha] vanilla-flavoured fudge

ΓΛΥΚΟ ΜΕΛΙΤΖΑΝΑΚΙ γλυκό μελιτζανάκι [gliko melitzanaki] dried small aubergine/eggplant in syrup

ΓΛΥΚΟ ΝΕΡΑΝΤΖΑΚΙ γλυκό νεραντζάκι [gliko nerantzaki] dried bitter orange in syrup

ΓΛΥΚΟ ΣΥΚΟ γλυκό σύκο [gliko siko] candied figs in syrup

ΓΛΥΚΟ ΣΥΚΟ ΦΡΕΣΚΟ γλυκό σύκο φρέσκο [gliko siko fresko] dried fig in syrup

ΓΛΥΚΟ ΤΡΙΑΝΤΑΦΥΛΛΟ γλυκό τριαντάφυλλο [gliko triandafilo] dried rose petals in syrup

ΓΛΩΣΣΑ γλώσσα [glosa] sole; tongue

ΓΛΩΣΣΕΣ ΤΗΓΑΝΗΤΕΣ γλώσσες τηγανητές [gloses tiganites] fried sole

ΓΟΥΡΟΥΝΟΠΟΥΛΟ ΣΤΟ ΦΟΥΡΝΟ ΜΕ ΠΑΤΑΤΕΣ γουρουνόπουλο στο φούρνο με πατάτες [gooroonopoolo sto foorno meh patates] oven-cooked pork with potatoes

ΓΡΑΒΙΕΡΑ γραβιέρα [gravi-era] hard cheese like gruyère

ΓΡΑΝΙΤΑ γρανίτα [granita] sorbet

ΓΡΑΝΙΤΑ ΛΕΜΟΝΙ γρανίτα λεμόνι [granita lemoni] lemon sorbet

ΓΡΑΝΙΤΑ ΜΠΑΝΑΝΑ γρανίτα μπανάνα [granita banana] banana sorbet

ΓΡΑΝΙΤΑ ΠΟΡΤΟΚΑΛΙ γρανίτα πορτοκάλι [granita portokali] orange sorbet

ΓΡΑΝΙΤΑ ΦΡΑΟΥΛΕΣ γρανίτα

φράουλες [granita fraooles] strawberry sorbet

ΔΑΜΑΣΚΗΝΑ δαμάσκηνα [thamaskina] prunes

ΔΑΜΑΣΚΗΝΟ δαμάσκηνο [thamaskino] plum

ΔΙΠΛΕΣ δίπλες [thiples] pancakes

ΕΛΑΙΟΛΑΔΟ ελαιόλαδο [eleolatho] olive oil

ΕΛΙΕΣ ελιές [eli-es] olives

ΕΝΤΟΣΘΙΑ ΑΡΝΙΟΥ ΛΑΔΟΡΙΓΑΝΗ εντόσθια αρνιού λαδορίγανη [endosthia arnioo lathorigani] lambs' intestines cooked in lemon and oil

ΕΠΙΔΟΡΠΙΟ επιδόρπιο [epithorpio] dessert

ΕΣΚΑΛΟΠ ΜΕ ΖΑΜΠΟΝ ΚΑΙ ΣΑΛΤΣΑ ΝΤΟΜΑΤΑΣ εσκαλόπ με ζαμπόν και σάλτσα ντομάτας [eskalop meh zabon keh saltsa domatas] escalope of veal with ham and tomato sauce

ΖΑΜΠΟΝ ζαμπόν [zabon] ham

ΖΑΧΑΡΗ ζάχαρη [zakhari] sugar

ΖΕΛΕ ζελέ [zeleh] jelly

ΖΥΜΑΡΙΚΑ ζυμαρικά [zimarika] pasta and rice

ΘΑΛΑΣΣΙΝΑ θαλασσινά [THalasina] seafood

ΚΑΒΟΥΡΙΑ καβούρια [kavooria] crab

ΚΑΚΑΒΙΑ κακαβιά [kakavia] mixed fish soup

ΚΑΚΑΒΙΑ ΨΑΡΟΣΟΥΠΑ κακαβιά ψαρόσουπα [kakavia psarosoopa] fish soup

ΚΑΛΑΜΑΡΑΚΙΑ καλαμαράκια [kalamarakia] baby squid

ΚΑΛΑΜΑΡΑΚΙΑ ΓΕΜΙΣΤΑ καλαμαράκια γεμιστά [kalamarakia yemista] stuffed baby squid

ΚΑΛΑΜΑΡΑΚΙΑ ΤΗΓΑΝΗΤΑ καλαμαράκια τηγανητά [kalamarakia tiganita] fried baby squid

ΚΑΛΑΜΑΡΙΑ καλαμάρια [kalamaria] squid

ΚΑΝΑΠΕ καναπέ [kanapeh] canapés

ΚΑΝΑΠΕ ΜΕ ΖΑΜΠΟΝ καναπέ με ζαμπόν [kanapeh meh zabon] ham canapés

ΚΑΝΑΠΕ ΜΕ ΚΡΕΑΣ ΨΗΤΟ καναπέ με κρέας ψητό [kanapeh meh kreas psito] meat canapés

ΚΑΝΑΠΕ ΜΕ ΜΑΥΡΟ ΧΑΒΙΑΡΙ καναπέ με μαύρο χαβιάρι [kanapeh meh mavro haviari] black caviar canapés

ΚΑΝΑΠΕ ΜΕ ΤΑΡΑΜΟΣΑΛΑΤΑ καναπέ με ταραμοσαλάτα [kanapeh meh taramosalata] taramosalata canapés

ΚΑΝΕΛΛΑ κανέλλα [kanela] cinnamon

ΚΑΝΕΛΛΟΝΙΑ ΓΕΜΙΣΤΑ κανελλόνια γεμιστά [kanelonia

yemista] stuffed canelloni

ΚΑΝΤΑΪΦΙ κανταΐ΄φι [kanda-ifi] shredded and rolled filo pastry in syrup

ΚΑΠΑΜΑΣ ΑΡΝΙ καπαμάς αρνί [kapamas arni] lamb cooked in spices and tomato sauce

ΚΑΠΝΙΣΤΟ καπνιστό [kapnisto] smoked

ΚΑΠΠΑΡΗ κάππαρη [kapari] caper

ΚΑΡΑΒΙΔΕΣ καραβίδες [karavithes] king prawns; crayfish

ΚΑΡΟΤΑ καρότα [karota] carrots

ΚΑΡΠΟΥΖΙ καρπούζι [karpoozi] watermelon

ΚΑΡΥΔΙ καρύδι [karithi] nut

ΚΑΡΥΔΟΠΙΤΤΑ καρυδόπιττα [karithopita] walnut cake; cake with nuts and syrup

ΚΑΡΧΑΡΙΑΣ καρχαρίας [karkharias] shark

ΚΑΣΕΡΙ κασέρι [kaseri] Cheddar-type cheese

ΚΑΣΤΑΝΑ κάστανα [kastana] chestnuts

ΚΑΣΤΑΝΑ ΓΛΑΣΕ κάστανα γλασέ [kastana glaseh] glazed chestnuts, marrons glacés

ΚΑΤΑΪΦΙ καταΐ΄φι [kata-ifi] shredded filo pastry with honey and nuts

ΚΑΤΑΛΟΓΟΣ κατάλογος [katalogos] menu

ΚΕΙΚ κέικ [cake] cake

ΚΕΙΚ ΚΑΝΕΛΛΑΣ κέικ κανέλλας [cake kanelas] cinammon cake

ΚΕΙΚ ΜΕ ΑΜΥΓΔΑΛΑ κέικ με αμύγδαλα [cake meh amigthala] almond cake

ΚΕΙΚ ΜΕ ΚΑΡΥΔΙΑ ΚΑΙ ΣΤΑΦΙΔΕΣ κέικ με καρύδια και σταφίδες [cake meh karithia keh stafithes] nut and sultana cake

ΚΕΙΚ ΣΟΚΟΛΑΤΑΣ κέικ σοκολάτας [cake sokolatas] chocolate cake

ΚΕΙΚ ΦΡΟΥΤΩΝ κέικ φρούτων [cake frooton] fruit cake

ΚΕΡΑΣΙΑ κεράσια [kerasia] cherries

ΚΕΦΑΛΟΤΥΡΙ κεφαλοτύρι [kefalotiri] very salty, hard cheese

ΚΕΦΤΕΔΕΣ κεφτέδες [keftethes] meatballs

ΚΕΦΤΕΔΕΣ ΜΕ ΣΑΛΤΣΑ κεφτέδες με σάλτσα [keftethes meh saltsa] meatballs in tomato sauce

ΚΕΦΤΕΔΕΣ ΣΤΟ ΦΟΥΡΝΟ κεφτέδες στο φούρνο [keftethes sto foorno] oven-cooked meatballs

ΚΕΦΤΕΔΕΣ ΤΗΓΑΝΗΤΟΙ κεφτέδες τηγανητοί [keftethes tiganiti] fried meatballs

ΚΙΜΑΣ κιμάς [kimas] minced meat

ΚΛΕΦΤΙΚΟ κλέφτικο [kleftiko] meat, potatoes and

vegetables cooked together in a pot or foil

ΚΟΚΚΙΝΙΣΤΟ κοκκινιστό [kokinisto] in tomato sauce

ΚΟΚΟΡΕΤΣΙ κοκορέτσι [kokoretsi] spit-roast rolled lamb offal

ΚΟΛΙΟΙ κολιοί [koli-i] mackerel

ΚΟΛΙΟΙ ΨΗΤΟΙ κολιοί ψητοί [koli-i psiti] fried mackerel

ΚΟΛΟΚΥΘΑΚΙΑ κολοκυθάκια [kolokiTHakia] courgettes/zucchini

ΚΟΛΟΚΥΘΑΚΙΑ ΓΕΜΙΣΤΑ ΜΕ ΚΙΜΑ κολοκυθάκια γεμιστά με κιμά [kolokiTHakia yemista meh kima] courgettes/zucchini stuffed with minced meat

ΚΟΛΟΚΥΘΑΚΙΑ ΓΕΜΙΣΤΑ ΜΕ ΡΥΖΙ κολοκυθάκια γεμιστά με ρύζι [kolokiTHakia yemista meh rizi] courgettes/zucchini stuffed with rice

ΚΟΛΟΚΥΘΑΚΙΑ ΓΙΑΧΝΙ κολοκυθάκια γιαχνί [kolokiTHakia yakhni] courgettes/zucchini and onions in a tomato sauce

ΚΟΛΟΚΥΘΑΚΙΑ ΛΑΔΕΡΑ κολοκυθάκια λαδερά [kolokiTHakia lathera] courgettes/zucchini cooked in oil

ΚΟΛΟΚΥΘΑΚΙΑ ΜΕ ΚΡΕΑΣ κολοκυθάκια με κρέας [kolokiTHakia meh kreas] courgette/zucchini and beef stew

ΚΟΛΟΚΥΘΑΚΙΑ ΜΕ ΠΑΤΑΤΕΣ κολοκυθάκια με πατάτες [kolokiTHakia meh patates] courgettes/zucchini with potatoes

ΚΟΛΟΚΥΘΑΚΙΑ ΜΟΥΣΑΚΑΣ κολοκυθάκια μουσακάς [kolokiTHakia moosakas] courgettes/zucchini with minced meat and béchamel

ΚΟΛΟΚΥΘΑΚΙΑ ΠΑΠΟΥΤΣΑΚΙΑ κολοκυθάκια παπουτσάκια [kolokiTHakia papootsakia] courgettes/zucchini with minced meat and onions

ΚΟΛΟΚΥΘΑΚΙΑ ΤΗΓΑΝΗΤΑ κολοκυθάκια τηγανητά [kolokiTHakia tiganita] fried courgettes/zucchini

ΚΟΛΟΚΥΘΟΚΕΦΤΕΔΕΣ κολοκυθοκεφτέδες [kolokiTHokeftethes] fried courgette/zucchini balls

ΚΟΛΟΚΥΘΟΤΥΡΟΠΙΤΤΑ κολοκυθοτυρόπιττα [kolokiTHotiropita] courgette/zucchini and cheese pie

ΚΟΜΠΟΣΤΑ κομπόστα [kobosta] fruit compote

ΚΟΤΑ κότα [kota] chicken

ΚΟΤΑ ΒΡΑΣΤΗ κότα βραστή [kota vrasti] boiled chicken

ΚΟΤΑ ΨΗΤΗ ΣΤΟ ΦΟΥΡΝΟ κότα ψητή στο φούρνο [kota psiti sto foorno] roast chicken

ΚΟΤΑ ΨΗΤΗ ΤΗΣ ΚΑΤΣΑΡΟΛΑΣ κότα ψητή της κατσαρόλας [kota psiti tis katsarolas] chicken casserole

ΚΟΤΑ ΨΗΤΗ ΤΗΣ ΣΟΥΒΛΑΣ **κότα ψητή της σούβλας** [kota psiti tis soovlas] spit-roast chicken

ΚΟΤΟΛΕΤΕΣ ΑΡΝΙΣΙΕΣ ΠΑΝΕ **κοτολέτες αρνίσιες πανέ** [kotoletes arnisi-es paneh] lamb cutlets

ΚΟΤΟΛΕΤΕΣ ΜΟΣΧΑΡΙΣΙΕΣ ΠΑΝΕ **κοτολέτες μοσχαρίσιες πανέ** [kotoletes moskharisi-es paneh] veal cutlets

ΚΟΤΟΠΙΤΤΑ **κοτόπιττα** [kotopita] chicken pie

ΚΟΤΟΠΟΥΛΟ **κοτόπουλο** [kotopoolo] chicken

ΚΟΤΟΠΟΥΛΟ ΓΙΟΥΒΕΤΣΙ ΜΕ ΧΥΛΟΠΙΤΤΕΣ **κοτόπουλο γιουβέτσι με χυλοπίττες** [kotopoolo yiovetsi meh hilopites] chicken with pasta

ΚΟΤΟΠΟΥΛΟ ΚΟΚΚΙΝΙΣΤΟ **κοτόπουλο κοκκινιστό** [kotopoolo kokinisto] chicken in tomato sauce

ΚΟΤΟΠΟΥΛΟ ΜΕ ΜΠΑΜΙΕΣ **κοτόπουλο με μπάμιες** [kotopoolo meh bami-es] chicken with okra

ΚΟΤΟΠΟΥΛΟ ΜΕ ΜΠΙΖΕΛΙΑ **κοτόπουλο με μπιζέλια** [kotopoolo meh bizelia] chicken with peas

ΚΟΤΟΠΟΥΛΟ ΠΑΝΕ **κοτόπουλο πανέ** [kotopoolo paneh] breaded chicken

ΚΟΤΟΠΟΥΛΟ ΠΙΛΑΦΙ **κοτόπουλο πιλάφι** [kotopoolo pilafi] chicken pilaf

ΚΟΤΟΠΟΥΛΟ ΤΗΣ ΣΟΥΒΛΑΣ **κοτόπουλο της σούβλας** [kotopoolo tis soovlas] spit-roast chicken

ΚΟΤΟΣΟΥΠΑ **κοτόσουπα** [kotosoopa] chicken soup

ΚΟΥΚΙΑ ΛΑΔΕΡΑ **κουκιά λαδερά** [kookia lathera] broad beans in tomato sauce

ΚΟΥΝΕΛΙ **κουνέλι** [kooneli] rabbit

ΚΟΥΝΕΛΙ ΜΕ ΣΑΛΤΣΑ **κουνέλι με σάλτσα** [kooneli meh saltsa] rabbit with tomato sauce

ΚΟΥΝΕΛΙ ΣΤΙΦΑΔΟ **κουνέλι στιφάδο** [kooneli stifatho] rabbit with onions

ΚΟΥΝΟΥΠΙΔΙ **κουνουπίδι** [koonoopithi] cauliflower

ΚΟΥΝΟΥΠΙΔΙ ΒΡΑΣΤΟ ΣΑΛΑΤΑ **κουνουπίδι βραστό σαλάτα** [koonopithi vrasto salata] boiled cauliflower salad

ΚΟΥΡΑΜΠΙΕΔΕΣ **κουραμπιέδες** [koorabi-ethes] Greek shortbread

ΚΟΥΡΑΜΠΙΕΔΕΣ ΜΕ ΑΜΥΓΔΑΛΟ **κουραμπιέδες με αμύγδαλο** [koorabi-ethes meh amigthalo] shortbread-type biscuits with sesame seeds and icing sugar

ΚΡΑΚΕΡΣ ΑΛΜΥΡΑ **κράκερς αλμυρά** [krakers almira] salted crackers

ΚΡΑΣΑΤΟ **κρασάτο** [krasato] cooked in wine sauce

ΚΡΕΑΣ κρέας [kreas] meat, usually beef

ΚΡΕΑΣ ΜΕ ΑΝΤΙΔΙΑ ΑΥΓΟΛΕΜΟΝΟ κρέας με αντίδια αυγολέμονο [kreas meh antithia avgolemono] beef with endives in egg and lemon sauce

ΚΡΕΑΣ ΜΕ ΦΑΣΟΛΙΑ ΞΕΡΑ κρέας με φασόλια ξερά [kreas meh fasolia xera] beef with butter beans

ΚΡΕΑΤΙΚΑ κρεατικά [kreh-atika] meat dishes

ΚΡΕΑΤΟΠΙΤΤΑ κρεατόπιττα [kreh-atopita] minced meat in filo pastry

ΚΡΕΜΑ κρέμα [krema] cream

ΚΡΕΜΑ ΚΑΡΑΜΕΛΕ κρέμα καραμελέ [krema karameleh] crème caramel

ΚΡΕΜΑ ΜΕ ΜΗΛΑ κρέμα με μήλα [krema meh mila] apples with cream

ΚΡΕΜΑ ΜΕ ΜΠΑΝΑΝΕΣ κρέμα με μπανάνες [krema meh bananes] bananas with cream

ΚΡΕΜΜΥΔΑΚΙΑ ΦΡΕΣΚΑ κρεμμυδάκια φρέσκα [kremithakia freska] spring onions

ΚΡΕΜΜΥΔΙΑ κρεμμύδια [kremithia] onions

ΚΡΕΜΜΥΔΟΣΟΥΠΑ κρεμμυδόσουπα [kremithosoopa] onion soup

ΚΡΕΠΑ κρέπα [krepa] pancake

ΚΡΟΚΕΤΕΣ κροκέτες [kroketes] croquettes

ΚΡΟΚΕΤΕΣ ΑΠΟ ΚΡΕΑΣ κροκέτες από κρέας [kroketes apo kreas] meat croquettes

ΚΡΟΚΕΤΕΣ ΜΕ ΑΥΓΑ ΚΑΙ ΤΥΡΙ κροκέτες με αυγά και τυρί [kroketes meh avga keh tiri] egg and cheese croquettes

ΚΡΟΚΕΤΕΣ ΜΠΑΚΑΛΙΑΡΟΥ κροκέτες μπακαλιάρου [kroketes bakaliaroo] cod croquettes

ΚΡΟΚΕΤΕΣ ΠΑΤΑΤΕΣ κροκέτες πατάτες [kroketes patates] potato croquettes

ΚΡΟΥΑΣΑΝ κρουασάν [croissants] croissants

ΚΥΔΩΝΙΑ κυδώνια [kithonia] quinces

ΚΥΔΩΝΟΠΑΣΤΟ κυδωνόπαστο [kithonopasto] thick jelly made from quince

ΚΥΝΗΓΙ κυνήγι [kiniyi] game

ΚΥΡΙΟ ΠΙΑΤΟ κύριο πιάτο [kirio piato] main course

ΚΩΚ κωκ [kok] cake with cream and chocolate topping

ΛΑΓΟΣ λαγός [lagos] hare

ΛΑΓΟΣ ΜΕ ΣΑΛΤΣΑ λαγός με σάλτσα [lagos meh saltsa] hare in tomato sauce

ΛΑΓΟΣ ΣΤΙΦΑΔΟ λαγός στιφάδο [lagos stifatho] hare and shallot stew

ΛΑΔΕΡΑ λαδερά [lathera] in olive oil and tomato sauce

ΛΑΔΙ λάδι [lathi] oil

ΛΑΔΟΛΕΜΟΝΟ λαδολέμονο [latholemono] olive oil and lemon dressing

ΛΑΔΟΞΥΔΟ λαδόξυδο [lathoxitho] oil and vinegar salad dressing

ΛΑΖΑΝΙΑ λαζάνια [lazania] lasagne

ΛΑΧΑΝΙΚΑ λαχανικά [lakhanika] vegetables

ΛΑΧΑΝΙΚΑ ΜΙΚΤΑ λαχανικά μικτά [lakhanika mikta] vegetables

ΛΑΧΑΝΑΚΙΑ ΒΡΥΞΕΛΛΩΝ λαχανάκια Βρυξελλών [lakhanakia vrixelon] Brussels sprouts

ΛΑΧΑΝΟ λάχανο [lakhano] cabbage

ΛΑΧΑΝΟ ΚΟΚΚΙΝΟ λάχανο κόκκινο [lakhano kokino] red cabbage

ΛΑΧΑΝΟ ΝΤΟΛΜΑΔΕΣ ΑΥΓΟΛΕΜΟΝΟ λάχανο ντολμάδες αυγολέμονο [lakhano dolmathes avgolemono] cabbage leaves stuffed with rice in egg and lemon sauce

ΛΑΧΑΝΟ ΝΤΟΛΜΑΔΕΣ λάχανο ντολμάδες [lakhano dolmathes] cabbage leaves stuffed with minced meat and rice

ΛΑΧΑΝΟ ΝΤΟΛΜΑΔΕΣ ΜΕ ΣΑΛΤΣΑ ΝΤΟΜΑΤΑΣ λάχανο ντολμάδες με σάλτσα ντομάτας [lakhano dolmathes meh saltsa domatas] vine leaves stuffed with rice in tomato sauce

ΛΑΧΑΝΟΣΑΛΑΤΑ λαχανοσαλάτα [lakhanosalata] cabbage salad

ΛΕΜΟΝΙ λεμόνι [lemoni] lemon

ΛΙΘΡΙΝΙ λιθρίνι [liTHrini] red snapper

ΛΙΘΡΙΝΙ ΨΗΤΟ λιθρίνι ψητό [liTHrini psito] grilled red snapper

ΛΟΥΚΑΝΙΚΑ λουκάνικα [lookanika] sausages

ΛΟΥΚΑΝΙΚΑ ΒΡΑΣΤΑ λουκάνικα βραστά [lookanika vrasta] boiled sausages

ΛΟΥΚΑΝΙΚΑ ΚΑΠΝΙΣΤΑ ΣΤΗ ΣΧΑΡΑ λουκάνικα καπνιστά στη σχάρα [lookanika kapnista sti skhara] grilled smoked sausages

ΛΟΥΚΑΝΙΚΑ ΤΗΓΑΝΗΤΑ λουκάνικα τηγανητά [lookanika tiganita] fried sausages

ΛΟΥΚΟΥΜΑΔΕΣ λουκουμάδες [lookoomathes] doughnuts

ΛΟΥΚΟΥΜΙΑ λουκούμια [lookoomia] Turkish delight

ΜΑΓΕΙΡΙΤΣΑ μαγειρίτσα [mayiritsa] traditional Easter soup made from lambs' intestines

ΜΑΓΙΑ μαγιά [maya] yeast

ΜΑΓΙΟΝΕΖΑ μαγιονέζα [mayoneza] mayonnaise

ΜΑΪΝΤΑΝΟΣ μαϊντανός [maindanos] parsley

ΜΑΚΑΡΟΝΑΚΙ ΚΟΦΤΟ **μακαρονάκι κοφτό** [makaronaki kofto] macaroni

ΜΑΚΑΡΟΝΙΑ **μακαρόνια** [makaronia] pasta

ΜΑΚΑΡΟΝΙΑ ΜΕ ΚΙΜΑ **μακαρόνια με κιμά** [makaronia meh kima] spaghetti bolognaise

ΜΑΚΑΡΟΝΙΑ ΜΕ ΦΡΕΣΚΟ ΒΟΥΤΥΡΟ ΚΑΙ ΠΑΡΜΕΖΑΝΑ **μακαρόνια με φρέσκο βούτυρο και παρμεζάνα** [makaronia meh fresko vootiro keh parmezana] spaghetti with butter and parmesan cheese

ΜΑΚΑΡΟΝΙΑ ΠΑΣΤΙΤΣΙΟ ΜΕ ΚΙΜΑ **μακαρόνια παστίτσιο με κιμά** [makaronia pastitsio meh kima] baked pasta dish with minced meat and béchamel

ΜΑΝΙΤΑΡΙΑ **μανιτάρια** [manitaria] mushrooms

ΜΑΝΙΤΑΡΙΑ ΤΗΓΑΝΗΤΑ **μανιτάρια τηγανητά** [manitaria tiganita] fried mushrooms

ΜΑΝΟΥΡΙ **μανούρι** [manoori] hard cheese

ΜΑΝΤΑΡΙΝΙ **μανταρίνι** [mandarini] satsuma, tangerine

ΜΑΡΓΑΡΙΝΗ **μαργαρίνη** [margarini] margarine

ΜΑΡΙΔΕΣ ΤΗΓΑΝΗΤΕΣ **μαρίδες τηγανητές** [marithes tiganites] small fried fish

ΜΑΡΜΕΛΑΔΑ **μαρμελάδα** [marmelatha] jam, marmalade

ΜΑΡΜΕΛΑΔΑ ΒΕΡΥΚΟΚΚΑ **μαρμελάδα βερύκοκκα** [marmelatha verikoka] apricot jam

ΜΑΡΜΕΛΑΔΑ ΠΟΡΤΟΚΑΛΙ **μαρμελάδα πορτοκάλι** [marmelatha portokali] orange jam

ΜΑΡΜΕΛΑΔΑ ΡΟΔΑΚΙΝΑ **μαρμελάδα ροδάκινα** [marmelatha pothakina] peach jam

ΜΑΡΜΕΛΑΔΑ ΦΡΑΟΥΛΕΣ **μαρμελάδα φράουλες** [marmelatha fraooles] strawberry jam

ΜΑΡΟΥΛΙ **μαρούλι** [marooli] lettuce

ΜΑΡΟΥΛΙΑ ΣΑΛΑΤΑ **μαρούλια σαλάτα** [maroolia salata] green salad

ΜΕ ΛΑΔΟΛΕΜΟΝΟ **με λαδολέμονο** [meh latholemono] with olive oil and lemon dressing

ΜΕΛΙ **μέλι** [meli] honey

ΜΕΛΙΤΖΑΝΕΣ **μελιτζάνες** [melidzanes] aubergines/eggplants

ΜΕΛΙΤΖΑΝΕΣ ΓΕΜΙΣΤΕΣ ΜΕ ΚΙΜΑ **μελιτζάνες γεμιστές με κιμά** [melitzanes yemistes meh kima] aubergines/eggplants stuffed with minced meat

ΜΕΛΙΤΖΑΝΕΣ ΓΙΑΧΝΙ **μελιτζάνες γιαχνί** [melitzanes yakhni] aubergines/eggplants with tomato and onions

ΜΕΛΙΤΖΑΝΕΣ ΙΜΑΜ

ΜΠΑΪΛΝΤΙ **μελιτζάνες ιμάμ μπαϊλντί** [melitzanes imam baildi] aubergines/eggplants with garlic and tomato

ΜΕΛΙΤΖΑΝΕΣ ΜΟΥΣΑΚΑ **μελιτζάνες μουσακά** [melidzanes moosaka] layers of aubergine/eggplant and minced meat topped with béchamel

ΜΕΛΙΤΖΑΝΕΣ ΠΑΠΟΥΤΣΑΚΙΑ **μελιτζάνες παπουτσάκια** [melidzaness papootsakia] stuffed aubergines/eggplants

ΜΕΛΙΤΖΑΝΕΣ ΤΗΓΑΝΗΤΕΣ **μελιτζάνες τηγανητές** [melitzanes tiganites] fried aubergines/eggplants

ΜΕΛΙΤΖΑΝΟΣΑΛΑΤΑ **μελιτζανοσαλάτα** [melidzanosalata] puréed aubergine/eggplant dip

ΜΕΛΟΜΑΚΑΡΟΝΑ **μελομακάρονα** [melomakarona] sweet cakes with cinammon, nuts and syrup

ΜΕΝΟΥ **μενού** [menoo] menu

ΜΕ ΣΑΛΤΣΑ **με σάλτσα** [meh saltsa] with sauce, usually tomato sauce

ΜΗΛΑ ΓΕΜΙΣΤΑ **μήλα γεμιστά** [mila yemista] stuffed apples with cinammon

ΜΗΛΟ **μήλο** [milo] apple

ΜΗΛΟΠΙΤΤΑ **μηλόπιττα** [milopita] apple pie

μισοψημένο [misopsimeno] medium (steak)

ΜΟΣΧΑΡΙ **μοσχάρι** [moskhari] veal; tender beef

ΜΟΣΧΑΡΙ ΒΡΑΣΤΟ **μοσχάρι βραστό** [moskhari vrasto] veal stew

ΜΟΣΧΑΡΙ ΚΟΚΚΙΝΙΣΤΟ **μοσχάρι κοκκινιστό** [moskhari kokinisto] veal in tomato sauce

ΜΟΣΧΑΡΙ ΜΕ ΑΡΑΚΑ **μοσχάρι με αρακά** [moskhari meh araka] veal with peas

ΜΟΣΧΑΡΙ ΜΕ ΚΡΙΘΑΡΑΚΙ **μοσχάρι με κριθαράκι** [moskhari meh kriTHaraki] veal with pasta

ΜΟΣΧΑΡΙ ΜΕ ΜΕΛΙΤΖΑΝΕΣ **μοσχάρι με μελιτζάνες** [moskhari meh melitzanes] veal with aubergines/eggplants

ΜΟΣΧΑΡΙ ΜΕ ΜΠΑΜΙΕΣ **μοσχάρι με μπάμιες** [moskhari meh bami-es] veal with okra

ΜΟΣΧΑΡΙ ΜΕ ΠΑΤΑΤΕΣ **μοσχάρι με πατάτες** [moskhari meh patates] veal with potatoes

ΜΟΣΧΑΡΙ ΜΕ ΠΑΤΑΤΕΣ ΣΤΟ ΦΟΥΡΝΟ **μοσχάρι με πατάτες στο φούρνο** [moskhari meh patates sto foorno] veal with potatoes cooked in the oven

ΜΟΣΧΑΡΙ ΜΕ ΠΟΥΡΕ **μοσχάρι με πουρέ** [moskhari meh pooreh] veal with mashed potatoes

ΜΟΣΧΑΡΙ ΜΕ ΦΑΣΟΛΑΚΙΑ **μοσχάρι με φασολάκια** [moskhari meh fasolakia] veal and green beans

ΜΟΣΧΑΡΙ ΡΟΣΜΠΙΦ **μοσχάρι ροσμπίφ** [moskhari rosbif] roast beef

ΜΟΣΧΑΡΙΣΙΟΣ ΚΙΜΑΣ **μοσχαρίσιος κιμάς** [moskharisios kimas] minced meat

ΜΟΣΧΑΡΙ ΣΝΙΤΖΕΛ ΜΕ ΠΑΤΑΤΕΣ ΤΗΓΑΝΗΤΕΣ **μοσχάρι σνίτζελ με πατάτες τηγανητές** [moskhari schnitzel meh patates tiganites] steak and chips/fries

ΜΟΣΧΑΡΙ ΣΝΙΤΖΕΛ ΜΕ ΠΟΥΡΕ **μοσχάρι σνίτζελ με πουρέ** [moskhari schnitzel meh patates pooreh] steak with mashed potatoes

ΜΟΣΧΑΡΙ ΨΗΤΟ **μοσχάρι ψητό** [moskhari psito] veal pot roast

ΜΟΥΣΑΚΑΣ **μουσακάς** [moosakas] moussaka – layers of vegetables and minced meat topped with béchamel sauce

ΜΟΥΣΑΚΑΣ ΠΑΤΑΤΕΣ **μουσακάς πατάτες** [moosakas patates] potatoes with minced meat and béchamel

ΜΟΥΣΤΑΡΔΑ **μουστάρδα** [moostartha] mustard

ΜΟΥΣΤΟΚΟΥΛΟΥΡΑ **μουστοκούλουρα** [moostokooloora] Greek biscuits

ΜΠΑΚΑΛΙΑΡΟΣ **μπακαλιάρος** [bakaliaros] cod; salt cod; haddock

ΜΠΑΚΑΛΙΑΡΟΣ ΚΡΟΚΕΤΕΣ **μπακαλιάρος κροκέτες** [bakaliaros krokètes] haddock croquettes

ΜΠΑΚΑΛΙΑΡΟΣ ΠΛΑΚΙ **μπακαλιάρος πλακί** [bakaliaros plaki] salted cod cooked in tomato sauce

ΜΠΑΚΑΛΙΑΡΟΣ ΤΗΓΑΝΗΤΟΣ **μπακαλιάρος τηγανητός** [bakaliaros tiganitos] fried salted cod

ΜΠΑΚΛΑΒΑΔΕΣ **μπακλαβάδες** [baklavathes] baklava – layers of thin pastry with nuts and syrup

ΜΠΑΚΛΑΒΑΔΕΣ ΜΕ ΚΑΡΥΔΙΑ **μπακλαβάδες με καρύδια** [baklavathes meh karithia] baklava – layers of thin pastry with walnuts and syrup

ΜΠΑΚΛΑΒΑΣ **μπακλαβάς** [baklavas] baklava – filo pastry with nuts and syrup

ΜΠΑΜΙΕΣ **μπάμιες** [bami-es] okra

ΜΠΑΜΙΕΣ ΛΑΔΕΡΕΣ **μπάμιες λαδερές** [bami-es latheres] okra in olive oil and tomato sauce

ΜΠΑΝΑΝΑ **μπανάνα** [banana] banana

ΜΠΑΡΜΠΟΥΝΙΑ **μπαρμπούνια** [barboonia] red mullet

ΜΠΑΡΜΠΟΥΝΙΑ ΠΑΝΕ **μπαρμπούνια πανέ** [barboonia paneh] breaded red mullet

ΜΠΑΧΑΡΙΚΟ μπαχαρικό [bakhariko] spice

ΜΠΕΖΕΔΕΣ μπεζέδες [bezethes] meringues with cream

ΜΠΕΙΚΟΝ μπέικον [bacon] bacon

ΜΠΕΙΚΟΝ ΚΑΠΝΙΣΤΟ μπέικον καπνιστό [bacon kapnisto] smoked bacon

ΜΠΕΣΑΜΕΛ ΣΑΛΤΣΑ μπεσαμέλ σάλτσα [besamel saltsa] béchamel sauce

ΜΠΙΖΕΛΙΑ μπιζέλια [bizelia] peas

ΜΠΙΣΚΟΤΑ μπισκότα [biskota] biscuits

ΜΠΙΣΚΟΤΑΚΙΑ ΑΛΜΥΡΑ μπισκοτάκια αλμυρά [biskotakia almira] savoury crackers

ΜΠΙΣΚΟΤΑ ΣΟΚΟΛΑΤΑΣ μπισκότα σοκολάτας [biskota sokolatas] chocolate biscuits

ΜΠΙΦΤΕΚΙ μπιφτέκι [bifteki] hamburger; grilled meatballs

ΜΠΟΝ ΦΙΛΕ μπον φιλέ [bon fileh] fillet steak

ΜΠΟΥΓΑΤΣΑ μπουγάτσα [boogatsa] puff pastry with various fillings

ΜΠΟΥΓΑΤΣΑ ΓΛΥΚΙΑ μπουγάτσα γλυκιά [boogatsa glikia] puff pastry with cream and icing sugar

ΜΠΟΥΡΕΚΑΚΙΑ μπουρεκάκια [boorekakia] cheese or minced meat pies

ΜΠΟΥΡΕΚΙ μπουρέκι [booreki] courgette, potato and cheese pie

ΜΠΡΙΑΜΙ μπριάμι [briami] ratatouille

ΜΠΡΙΑΜΙ ΜΕ ΚΟΛΟΚΥΘΑΚΙΑ μπριάμι με κολοκυθάκια [briami meh kolokiTHakia] courgettes/zucchini cooked with potatoes in the oven

ΜΠΡΙΖΟΛΑ μπριζόλα [brizola] chop; steak

ΜΠΡΙΖΟΛΑ ΜΟΣΧΑΡΙΣΙΑ μπριζόλα μοσχαρίσια [brizola moskharisia] beef steak

ΜΠΡΙΖΟΛΕΣ μπριζόλες [brizoles] chops; steaks

ΜΠΡΙΖΟΛΕΣ ΒΟΔΙΝΕΣ ΣΤΗ ΣΧΑΡΑ μπριζόλες βοδινές στη σχάρα [brizoles vothines sti skhara] grilled T-bone steak

ΜΠΡΙΖΟΛΕΣ ΣΤΟ ΤΗΓΑΝΙ μπριζόλες στο τηγάνι [brizoles sto tigani] fried T-bone steak

ΜΠΡΙΖΟΛΕΣ ΧΟΙΡΙΝΕΣ μπριζόλες χοιρινές [brizoles khirines] pork chops

ΜΠΡΙΖΟΛΕΣ ΧΟΙΡΙΝΕΣ ΣΤΗ ΣΧΑΡΑ μπριζόλες χοιρινές στη σχάρα [brizoles khirines sti skhara] charcoal-grilled pork chops

ΜΠΡΟΚΟΛΟ μπρόκολο [brokolo] broccoli

ΜΥΑΛΑ μυαλά [miala] brains

ΜΥΑΛΑ ΠΑΝΕ μυαλά πανέ [miala paneh] breaded cows' brains

ΜΥΔΙΑ μύδια [mithia] mussels

ΜΥΔΙΑ ΤΗΓΑΝΗΤΑ μύδια τηγανητά [mithia tiganita] fried mussels

ΝΕΦΡΑ νεφρά [nefra] kidneys

ΝΕΦΡΑ ΨΗΤΑ/ΤΗΓΑΝΗΤΑ νεφρά ψητά/τηγανητά [nefra psita/tiganita] grilled/fried kidneys

ΝΤΟΛΜΑΔΑΚΙΑ ντολμαδάκια [dolmathakia] vine leaves stuffed with minced meat, rice and herbs

ΝΤΟΛΜΑΔΕΣ ντολμάδες [dolmathes] vine or cabbage leaves stuffed with minced meat and/or rice

ΝΤΟΛΜΑΔΕΣ ΑΥΓΟΛΕΜΟΝΟ ΜΕ ΚΙΜΑ ντολμάδες αυγολέμονο με κιμά [dolmathes avgolemono meh kima] vine leaves with rice and minced meat in egg and lemon sauce

ΝΤΟΛΜΑΔΕΣ ΓΙΑΛΑΝΤΖΙ ντολμάδες γιαλαντζί [dolmathes yialantzi] vine leaves stuffed with rice

ΝΤΟΜΑΤΕΣ ντομάτες [domates] tomatoes

ΝΤΟΜΑΤΕΣ ΓΕΜΙΣΤΕΣ ΜΕ ΚΙΜΑ ντομάτες γεμιστές με κιμά [domates yemistes meh kima] stuffed tomatoes with minced meat

ΝΤΟΜΑΤΕΣ ΓΕΜΙΣΤΕΣ ΜΕ ΡΥΖΙ ντομάτες γεμιστές με ρύζι [domates yemistes meh rizi] tomatoes stuffed with rice

ΝΤΟΜΑΤΕΣ ΓΕΜΙΣΤΕΣ ντομάτες γεμιστές [domates yemistes] stuffed tomatoes

ΝΤΟΜΑΤΟΣΑΛΑΤΑ ντοματοσαλάτα [domatosalata] tomato salad

ΝΤΟΜΑΤΟΣΟΥΠΑ ντοματόσουπα [domatosoopa] tomato soup

ΝΤΟΝΑΤΣ ντόνατς [doughnuts] doughnuts

ΞΗΡΟΙ ΚΑΡΠΟΙ ξηροί καρποί [xiri karpi] nuts, dried fruit

ΞΙΦΙΑΣ ξιφίας [xifias] swordfish

ΞΥΔΙ ξύδι [xithi] vinegar

ΟΜΕΛΕΤΑ ομελέτα [omeleta] omelette

ΟΜΕΛΕΤΑ ΛΟΥΚΑΝΙΚΑ ομελέτα λουκάνικα [omeleta lookanika] omelette with sausages

ΟΡΕΚΤΙΚΑ ορεκτικά [orektika] hors d'oeuvres, starters

ΟΣΤΡΑΚΟΕΙΔΗ οστρακοειδή [ostrako-ithi] shellfish

ΠΑΓΩΤΟ παγωτό [pagoto] ice cream

ΠΑΓΩΤΟ ΒΕΡΥΚΟΚΚΟ παγωτό βερύκοκκο [pagoto verikoko] apricot ice cream

ΠΑΓΩΤΟ ΚΟΚΤΑΙΗΛ παγωτό κοκταίηλ [pagoto cocktail] ice cream cocktail

ΠΑΓΩΤΟ ΚΡΕΜΑ παγωτό

κρέμα [pagoto krema] vanilla ice cream

ΠΑΓΩΤΟ ΜΕ ΣΑΝΤΙΓΥ **παγωτό με σαντιγύ** [pagoto meh sandiyī] ice cream with whipped cream

ΠΑΓΩΤΟ ΜΟΚΚΑ **παγωτό μόκκα** [pagoto moka] coffee-flavoured ice cream

ΠΑΓΩΤΟ ΜΠΑΝΑΝΑ **παγωτό μπανάνα** [pagoto banana] banana ice cream

ΠΑΓΩΤΟ ΠΑΡΦΑΙ **παγωτό παρφαί** [pagoto parfeh] ice cream parfait

ΠΑΓΩΤΟ ΠΡΑΛΙΝΑ **παγωτό πραλίνα** [pagoto pralina] praline ice cream

ΠΑΓΩΤΟ ΣΟΚΟΛΑΤΑ **παγωτό σοκολάτα** [pagoto sokolata] chocolate ice cream

ΠΑΓΩΤΟ ΦΡΑΟΥΛΑ **παγωτό φράουλα** [pagoto fraoola] strawberry ice cream

ΠΑΓΩΤΟ ΦΥΣΤΙΚΙ **παγωτό φυστίκι** [pagoto fistikī] pistachio ice cream

ΠΑΞΙΜΑΔΙ **παξιμάδι** [paximathī] dried, hard bread

ΠΑΝΤΖΑΡΙ **παντζάρι** [pandzarī] beetroot

ΠΑΠΙΑ **πάπια** [papia] duck

ΠΑΠΡΙΚΑ **πάπρικα** [paprika] paprika

ΠΑΡΜΕΖΑΝΑ **παρμεζάνα** [parmezana] parmesan

ΠΑΣΤΑ **πάστα** [pasta] cake

ΠΑΣΤΑ ΑΜΥΓΔΑΛΟΥ **πάστα αμυγδάλου** [pasta amigthaloo] almond gâteau

ΠΑΣΤΑ ΚΟΡΜΟΣ **πάστα κορμός** [pasta kormos] chocolate log

ΠΑΣΤΑ ΝΟΥΓΚΑΤΙΝΑ **πάστα νουγκατίνα** [pasta noogatin] cream gâteau

ΠΑΣΤΑ ΣΟΚΟΛΑΤΙΝΑ **πάστα σοκολατίνα** [pasta sokolatina] chocolate gâteau

ΠΑΣΤΑ ΦΡΑΟΥΛΑ **πάστα φράουλα** [pasta fraoola] strawberry gâteau

ΠΑΣΤΙΤΣΙΟ **παστίτσιο** [pastitsio] macaroni cheese or lasagne-type dish, with minced meat and white sauce

ΠΑΣΤΙΤΣΙΟ ΛΑΖΑΝΙΑ **παστίτσιο λαζάνια** [pastitsio lazania] lasagne

ΠΑΣΤΙΤΣΙΟ ΜΑΚΑΡΟΝΙΑ ΜΕ ΚΙΜΑ **παστίτσιο μακαρόνια με κιμά** [pastitsio makaronia meh kima] baked pasta dish with minced meat and béchamel

ΠΑΣΤΟ **παστό** [pasto] salted

ΠΑΤΑΤΕΣ **πατάτες** [patates] potatoes

ΠΑΤΑΤΕΣ ΓΑΡΝΙΤΟΥΡΑ **πατάτες γαρνιτούρα** [patates garnitoora] potatoes

ΠΑΤΑΤΕΣ ΓΙΑΧΝΙ **πατάτες γιαχνί** [patates yakhnī] potatoes cooked with onion and tomato

ΠΑΤΑΤΕΣ ΚΑΙ ΚΟΛΟΚΥΘΑΚΙΑ ΣΤΟ

ΦΟΥΡΝΟ πατάτες και κολοκυθάκια στο φούρνο [patates keh kolokiTHakia sto foorno] potatoes, courgettes/zucchini and tomatoes baked in the oven

ΠΑΤΑΤΕΣ ΚΟΛΟΚΥΘΙΑ ΜΟΥΣΑΚΑΣ πατάτες κολοκύθια μουσακάς [patates kolokiTHia moosakas] potatoes with courgettes/zucchini, minced meat and cheese sauce

ΠΑΤΑΤΕΣ ΠΟΥΡΕ πατάτες πουρέ [patates pooreh] mashed potatoes

ΠΑΤΑΤΕΣ ΡΙΓΑΝΑΤΕΣ πατάτες ριγανάτες στο φούρνο [patates riganates sto foorno] oven-cooked potatoes with oregano

ΠΑΤΑΤΕΣ ΣΟΥΦΛΕ πατάτες σουφλέ [patates soofleh] potato soufflé

ΠΑΤΑΤΕΣ ΣΤΟ ΦΟΥΡΝΟ ΡΙΓΑΝΑΤΕΣ πατάτες στο φούρνο ριγανάτες [patates sto foorno riganates] potatoes baked in the oven with oregano, lemon and olive oil

ΠΑΤΑΤΕΣ ΤΗΓΑΝΙΤΕΣ πατάτες τηγανιτές [patates tiganites] chips, French fries

ΠΑΤΑΤΕΣ ΤΣΙΠΣ πατάτες τσιπς [patates tsips] chips, French fries

ΠΑΤΑΤΟΣΑΛΑΤΑ πατατοσαλάτα [patatosalata] potato salad

ΠΑΤΖΑΡΙΑ πατζάρια [patzaria] beetroot

ΠΑΤΣΑΣ πατσάς [patsas] tripe; soup made from lambs' intestines

ΠΑΤΣΑΣ ΣΟΥΠΑ πατσάς σούπα [patsas soopa] tripe soup

ΠΕΠΟΝΙ πεπόνι [peponi] melon

ΠΕΣΤΡΟΦΑ πέστροφα [pestrofa] trout

ΠΕΣΤΡΟΦΑ ΨΗΤΗ πέστροφα ψητή [pestrofa psiti] grilled trout

ΠΗΧΤΗ πηχτή [pikhti] potted meat

ΠΙΛΑΦΙ πιλάφι [pilafi] rice

ΠΙΛΑΦΙ ΜΕ ΓΑΡΙΔΕΣ πιλάφι με γαρίδες [pilafi meh garithes] shrimp pilaf

ΠΙΛΑΦΙ ΜΕ ΜΥΔΙΑ πιλάφι με μύδια [pilafi meh mithia] pilaf with mussels

ΠΙΛΑΦΙ ΜΕ ΣΑΛΤΣΑ ΝΤΟΜΑΤΑ πιλάφι με σάλτσα ντομάτα [pilafi meh saltsa domata] pilaf with tomato sauce

ΠΙΛΑΦΙ ΤΑΣ-ΚΕΜΠΑΠ πιλάφι τας-κεμπάπ [pilafi tas kebab] rice with cubes of beef in tomato sauce

ΠΙΠΕΡΙ πιπέρι [piperi] pepper (spice)

ΠΙΠΕΡΙΕΣ πιπεριές [piperi-es] peppers

ΠΙΠΕΡΙΕΣ ΓΕΜΙΣΤΕΣ ΜΕ ΚΙΜΑ πιπεριές γεμιστές με

κιμά [piperi-es yemistes meh kima] peppers stuffed with minced meat

ΠΙΠΕΡΙΕΣ ΓΕΜΙΣΤΕΣ ΜΕ ΡΥΖΙ **πιπεριές γεμιστές με ρύζι** [piperi-es yemistes meh rizi] peppers stuffed with rice

ΠΙΠΕΡΙΕΣ ΓΕΜΙΣΤΕΣ **πιπεριές γεμιστές** [piperi-es yemistes] stuffed peppers

ΠΙΠΕΡΙΕΣ ΚΟΚΚΙΝΕΣ **πιπεριές κόκκινες** [piperi-es kokines] red peppers

ΠΙΠΕΡΙΕΣ ΠΡΑΣΙΝΕΣ **πιπεριές πράσινες** [piperi-es prasines] green peppers

ΠΙΡΟΣΚΙ **πιροσκί** [piroski] minced meat or sausage rolls

ΠΙΤΣΑ **πίτσα** [pizza] pizza

ΠΙΤΣΑ ΜΕ ΖΑΜΠΟΝ **πίτσα με ζαμπόν** [pizza meh zabon] ham pizza

ΠΙΤΣΑ ΜΕ ΜΑΝΙΤΑΡΙΑ **πίτσα με μανιτάρια** [pizza meh manitaria] mushroom pizza

ΠΙΤΣΑ ΜΕ ΝΤΟΜΑΤΑ ΤΥΡΙ **πίτσα με ντομάτα τυρί** [pizza meh domata tiri] cheese and tomato pizza

ΠΙΤΣΑ ΣΠΕΣΙΑΛ **πίτσα σπέσιαλ** [pizza special] special pizza

ΠΙΤΤΑ **πίττα** [pita] pie

ΠΙΤΤΑ ΜΕ ΚΙΜΑ **πίττα με κιμά** [pita meh kima] minced meat pie

ΠΛΑΚΙ **πλακί** [plaki] baked in the oven in a tomato sauce

πολύ ψημένο [poli psimeno] overdone

ΠΟΡΤΟΚΑΛΙ **πορτοκάλι** [portokali] orange

ΠΟΥΛΕΡΙΚΑ **πουλερικά** [poulerika] poultry

ΠΟΥΤΙΓΚΑ **πουτίγκα** [pootiga] pudding

ΠΟΥΤΙΓΚΑ ΜΕ ΑΝΑΝΑ **πουτίγκα με ανανά** [pootiga meh anana] pineapple pudding

ΠΟΥΤΙΓΚΑ ΜΕ ΚΑΡΥΔΙΑ **πουτίγκα με καρύδια** [pootiga meh karithia] walnut pudding

ΠΟΥΤΙΓΚΑ ΜΕ ΣΤΑΦΙΔΕΣ **πουτίγκα με σταφίδες** [pootiga meh stafithes] sultana pudding

ΠΡΑΣΑ **πράσα** [prasa] leeks

ΠΡΑΣΟΠΙΤΤΑ **πρασόπιττα** [prasopita] leek pie

ΠΡΩΤΟ ΠΙΑΤΟ **πρώτο πιάτο** [proto piato] starter

ΡΑΒΑΝΙ **ραβανί** [ravani] very sweet sponge cake

ΡΑΒΙΟΛΙΑ **ραβιόλια** [raviolia] ravioli

ΡΙΓΑΝΗ **ρίγανη** [rigani] oregano

ΡΟΔΑΚΙΝΟ **ροδάκινο** [rothakino] peaches

ΡΟΣΜΠΙΦ ΑΡΝΙ ΜΟΣΧΑΡΙ **ροσμπίφ αρνί μοσχάρι** [rozbif arni moskhari] roast beef, veal or lamb

ΡΥΖΙ **ρύζι** [rizi] rice

ΡΥΖΟΓΑΛΟ **ρυζόγαλο** [rizogalo] rice pudding

ΡΩΣΙΚΗ ΣΑΛΑΤΑ ρώσικη σαλάτα [rosiki salata] Russian salad

ΣΑΛΑΜΙ σαλάμι [salami] salami

ΣΑΛΑΤΑ σαλάτα [salata] salad

ΣΑΛΑΤΑ ΑΜΠΕΛΟΦΑΣΟΥΛΑ σαλάτα αμπελοφάσουλα [salata abelofasoola] runner bean salad

ΣΑΛΑΤΑ ΚΟΥΝΟΥΠΙΔΙ ΒΡΑΣΤΟ σαλάτα κουνουπίδι βραστό [salata koonoopithi vrasto] boiled cauliflower salad

ΣΑΛΑΤΑ ΜΑΡΟΥΛΙΑ σαλάτα μαρούλια [salata maroolia] lettuce salad

ΣΑΛΑΤΑ ΝΤΟΜΑΤΕΣ ΚΑΙ ΑΓΓΟΥΡΙΑ σαλάτα ντομάτες και αγγούρια [salata domates keh agooria] tomato and cucumber salad

ΣΑΛΑΤΑ ΝΤΟΜΑΤΕΣ-ΠΙΠΕΡΙΕΣ σαλάτα ντομάτες-πιπεριές [salata domates piperies] tomato and green pepper salad

ΣΑΛΑΤΑ ΣΠΑΡΑΓΓΙΑ σαλάτα σπαράγγια [salata sparagia] asparagus salad

ΣΑΛΑΤΑ ΦΑΣΟΛΙΑ ΞΗΡΑ σαλάτα φασόλια ξηρά [salata fasolia xira] butter bean salad

ΣΑΛΑΤΑ ΧΟΡΤΑ ΒΡΑΣΜΕΝΑ σαλάτα χόρτα βρασμένα [salata khorta vrasmena] chicory salad

ΣΑΛΑΤΑ ΧΩΡΙΑΤΙΚΗ σαλάτα χωριάτικη [salata khoriatiki] Greek salad – tomatoes, cucumber, peppers, feta, olives and boiled eggs with olive oil and vinegar dressing

ΣΑΛΙΓΚΑΡΙΑ σαλιγκάρια [saligaria] snails

ΣΑΛΤΣΑ σάλτσα [saltsa] sauce

ΣΑΛΤΣΑ ΜΠΕΣΑΜΕΛ σάλτσα μπεσαμέλ [saltsa besamel] béchamel sauce

ΣΑΛΤΣΑ ΝΤΟΜΑΤΑ σάλτσα ντομάτα [saltsa domata] tomato sauce

ΣΑΜΑΛΙ σάμαλι [samali] semolina cake with honey

ΣΑΝΤΙΓΥ σαντιγύ [sandiyi] whipped cream

ΣΑΝΤΟΥΙΤΣ σάντουιτς [sandwich] sandwich

ΣΑΡΔΕΛΛΕΣ σαρδέλλες [sartheles] sardines

ΣΑΡΔΕΛΛΕΣ ΛΑΔΙΟΥ σαρδέλλες λαδιού [sartheles lathioo] sardines in oil

ΣΕΛΙΝΟ σέλινο [selino] celery

ΣΙΜΙΓΔΑΛΙ σιμιγδάλι [simigthali] semolina

ΣΙΡΟΠΙ σιρόπι [siropi] syrup

ΣΚΟΡΔΑΛΙΑ σκορδαλιά [skorthalia] thick garlic sauce

ΣΚΟΡΔΑΛΙΑ ΜΕ ΨΩΜΙ σκορδαλιά με ψωμί [skorthalia meh psomi] thick garlic sauce made with bread

ΣΚΟΡΔΟ σκόρδο [skortho] garlic

ΣΟΚΟΛΑΤΑΚΙΑ σοκολατάκια [sokolatakia] little chocolate cakes; milk chocolates

ΣΟΛΟΜΟΣ σολομός [solomos] salmon

ΣΟΛΟΜΟΣ ΚΑΠΝΙΣΤΟΣ σολομός καπνιστός [solomos kapnistos] smoked salmon

ΣΟΥΒΛΑΚΙΑ σουβλάκια [soovlakia] meat grilled on a skewer, served in pitta bread

ΣΟΥΒΛΑΚΙΑ ΑΠΟ ΚΡΕΑΣ ΑΡΝΙΣΙΟ σουβλάκια από κρέας αρνίσιο [soovlakia apo kreas arnisio] lamb souvlaki/kebab

ΣΟΥΒΛΑΚΙΑ ΑΠΟ ΚΡΕΑΣ ΜΟΣΧΑΡΙΣΙΟ σουβλάκια από κρέας μοσχαρίσιο [soovlakia apo kreas moskharisio] veal souvlaki/kebab

ΣΟΥΒΛΑΚΙΑ ΑΠΟ ΚΡΕΑΣ ΧΟΙΡΙΝΟ σουβλάκια από κρέας χοιρινό [soovlakia apo kreas khirino] pork souvlaki/kebab

ΣΟΥΒΛΑΚΙΑ ΝΤΟΝΕΡ ΜΕ ΠΙΤΤΑ σουβλάκια ντονέρ με πίττα [soovlaki doner meh pita] donner kebab with pitta bread

ΣΟΥΒΛΑΚΙ ΚΑΛΑΜΑΚΙ σουβλάκι καλαμάκι [soovlaki kalamaki] shish kebab

ΣΟΥΠΑ σούπα [soopa] soup

ΣΟΥΠΑ ΠΑΤΣΑΣ σούπα πατσάς [soopa patsas] tripe soup

ΣΟΥΠΑ ΡΕΒΥΘΙΑ σούπα ρεβύθια [soopa revîTHia] chickpea soup

ΣΟΥΠΑ ΤΡΑΧΑΝΑΣ σούπα τραχανάς [soopa trakhanas] milk broth with flour

ΣΟΥΠΑ ΦΑΚΕΣ σούπα φακές [soopa fakes] lentil soup

ΣΟΥΠΑ ΦΑΣΟΛΙΑ σούπα φασόλια [soopa fasolia] bean soup

ΣΟΥΠΑ ΨΑΡΙ σούπα ψάρι [soopa psari] fish soup

ΣΟΥΠΑ ΨΑΡΙ ΑΥΓΟΛΕΜΟΝΟ σούπα ψάρι αυγολέμονο [soopa psari avgolemono] fish soup with egg and lemon

ΣΟΥΠΕΣ σούπες [soopes] soups

ΣΟΥΠΙΕΣ σουπιές [soopi-es] cuttlefish

ΣΟΥΠΙΕΣ ΜΕ ΣΠΑΝΑΚΙ σουπιές με σπανάκι [soopi-es meh spanaki] cuttlefish and spinach stew

ΣΟΥΠΙΕΣ ΤΗΓΑΝΗΤΕΣ σουπιές τηγανητές [soopi-es tiganites] fried cuttlefish

ΣΟΥΣΑΜΙ σουσάμι [soosami] sesame

ΣΟΥΤΖΟΥΚΑΚΙΑ σουτζουκάκια [sootzookakia] spicy meatballs in red sauce

ΣΟΥΦΛΕ σουφλέ [soofleh] soufflé

ΣΠΑΓΓΕΤΟ ΜΕ ΦΡΕΣΚΟ ΒΟΥΤΥΡΟ ΚΑΙ ΠΑΡΜΕΖΑΝΑ σπαγγέτο με φρέσκο βούτυρο και παρμεζάνα [spageto meh fresko vootiro keh parmezana] spaghetti with butter and parmesan cheese

ΣΠΑΝΑΚΙ σπανάκι [spanaki] spinach

ΣΠΑΝΑΚΟΠΙΤΤΑ σπανακόπιττα [spanakopita] spinach (and sometimes feta) in filo pastry

σπάνιος [spanios] rare (steak)

ΣΠΑΡΑΓΓΙΑ ΣΑΛΑΤΑ σπαράγγια σαλάτα [sparagia salata] asparagus salad

ΣΠΕΣΙΑΛΙΤΕ σπεσιαλιτέ [spesialiteh] speciality

ΣΠΛΗΝΑΝΤΕΡΟ σπληνάντερο [splinandero] intestines stuffed with spleen

ΣΤΑΦΙΔΕΣ σταφίδες [stafithes] dried fruit

ΣΤΑΦΙΔΟΨΩΜΟ σταφιδόψωμο [stafithopsomo] bread with raisins

ΣΤΑΦΥΛΙΑ σταφύλια [stafilia] grapes

ΣΤΙΦΑΔΟ στιφάδο [stifatho] chopped meat with onions; hare or rabbit stew with onions

ΣΤΟ ΦΟΥΡΝΟ στο φούρνο [sto foorno] baked in the oven

ΣΤΡΕΙΔΙΑ στρείδια [strithia] oysters

ΣΥΚΑ σύκα [sika] figs

ΣΥΚΩΤΑΚΙΑ συκωτάκια [sikotakia] liver

ΣΥΚΩΤΑΚΙΑ ΜΑΡΙΝΑΤΑ συκωτάκια μαρινάτα [sikotakia marinata] liver cooked in rosemary

ΣΥΚΩΤΑΚΙΑ ΠΙΛΑΦΙ συκωτάκια πιλάφι [sikotakia pilafi] liver pilaf

ΣΥΚΩΤΑΚΙΑ ΣΤΗ ΣΧΑΡΑ συκωτάκια στη σχάρα [sikotakia sti skhara] grilled liver

ΣΥΚΩΤΑΚΙΑ ΤΗΓΑΝΗΤΑ συκωτάκια τηγανητά [sikotakia tiganita] fried liver

ΣΥΚΩΤΙ ΨΗΤΟ συκώτι ψητό [sikoti psito] charcoal-grilled liver

ΣΥΝΑΓΡΙΔΑ ΨΗΤΗ συναγρίδα ψητή [sinagritha psiti] grilled sea bream

ΣΦΥΡΙΔΑ ΒΡΑΣΤΗ σφυρίδα βραστή [sriritha vrasti] boiled pike

ΣΩΤΕ σωτέ [soteh] lightly fried, sautéed

ΤΑΡΑΜΑΣ ταραμάς [taramas] cod roe

ΤΑΡΑΜΟΚΕΦΤΕΔΕΣ ταραμοκεφτέδες [taramokeftethes] roe pâté balls with spices

ΤΑΡΑΜΟΣΑΛΑΤΑ ταραμοσαλάτα [taramosalata] cod roe dip

ΤΑΡΤΑ τάρτα [tarta] tart

ΤΑΡΤΑ ΜΕ ΚΕΡΑΣΙΑ τάρτα με κεράσια [tarta meh kerasia] cherry tart

ΤΑΡΤΑ ΜΕ ΚΡΕΜΑ ΚΑΙ ΑΜΥΓΔΑΛΑ τάρτα με κρέμα και αμύγδαλα [tarta meh krema keh amigthala] cream and almond tart

ΤΑΡΤΑ ΜΕ ΚΡΕΜΑ ΚΑΙ ΚΑΡΥΔΙΑ **τάρτα με κρέμα και καρύδια** [tarta meh krema keh karithia] walnut and cream tart

ΤΑΡΤΑ ΜΕ ΦΡΑΟΥΛΕΣ **τάρτα με φράουλες** [tarta meh fraooles] strawberry tart

ΤΑΡΤΑ ΜΗΛΟΥ **τάρτα μήλου** [tarta miloo] apple tart

ΤΑΣ-ΚΕΜΠΑΠ **τασ-κεμπάπ** [tas kebab] spicy lamb cutlets

ΤΑΣ-ΚΕΜΠΑΠ ΠΙΛΑΦΙ **τας-κεμπάπ πιλάφι** [tas kebab pilafi] spicy lamb cutlets pilaf

ΤΖΑΤΖΙΚΙ **τζατζίκι** [dzadziki] yoghurt, cucumber and garlic dip

ΤΗΓΑΝΗΤΟΣ **τηγανητός** [tiganitos] fried

ΤΗΓΑΝΙΤΕΣ **τηγανίτες** [tiganites] pancakes

ΤΗΣ ΚΑΤΣΑΡΟΛΑΣ **της κατσαρόλας** [tis katsarolas] casseroled

ΤΗΣ ΣΟΥΒΛΑΣ **της σούβλας** [tis soovlas] roast on a spit

ΤΗΣ ΣΧΑΡΑΣ **της σχάρας** [tis skharas] grilled over charcoal

ΤΟΝΝΟΣ **τόννος** [tonos] tuna

ΤΟΝΝΟΣΑΛΑΤΑ **τοννοσαλάτα** [tonosalata] tuna salad

ΤΟΣΤ **τοστ** [tost] toasted sandwich

ΤΟΣΤ ΚΛΑΜΠ **τοστ κλαμπ** [tost club] toasted club sandwich

ΤΟΣΤ ΜΕ ΑΥΓΟ **τοστ με αυγό** [tost meh avgo] toasted egg sandwich

ΤΟΣΤ ΜΕ ΖΑΜΠΟΝ **τοστ με ζαμπόν** [tost meh zabon] toasted ham sandwich

ΤΟΣΤ ΜΕ ΚΟΤΟΠΟΥΛΟ **τοστ με κοτόπουλο** [tost meh kotopoolo] toasted chicken sandwich

ΤΟΣΤ ΜΕ ΚΡΕΑΣ **τοστ με κρέας** [tost meh kreas] toasted meat sandwich

ΤΟΣΤ ΜΕ ΜΠΙΦΤΕΚΙ **τοστ με μπιφτέκι** [tost meh bifteki] toasted hamburger

ΤΟΣΤ ΜΕ ΤΥΡΙ **τοστ με τυρί** [tost meh tiri] toasted cheese sandwich

ΤΟΥ ΑΤΜΟΥ **του ατμού** [too atmoo] steamed

ΤΟΥΡΣΙ **τουρσί** [toorsi] pickled

ΤΟΥΡΤΑ **τούρτα** [toorta] gâteau

ΤΟΥΡΤΑ ΑΜΥΓΔΑΛΟΥ **τούρτα αμυγδάλου** [toorta amigthaloo] almond gâteau

ΤΟΥΡΤΑ ΚΡΕΜΑ ΜΕ ΦΡΑΟΥΛΕΣ **τούρτα κρέμα με φράουλες** [toorta krema meh fraooles] strawberry cream gâteau

ΤΟΥΡΤΑ ΜΟΚΚΑ **τούρτα μόκκα** [toorta moka] coffee gâteau

ΤΟΥΡΤΑ ΝΟΥΓΚΑΤΙΝΑ **τούρτα νουγκατίνα** [toorta noogatina] nougat gâteau

ΤΟΥΡΤΑ ΣΑΝΤΙΓΥ **τούρτα σαντιγύ** [toorta sandiyi] whipped cream gâteau

ΤΟΥΡΤΑ ΣΟΚΟΛΑΤΑΣ τούρτα σοκολάτας [**too**rta sokolatas] chocolate gâteau

ΤΡΟΥΦΑΚΙΑ τρουφάκια [troofakia] small chocolate fudge cake

ΤΣΙΠΟΥΡΕΣ τσιπούρες [tsip**oo**res] sea bream

ΤΣΙΠΟΥΡΕΣ ΨΗΤΕΣ τσιπούρες ψητές [tsip**oo**res psites] roast sea bream

ΤΣΙΠΣ τσιπς [tsips] crisps, (US) potato chips

ΤΣΟΥΡΕΚΙ τσουρέκι [tsoo**re**ki] light sponge

ΤΣΟΥΡΕΚΙΑ τσουρέκια [tsoo**re**kia] sweet bread with fresh butter (Christmas/Easter dish)

ΤΥΡΙ τυρί [tiri] cheese

ΤΥΡΙΑ τυριά [tiria] cheese

ΤΥΡΟΠΙΤΤΑ τυρόπιτα [tir**o**pita] cheese and egg in filo pastry

ΤΥΡΟΠΙΤΤΑΚΙΑ τυροπιτάκια [tiropit**a**kia] small cheese pies

ΦΑΒΑ φάβα [fava] chick pea soup

ΦΑΚΕΣ φακές [fak**e**s] lentil soup

ΦΑΣΟΛΑΔΑ φασολάδα [fasolatha] bean soup with celery, carrots and tomatoes

ΦΑΣΟΛΑΚΙΑ φασολάκια [fasol**a**kia] green beans

ΦΑΣΟΛΑΚΙΑ ΛΑΔΕΡΑ φασολάκια λαδερά [fasol**a**kia lathera] green beans in olive oil and tomato sauce

ΦΑΣΟΛΑΚΙΑ ΦΡΕΣΚΑ ΓΙΑΧΝΙ φασολάκια φρέσκα γιαχνί [fasol**a**kia fr**e**ska yakhni] runner beans with onion and tomato

ΦΑΣΟΛΑΚΙΑ ΦΡΕΣΚΑ ΣΑΛΑΤΑ φασολάκια φρέσκα σαλάτα [fasol**a**kia fr**e**ska sal**a**ta] runner bean salad

ΦΑΣΟΛΙΑ φασόλια [fas**o**lia] beans

ΦΑΣΟΛΙΑ ΓΙΓΑΝΤΕΣ ΓΙΑΧΝΙ φασόλια γίγαντες γιαχνί [fas**o**lia yigandes yakhni] butter beans with onion and tomato

ΦΑΣΟΛΙΑ ΓΙΓΑΝΤΕΣ ΣΤΟ ΦΟΥΡΝΟ φασόλια γίγαντες στο φούρνο [fas**o**lia yigandes sto foorno] oven-cooked butter beans

ΦΑΣΟΛΙΑ ΓΙΓΑΝΤΕΣ φασόλια γίγαντες [fas**o**lia yigandes] large dried beans in tomato sauce

ΦΑΣΟΛΙΑ ΣΟΥΠΑ φασόλια σούπα [fas**o**lia s**oo**pa] bean soup

ΦΕΤΑ φέτα [feta] feta cheese

ΦΙΛΕ ΜΙΝΙΟΝ φιλέ μινιόν [file**h** minion] thin fillet steak

ΦΙΛΕΤΟ φιλέτο [file**to**] fillet steak

ΦΛΟΓΕΡΕΣ ΜΕ ΚΡΕΜΑ φλογέρες με κρέμα [floy**e**res meh kr**e**ma] round sweets filled with cream

ΦΟΝΤΑΝ φοντάν [fondan] sweets

ΦΟΝΤΑΝ ΑΜΥΓΔΑΛΟΥ φοντάν αμυγδάλου [fondan amigthaloo] almond sweets

ΦΟΝΤΑΝ ΑΠΟ ΚΑΡΥΔΑ φοντάν από καρύδα [fondan apo karitha] coconut sweets

ΦΟΝΤΑΝ ΑΠΟ ΚΑΡΥΔΙΑ φοντάν από καρύδια [fondan apo karithia] walnut sweets

ΦΟΝΤΑΝ ΙΝΔΙΚΗΣ ΚΑΡΥΔΑΣ φοντάν ινδικής καρύδας [fondan inthikis karithas] coconut sweets

ΦΟΝΤΑΝ ΠΟΡΤΟΚΑΛΙΟΥ φοντάν πορτοκαλιού [fondan portokali-**oo**] orange sweets

ΦΟΥΝΤΟΥΚΙΑ φουντούκια [foond**oo**kia] hazelnuts

ΦΡΑΟΥΛΕΣ φράουλες [fra-ooles] strawberries

ΦΡΑΟΥΛΕΣ ΜΕ ΣΑΝΤΙΓΥ φράουλες με σαντιγύ [fra-ooles meh sandiyi] strawberries with whipped cream

ΦΡΙΚΑΣΕ ΑΡΝΙ φρικασέ αρνί [frikas**eh** arni] lamb cooked in lettuce with cream sauce

ΦΡΟΥΙ-ΓΚΛΑΣΕ φρουί-γκλασέ [froo**i**-glas**eh**] dried assorted fruits with sugar

ΦΡΟΥΤΑ φρούτα [fro**o**ta] fruit

ΦΡΟΥΤΟΣΑΛΑΤΑ φρουτοσαλάτα [frootosalata] fruit salad

ΦΡΥΓΑΝΙΑ φρυγανιά [frigania] toast

ΦΡΥΓΑΝΙΕΣ φρυγανιές [frigani-es] French toast

ΦΥΛΛΟ ΠΙΤΤΑΣ φύλλο πίττας [filo pitas] filo pastry

ΦΥΣΤΙΚΙΑ φυστίκια [fistikia] peanuts

ΦΥΣΤΙΚΙΑ ΑΙΓΙΝΗΣ φυστίκια Αιγίνης [fistikia Eyinis] pistachios

ΧΑΒΙΑΡΙ χαβιάρι [khaviari] caviar

ΧΑΛΒΑΣ χαλβάς [khalvas] halva, sweet made from semolina, sesame seeds, nuts and honey

ΧΑΜΠΟΥΡΓΚΕΡ χάμπουργκερ [khamburger] hamburger

ΧΗΝΑ χήνα [khina] goose

ΧΟΙΡΙΝΟ χοιρινό [khirino] pork

ΧΟΙΡΙΝΟ ΜΕ ΣΕΛΙΝΟ χοιρινό με σέλινο [khirino meh selino] pork casserole with celery

ΧΟΙΡΙΝΟ ΠΑΣΤΟ χοιρινό παστό [khirino pasto] salted pork

ΧΟΙΡΙΝΟ ΣΟΥΒΛΑΣ χοιρινό σούβλας [khirino soovlas] pork on the spit

ΧΟΙΡΙΝΟ ΣΤΗ ΣΧΑΡΑ χοιρινό στη σχάρα [khirino sti skhara] grilled pork

ΧΟΙΡΙΝΟ ΦΟΥΡΝΟΥ ΜΕ ΠΑΤΑΤΕΣ χοιρινό φούρνου με πατάτες [khirino foornoo meh patates] roast pork with potatoes

ΧΟΡΤΑ ΒΡΑΣΜΕΝΑ ΣΑΛΑΤΑ **χόρτα βρασμένα σαλάτα** [khorta vrasmena salata] boiled chicory salad

ΧΟΡΤΑΡΙΚΑ **χορταρικά** [khortarika] vegetables

ΧΟΡΤΟΣΟΥΠΑ **χορτόσουπα** [khortosoopa] vegetable soup

ΧΤΑΠΟΔΑΚΙ ΞΥΔΑΤΟ **χταποδάκι ξυδάτο** [khtapothaki xithato] pickled octopus

ΧΤΑΠΟΔΙ **χταπόδι** [khtapothi] octopus

ΧΤΑΠΟΔΙ ΒΡΑΣΤΟ **χταπόδι βραστό** [khtapothi vrasto] boiled octopus

ΧΤΑΠΟΔΙ ΚΡΑΣΑΤΟ **χταπόδι κρασάτο** [khtapothi krasato] octopus in wine

ΧΤΑΠΟΔΙ ΜΕ ΜΑΚΑΡΟΝΑΚΙ **χταπόδι με μακαρονάκι** [khtapothi meh makaronaki] octopus with macaroni

ΧΤΑΠΟΔΙ ΠΙΛΑΦΙ **χταπόδι πιλάφι** [khtapothi pilafi] octopus pilaf

ΧΤΑΠΟΔΙ ΣΤΙΦΑΔΟ **χταπόδι στιφάδο** [khtapothi stifatho] octopus with small onions

ΧΥΛΟΠΙΤΕΣ **χυλοπίτες** [khilopites] tagliatelle

ΧΥΛΟΠΙΤΕΣ ΜΕ ΒΟΥΤΥΡΟ ΚΑΙ ΤΥΡΙ **χυλοπίτες με βούτυρο και τυρί** [khilopites meh vootiro keh tiri] tagliatelle with butter and cheese

ΧΥΛΟΠΙΤΕΣ ΜΕ ΚΙΜΑ **χυλοπίτες με κιμά** [khilopites meh kima] tagliatelle with minced meat sauce

ΧΥΛΟΠΙΤΕΣ ΜΕ ΚΟΤΟΠΟΥΛΟ **χυλοπίτες με κοτόπουλο** [khilopites meh kotopoolo] tagliatelle with chicken

ΧΩΡΙΑΤΙΚΗ ΣΑΛΑΤΑ **χωριάτικη σαλάτα** [khoriatiki salata] Greek salad – tomatoes, cucumber, peppers, feta, olives and boiled eggs with olive oil and vinegar dressing

ΨΑΡΙ **ψάρι** [psari] fish

ΨΑΡΙ ΒΡΑΣΤΟ ΜΑΓΙΟΝΕΖΑ **ψάρι βραστό μαγιονέζα** [psari vrasto mayoneza] steamed fish with mayonnaise

ΨΑΡΙΑ **ψάρια** [psaria] fish

ΨΑΡΙΑ ΓΛΩΣΣΕΣ ΒΡΑΣΤΕΣ ΜΕ ΑΥΓΟΛΕΜΟΝΟ **ψάρια γλώσσες βραστές με αυγολέμονο** [psaria gloses vrastes meh avgolemono] steamed sole with oil and lemon

ΨΑΡΙΑ ΜΑΡΙΝΑΤΑ **ψάρια μαρινάτα** [psaria marinata] marinated fish

ΨΑΡΙΑ ΤΗΓΑΝΗΤΑ **ψάρια τηγανητά** [psaria tiganita] fried fish

ΨΑΡΙΑ ΨΗΤΑ ΣΤΗ ΣΧΑΡΑ **ψάρια ψητά στη σχάρα** [psaria psita sti skhara] charcoal-grilled fish

ΨΑΡΟΣΟΥΠΑ **ψαρόσουπα** [psarosoopa] fish soup

ΨΗΤΟ ψητό [psito] grilled over charcoal; oven-roasted

ΨΗΤΟ ΣΤΗ ΣΧΑΡΑ ψητό στη σχάρα [psito sti skhara] grilled

ΨΩΜΑΚΙ ψωμάκι [psomaki] roll

ΨΩΜΙ ψωμί [psomi] bread

ΨΩΜΙ ΑΣΠΡΟ ψωμί άσπρο [psomi aspro] white bread

ΨΩΜΙ ΓΙΑ ΤΟΣΤ ψωμί για τοστ [psomi ya tost] sliced bread

ΨΩΜΙ ΜΑΥΡΟ ψωμί μαύρο [psomi mavro] brown bread

ΩΜΟΣ ωμός [omos] raw

Menu Reader: Drink

Essential Terms

beer i bira
bottle to bookali
brandy to koniak
coffee o kafes
cup: a cup of ... ena flidzani ...
fruit juice o khimos frooton
gin to tzin
a gin and tonic ena tzin meh tonik
glass: a glass of ... ena potiri ...
milk to gala
mineral water to emfialomeno nero
orange juice i portokalatha
red wine to kokino krasi
rosé to rozeh
soda (water) i sotha
soft drink to anapsiktiko
sugar i zakhari
tea to tsa-i
tonic (water) to tonik
vodka i votka
water to nero
whisky to whisky
white wine to aspro krasi
wine to kras
wine list o katalogos ton krasion

another ..., please ali mia ..., parakalo

ΑΕΡΙΟΥΧΟ αεριούχο [aeriookho] fizzy

ΑΛΚΟΟΛ αλκοόλ [alko-**ol**] alcohol

ΑΝΑΝΑΣ ΧΥΜΟΣ ανανάς χυμός [ananas khimos] pineapple juice

ΑΝΑΨΥΚΤΙΚΟ αναψυκτικό [anapsiktiko] soft drink

ΑΠΕΡΙΤΙΦ απεριτίφ [aperitif] aperitif

ΑΣΠΡΟ ΚΡΑΣΙ άσπρο κρασί [aspro krasi] white wine

ΒΟΤΚΑ βότκα [votka] vodka

ΒΥΣΣΙΝΑΔΑ βυσσινάδα [visinatha] black cherry juice

ΓΑΛΑ γάλα [gala] milk

ΓΑΛΑ ΚΑΚΑΟ γάλα κακάο [gala kakao] chocolate milk

ΓΑΛΛΙΚΟΣ ΚΑΦΕΣ γαλλικός καφές [galikos kafes] filter coffee; French coffee

ΓΛΥΚΟ ΚΡΑΣΙ γλυκό κρασί [gliko krasi] sweet wine

ΕΛΛΗΝΙΚΟΣ ΚΑΦΕΣ ελληνικός καφές [elinikos kafes] Greek coffee

ΖΕΣΤΗ ΣΟΚΟΛΑΤΑ ζεστή σοκολάτα [zesti sokolata] hot chocolate

ΚΑΚΑΟ κακάο [kakao] cocoa

ΚΑΤΑΛΟΓΟΣ ΚΡΑΣΙΩΝ κατάλογος κρασιών [katalogos krasion] wine list

ΚΑΦΕΣ καφές [kafes] coffee

ΚΑΦΕΣ ΜΕΤΡΙΟΣ καφές μέτριος [kafes metrios] medium-sweet Greek coffee

ΚΑΦΕΣ ΒΑΡΥΣ ΓΛΥΚΟΣ καφές βαρύς γλυκός [kafes varis glikos] sweet Greek coffee

ΚΑΦΕΣ ΜΕ ΓΑΛΑ καφές με γάλα [kafes meh gala] coffee with milk

ΚΟΚΑ ΚΟΛΑ κόκα κόλα [koka kola] Coca-Cola®

ΚΟΚΚΙΝΟ ΚΡΑΣΙ κόκκινο κρασί [kokino krasi] red wine

ΚΟΚΤΕΗΛ κοκτέηλ [kokteil] cocktail

ΚΟΝΙΑΚ κονιάκ [koniak] brandy

ΚΡΑΣΙ κρασί [krasi] wine

ΚΡΑΣΙ ΑΣΠΡΟ κρασί άσπρο [krasi aspro] white wine

ΚΡΑΣΙ ΚΟΚΚΙΝΟ κρασί κόκκινο [krasi kokino] red wine

ΚΡΑΣΙ ΜΑΥΡΟΔΑΦΝΗ κρασί μαυροδάφνη [krasi mavrothafni] sweet red wine

ΚΡΑΣΙ ΡΕΤΣΙΝΑ κρασί ρετσίνα [krasi retsina] retsina

ΚΡΑΣΙ ΡΟΖΕ κρασί ροζέ [krasi rozeh] rosé wine

ΚΡΑΣΙ ΤΟΥ ΜΑΓΑΖΙΟΥ κρασί του μαγαζιού [krasi too magazi-**oo**] house wine

ΛΕΜΟΝΑΔΑ λεμονάδα [lemonatha] lemonade

ΛΙΚΕΡ λικέρ [liker] liqueur

ΜΕΤΑΛΛΙΚΟ ΝΕΡΟ μεταλλικό νερό [metaliko nero] mineral water
ΜΗΛΟΧΥΜΟΣ μηλοχυμός [milokhimos] apple juice
ΜΠΥΡΑ μπύρα [bira] beer, lager

ΝΕΣΚΑΦΕ νέσκαφέ [neskafeh] Nescafé®, instant coffee
ΝΕΣΚΑΦΕ ΦΡΑΠΕ νέσκαφέ φραπέ [neskafeh frapeh] iced coffee
ΝΕΡΟ νερό [nero] water
ΝΤΟΜΑΤΑ ΧΥΜΟΣ ντομάτα χυμός [domata khimos] tomato juice

ΟΥΖΟ ούζο [oozo] ouzo
ΟΥΙΣΚΥ ουίσκυ whisky, scotch

παγακι παγάκι [pagaki] ice cube
ΠΑΓΟΣ πάγος [pagos] ice
ΠΟΡΤΟΚΑΛΑΔΑ πορτοκαλάδα [portokalatha] orange juice
ΠΟΡΤΟΚΑΛΙ ΧΥΜΟΣ πορτοκάλι χυμός [portokali khimos] orange juice
ΠΟΤΑ ποτά [pota] drinks

ΡΑΚΗ ρακή [raki] strong spirit, eau-de-vie
ΡΕΤΣΙΝΑ ρετσίνα [retsina] retsina
ΡΟΖΕ ΚΡΑΣΙ ροζέ κρασί [rozeh krasi] rosé wine
ΡΟΥΜΙ ρούμι [roomi] rum

ΣΤΑΦΥΛΙ ΧΥΜΟΣ σταφύλι χυμός [stafili khimos] grape juice

TZIN τζιν [tzin] gin
TZIN ΜΕ TONIK τζιν με τόνικ [tzin meh tonik] gin and tonic
ΤΣΑΙ τσάι [tsa-i] tea
ΤΣΑΙ ΜΕ ΛΕΜΟΝΙ τσάι με λεμόνι [tsa-i meh lemoni] lemon tea
ΤΣΙΠΟΥΡΟ τσίπουρο [tsipooro] type of ouzo

ΦΡΑΠΕ φραπέ [frapeh] iced coffee

ΧΥΜΟΣ χυμός [khimos] juice
ΧΩΡΙΣ ΚΑΦΕΪΝΗ χωρίς καφεΐνη [khoris kafeini] decaffeinated

How the Language Works

The Greek Alphabet

Set out below is the Greek alphabet, the names of the Greek letters, and the system of transliteration used in this book:

Α, α	**a**lfa	a as in c**a**t
Β, β	v**i**ta	v as in **v**et
Γ, γ	g**a**ma	y as in **y**es, except before consonants and a or o, when it's a throaty version of the g in **g**ap
Δ, δ	th**e**lta	th as in **th**en
Ε, ε	**e**psilon	e as in g**e**t
Ζ, ζ	z**i**ta	z
Η, η	**i**ta	i as in sk**i**
Θ, θ	th**i**ta	as the th in **th**eme (represented by th)
Ι, ι	y**o**ta	i as in b**i**t
Κ, κ	k**a**pa	k
Λ, λ	l**a**mtha	l
Μ, μ	mi	m
Ν, ν	ni	n
Ξ, ξ	ksi	x
Ο, ο	**o**mikron	o as in h**o**t
Π, π	pi	p
Ρ, ρ	ro	r
Σ, σ, ς*	s**i**gma	s
Τ, τ	taf	t
Υ, υ	**i**psilon	long i, indistinguishable from **i**ta
Φ, φ	fi	f
Χ, χ	khi	h as in **h**at or harsh ch in the Scottish word lo**ch** (represented by kh)
Ψ, ψ	psi	ps as in li**ps**
Ω, ω	om**e**ga	o as in h**o**t, indistinguishable from **o**mikron

* this letter is used only at the end of a word in lower case

Combinations and diphthongs:

ΑΙ, αι	e as in g**e**t
ΑΥ, αυ	av or af depending on following consonant
ΕΙ, ει	long i, exactly like **i**ta
ΟΙ, οι	long i, exactly like **i**ta
ΕΥ, ευ	ev or ef depending on following consonant
ΟΥ, ου	oo as in m**oo**n
ΓΓ, γγ	ng as in a**ng**le
ΓΚ, γκ	g as in **g**oat at the beginning of a word; ng in the middle
ΜΠ, μπ	b as in bar and sometimes mb as in e**mb**assy in the middle of a word
ΝΤ, ντ	d at the beginning of a word and sometimes nd as in e**nd** in the middle
ΤΣ, τσ	ts as in hi**ts**

Pronunciation

Throughout this book Greek words have been transliterated into romanized form (see **The Greek Alphabet** page 209) so that they can be read as though they were English, bearing in mind the notes on pronunciation given below:

a	as in c**a**t
e	as in g**e**t
eh	represents e at end of a word; should always be pronounced as in g**e**t
g	as in **g**oat
i	as in sk**i**
kh	like the ch in the Scottish way of saying lo**ch**
o	as in h**o**t
th	as in **th**en
TH	as in **th**eme

Letters given in bold type indicate the part of the word to be stressed. When two vowels (such as 'ea') are next to each other in the pronunciation, both should be pronounced, as for example in the word: amfiTH**e**atro (amphitheatre).

Abbreviations

acc	accusative case	neut	neuter
adj	adjective	nom	nominative case
fam	familiar	pl	plural
fem	feminine	pol	polite
gen	genitive case	sing	singular
masc	masculine		

Note

An asterisk (*) next to a word in the dictionaries means that you should refer to the **How the Language Works** section for further information.

Nouns and Articles

Articles

Greek nouns have one of three genders – masculine, feminine or neuter. The indefinite article (a, an) for each gender is:

masc	fem	neut
ένας	μία	ένα
enas	mi**a**	**e**na

ένας άνδρας	μία γυναίκα	ένα παιδί
enas **a**nthras	mi**a** yin**e**ka	**e**na peth**i**
a man	a woman	a child

The definite article (the) is:

	masc	fem	neut
sing	ο	η	το
	o	i	to

	masc	fem	neut
plural	οι	οι	τα
	i	i	ta

ο πατέρας	οι πατεράδες
o pat**e**ras	i pater**a**thes
the father	the fathers

το μωρό	τα μωρά
to mor**o**	ta mor**a**
the baby	the babies

η χώρα	οι χώρες
i kh**o**ra	i kh**o**res
the country	the countries

η μητέρα	οι μητέρες
i mit**e**ra	i mit**e**res
the mother	the mothers

ο δρόμος	οι δρόμοι
o thr**o**mos	i thr**o**mi
the street	the streets

το βουνό	τα βουνά
o voon**o**	ta voon**a**
the mountain	the mountains

Cases

There are three main cases in Greek – nominative, genitive and accusative. The forms of articles, nouns, adjectives and most pronouns change according to their gender, number and case. The indefinite article (a, an) declines as follows:

sing	masc	fem	neut
nom	έναι	μία	ένα
	enas	mi**a**	**e**na
gen	ενός	μιάς	ενός
	en**o**s	mi**a**s	en**o**s
acc	ένα(ν)*	μία	ένα
	ena(n)	mi**a**	**e**na

The definite article (the) declines as follows:

sing	masc	fem	neut
nom	ο	η	το
	o	i	to
gen	του	της	του
	too	tis	too
acc	το(ν)*	τη(ν)*	το
	to(n)	ti(n)	to

*The forms έναν and τον/την should be used before nouns beginning with a vowel.

plural	masc	fem	neut
nom	οι	οι	τα
	i	i	ta
gen	των	των	των
	ton	ton	ton
acc	τους	τις	τα
	toos	tis	ta

Nominative Case

The nominative case is used for the subject of sentences:

το δωμάτιό μου είναι μικρό
to thomatio moo ineh mikro
my room is small

ο Γιάννης διαβάζει ένα βιβλίο
o Yanis thiavazi ena vivlio
John is reading a book

Genitive Case

The genitive case is used to indicate possession and to translate 'of':

αυτό είναι το αυτοκίνητο του Γιώργου
afto ineh to aftokinito too Yorgoo
this is George's car

ο σκύλος του γείτονα
o skilos too yitona
the neighbour's dog

Accusative Case

The accusative case is used for direct objects:

μπορείτε να μας φέρετε το λογαριασμό, παρακαλώ;
boriteh na mas fereteh to logariasmo, parakalo?
could you bring us the bill, please?

έχασα το λεωφορείο
ekhasa to leoforio
I missed the bus

The accusative case is also used with some prepositions (to, from, with etc):

αυτή πήγε στην παραλία
afti piyeh stin paralia
she has gone to the beach

αυτός είναι από τη Σκωτία
aftos ineh apo ti Skotia
he comes from Scotland

αυτοί πηγαίνουν με τα πόδια
afti piyenoon meh ta pothia
they are going on foot

προτιμάμε να ταξιδεύουμε με το τρένο
protimameh na taxithevoomeh meh to treno
we prefer to travel by train

Vocative Case

Another case in Greek is the vocative case, which is used to address someone directly. The vocative has the same endings as the nominative case, apart from masculine nouns and names where the final ς is dropped:

Μαρία, πού είναι ο Γιάννης;	Γιάννη, πού είναι η Μαρία;
Maria, poo ineh o Yanis?	Yani, poo ineh i Maria?
Mary, where is John?	John, where is Mary?

Noun Endings

The endings of nouns change according to whether they are singular or plural and depending on whether they are in the nominative, genitive or accusative cases.

Masculine Nouns

Masculine nouns usually have one of three endings:

	-ας	-ης	-ος
	ο χειμώνας	ο εργάτης	ο δάσκαλος
	the winter	the workman	the teacher
sing			
nom	ο χειμώνας	ο εργάτης	ο δάσκαλος
	o khimonas	o ergatis	o thaskalos
gen	του χειμώνα	του εργάτη	του δασκάλου
	too khimona	too ergati	too thaskaloo
acc	το χειμώνα	τον εργάτη	τον δάσκαλο
	to khimona	ton ergati	ton thaskalo

plural			
nom	οι χειμώνες i khim**o**nes	οι εργάτες i erg**a**tes	οι δάσκαλοι i th**a**skali
gen	των χειμώνων ton khim**o**non	των εργατών ton erga**to**n	των δασκάλων ton thask**a**lon
acc	τους χειμώνες toos khim**o**nes	τους εργάτες toos erg**a**tes	τους δασκάλους toos thask**a**loos

A few masculine nouns end in:

-άς, -ές or -ούς

but for these only the plural differs from the above endings:

ο ψαράς o psar**a**s fisherman	οι ψαράδες i psar**a**thes fishermen
ο παπάς o pap**a**s the priest	οι παπάδες i pap**a**thes the priests
ο καφές o kaf**e**s the coffee	οι καφέδες i kaf**e**thes the coffees
ο καναπές o kanap**e**s the couch	οι καναπέδες i kanap**e**thes the couches
ο παππούς o pap**oo**s the grandfather	οι παππούδες i pap**oo**thes the grandfathers

Feminine Nouns

Feminine nouns either end in:

-α or -η

η γλώσσα the tongue, the language	η νίκη the victory

sing		
nom	η γλώσσα	η νίκη
	i **glo**sa	i **ni**ki
gen	της γλώσσας	της νίκης
	tis **glo**sas	tis **ni**kis
acc	τη γλώσσα	τη νίκη
	ti **glo**sa	ti **ni**ki
plural		
nom	οι γλώσσες	οι νίκες
	i **glo**ses	i **ni**kes
gen	των γλωσσών	των νικών
	ton **glo**son	ton **ni**kon
acc	τις γλώσσες	τις νίκες
	tis **glo**ses	tis **ni**kes

Some irregular feminine nouns ending in -η take the plural ending -εις, for example:

η λέξη	οι λέξεις
i **le**xi	i **le**xis
the word	the words
η απόφαση	οι αποφάσεις
i **apo**fasi	i **apo**fasis
the decision	the decisions

Feminine nouns ending in -ος decline like masculine nouns. For example:

η έξοδος	η είσοδος
i **e**xothos	i **i**sothos
the exit	the entrance

Neuter Nouns

Neuter nouns have one of the following endings:

-ο, -ι or -μα

		το δέντρο the tree	το ψωμί the bread, the loaf	το όνομα the name
sing	nom	το δέντρο to th**e**ndro	το ψωμί to psom**i**	το όνομα to **o**noma
	gen	του δέντρου too th**e**ndroo	του ψωμιού too psomi-**oo**	του ονόματος too on**o**matos
	acc	το δέντρο to th**e**ndro	το ψωμί to psom**i**	το όνομα to **o**noma
plural	nom	τα δέντρα ta th**e**ndra	τα ψωμιά ta psom**ia**	τα ονόματα ta on**o**mata
	gen	των δέντρων ton th**e**ndron	των ψωμιών ton psom**io**n	των ονομάτων ton onom**a**ton
	acc	τα δέντρα ta th**e**ndra	τα ψωμιά ta psom**ia**	τα ονόματα ta on**o**mata

Several neuter nouns end in -ος:

το είδος to **i**thos the kind	τα είδη ta **i**thi the kinds	το μέγεθος to me**y**eTHos the size	τα μεγέθη ta mey**e**THi the sizes

Adjectives and Adverbs

Most adjectives also change as follows according to gender and number:

masc	fem	neut	masc	fem	neut
ακριβός expensive			γλυκός sweet		
ακριβός akriv**o**s	ακριβή akriv**i**	ακριβό akriv**o**	γλυκός glik**o**s	γλυκιά glik**ia**	γλυκό glik**o**
όμορφος beautiful			ελαφρύς light		
όμορφος **o**morfos	όμορφη **o**morfi	όμορφο **o**morfo	ελαφρύς elafr**i**s	ελαφριά elafr**ia**	ελαφρύ elafr**i**

Adjective endings follow the pattern of the corresponding noun endings. Adjectives should agree with their nouns in gender, number, and case:

ο καλός φίλος	έχω μερικούς καλούς φίλους
o kalos filos	ekho merikoos kaloos filoos
the good friend	I have some good friends
η όμορφη πόλη	είδαμε ένα ωραίο έργο
i omorfi poli	ithameh enah oreo ergo
the beautiful town	we saw a good film

The most common irregular adjective is:

ο πολύς a lot of, much, many

	sing	plural
masc	ο πολύς	οι πολλοί
	o polis	i poli
fem	η πολλή	οι πολλές
	i poli	i poles
neut	το πολύ	τα πολλά
	to poli	ta pola

Comparatives

The comparative is formed by putting the word πιό [pio] 'more' in front of the adjective:

αυτό το ξενοδοχείο είναι πιό/λιγότερο ακριβό από εκείνο
afto to xenothokhio ineh pio/ligotero akrivo apo ekino
this hotel is more/less expensive than that one

είναι πιό ήσυχα εδώ
ineh pio isikha etho
it's quieter here

Superlatives

Superlatives are formed by putting the definite article in front of the comparative:

η Ομόνοια είναι η πιό διάσημη πλατεία στην Αθήνα
i Omoni-a ineh i pio thiasimi plati-a stin ATHina
Omonia Square is the most famous square in Athens

αυτός ο δρόμος είναι ο λιγότερο επικίνδυνος
aftos o thromos ineh o ligotero epikinthinos
this road is the least dangerous

η ταβέρνα Ο Γιάννης είναι η πιο δημοφιλής ταβέρνα στη Μυτιλήνη
i taverna O Yanis ineh i pio thimofilis taverna sti Mitilini
the O Yanis taverna is the most popular in Mitilini

'As ... as' is translated as τόσο ... όσο:

αυτό το εστιατόριο είναι τόσο ακριβό όσο και το άλλο
afto to estiatorio ineh toso akrivo oso keh to alo
this restaurant is as expensive as that one

αυτή η πόλη δεν είναι τόσο ενδιαφέρουσα όσο νόμιζα
afti i poli then ineh toso enthiaferoosa oso nomiza
this town is not as interesting as I thought

The following common adjectives have irregular comparatives and superlatives:

κακός kakos bad	χειρότερος khiroteros worse	χείριστος khiristos worst
καλός kalos good	καλύτερος kaliteros better	κάλλιστος kalistos best
μικρός mikros small	μικρότερος mikroteros smaller	ελάχιστος elakhistos smallest

μεγάλος **mega**los big	μεγαλύτερος mega**li**teros bigger	μέγιστος me**yi**stos biggest
λίγος **li**gos few	λιγότερος lig**o**teros fewer	ελάχιστος e**la**khistos fewest
πολύς **po**lis a lot of	περισσότερος peris**o**teros a lot more of	

Adverbs

If the adjective ends in -ος, remove this ending and add -α to create the adverb:

adjective	adverb	adjective	adverb
καλός kal**o**s good	καλά kal**a** well	ωραίος ore**o**s nice	ωραία ore**h**-a nicely
κακός kak**o**s bad	κακά kak**a** badly	τυχερός tikher**o**s lucky	τυχερά tikher**a** luckily

If the adjective ends in -ης, remove this ending and add -ως to create the adverb:

adjective	adverb
συνεχής sinekh**i**s continuous	συνεχώς sinekh**o**s continuously
ακριβής akriv**i**s precise	ακριβώς akriv**o**s precisely
διεθνής thi-eTHn**i**s international	διεθνώς thi-eTHn**o**s internationally

Possessive Adjectives

my	μου	moo	its	του	too
your (sing, fam)	σου	soo	our	μας	mas
his	του	too	your (pl, pol)	σας	sas
her	της	tis	their	τους	toos

Possessive adjectives do not change according to case, gender or number. They follow the noun they refer to, but note that the definite article is placed in front of the noun:

το διαβατήριό μου	τα λεφτά τους	το βιβλίο της
to thiavat**i**rio moo	ta lef**ta** toos	to vivl**io** tis
my passport	their money	her book

Pronouns

Possessive Pronouns

Possessive pronouns (mine, hers etc) are formed by placing the word δικός in front of the possessive. δικός declines like an adjective, agreeing with the object possessed in case, gender and number:

	masc	fem	neut
mine	δικός μου thik**o**s moo	δική μου thik**i** moo	δικό μου thik**o** moo
yours (sing, fam)	δικός σου thik**o**s soo	δική σου thik**i** soo	δικό σου thik**o** soo
his	δικός του thik**o**s too	δική του thik**i** too	δικό του thik**o** too
hers	δικός της thik**o**s tis	δική της thik**i** tis	δικό της thik**o** tis
its	δικός του thik**o**s too	δική του thik**i** too	δικό του thik**o** too
ours	δικός μας thik**o**s mas	δική μας thik**i** mas	δικό μας thik**o** mas
yours (pl, pol)	δικός σας thik**o**s sas	δική σας thik**i** sas	δικό σας thik**o** sas
theirs	δικός τους thik**o**s toos	δική τους thik**i** toos	δικό τους thik**o** toos

Plurals take the usual adjective endings:

αυτές είναι οι δικές μας
aftes ineh i thikes mas
these are ours

Personal Pronouns

nom	gen	acc
εγώ [ego] I	μου [moo] me	με/εμένα [meh/emena] me
εσύ [esi] you*	σου [soo] you	σε/εσένα [seh/esena] you
αυτός [aftos] he	του [too] him	τον [ton] him
αυτή [afti] she	της [tis] her	την [tin] her
αυτό [afto] it	του [too] it	το [to] it
εμείς [emis] we	μας [mas] us	μας/εμάς [mas/emas] us
εσείς [esis] you**	σας/εσάς [sas/esas] you	σας/εσάς [sas/esas] you
αυτοί [afti] they (m)	τους [toos] them	τους/αυτούς [toos/aftoos] them
αυτές [aftes] they (f)	τους [toos] them	τις/αυτές [tis/aftes] them
αυτά [afta] they (n)	τους [toos] them	τα/αυτά [ta/afta] them

* εσύ is used when speaking to one person and is the familiar form generally used when speaking to family, friends and children.

** εσείς is the polite form which can be used to address one person or several people.

αυτή του έδωσε τα χρήματα
afti too ethoseh ta khrimata
she gave him the money

εγώ τους είδα να το κλέβουν
ego toos itha na to klevoon
I saw them stealing it

Where two forms are given for the accusative, the second is used after prepositions:

θα πάω μαζί με αυτές
THa pao mazi meh aftes
I will go with them

αυτό είναι ένα δώρο γιά εσένα
afto ineh ena thoro ya esena
this is a present for you

In Greek the subject pronoun (nominative) is usually omitted:

έφυγε χθές
efiyeh khTH**es**
he left yesterday

θα ήθελα να παραγγείλω
THa **i**THela na parang**i**lo
I'd like to order

Although it may be retained for emphasis:

αυτή ήταν πρώτη
af**ti i**tan pr**o**ti
SHE was first

εσύ φταίς
esi ftes
YOU are to blame

αυτός έκλεψε το πορτοφόλι μου
af**tos e**klepseh to portof**o**li moo
HE stole my wallet

Examples using pronouns in genitive and accusative:

το πήρε από την τσάντα μου
to p**i**reh ap**o** tin ts**a**nda moo
he took it from my bag

εσύ τους το έδωσες;
esi toos to **e**thoses?
did YOU give it to them?

την πήρα μαζί μου
tin p**i**ra maz**i** moo
I took her with me

τα αγόρασε χθες
ta ag**o**raseh khTH**es**
she bought them yesterday

θα σου τον συστήσω
THa soo ton sist**i**so
I shall introduce you to him

την είδα
tin **i**tha
I saw her

δε σε ακούω καλά
theh seh ak**oo**-o kal**a**
I cannot hear you very well

Verbs

The form of the verb given in dictionaries is usually the first person singular of the present tense. This is the basic form (equivalent to the infinitive) and the endings are either -ω (active verbs) or -μαι (passive verbs).

Although there are two categories of Greek verbs (active and passive), many verbs that are not passive in English are considered passive in Greek.

Present Tense

Present tense endings for verbs ending in -ω depend on whether or not the stress falls on the last syllable:

	stress not on last syllable	stress on last syllable	
	αγοράζω buy	πουλώ sell	μπορώ be able
I	αγοράζ-ω agora**z**o	πουλ-ώ poolo	μπορ-ώ boro
you	αγοράζ-εις agora**z**is	πουλ-άς poolas	μπορ-είς boris
he/she	αγοράζ-ει agora**z**i	πουλ-ά poola	μπορ-εί bori
we	αγοράζ-ουμε agora**z**oomeh	πουλ-άμε poolameh	μπορ-ούμε boroomeh
you	αγοράζ-ετε agora**z**eteh	πουλ-άτε poolateh	μπορ-είτε boriteh
they	αγοράζ-ουν agora**z**oon	πουλ-ούν pooloon	μπορ-ούν boroon

πόσο το πουλάς;
poso to poolas?
how much are you selling it for?

το αγοράζω για χίλιες δραχμές
to agorazo ya khili-es thrakhmes
I am buying it for 1,000 drachmas

δεν μπορεί να περπατήσει
then bori na perpatisi
he can't walk

Passive verbs ending in -μαι take the following endings:

ντώνομαι be dressed, dress (oneself)

I	ντών-ομαι [dinomeh]
you	ντών-εσαι [dineseh]
he/she	ντών-εται [dineteh]
we	ντυν-όμαστε [dinomasteh]
you	ντών-εστε [dinesteh]
they	ντών-ονται [dinondeh]

The verbs 'to be' and 'to have' are irregular:

είμαι I am [imeh]	είμαστε we are [imasteh]
είσαι you are [iseh]	είσαστε/είστε you are [isasteh/isteh]
είναι he/she/it is [ineh]	είναι they are [ineh]
έχω I have [ekho]	έχουμε we have [ekhoomeh]
έχεις you have [ekhis]	έχετε you have [ekheteh]
έχει he/she/it has [ekhi]	έχουν they have [ekhoon]

Past Simple Tense

To describe an action that has taken place in the past, use the past simple tense in Greek. To form this, take the basic form of the verb and add the following endings. Note that in the simple past, the stress moves back one syllable and sometimes changes have to be made to the form of the verb which comes before these endings. For example, where necessary, the letter ε is added to the beginning of the verb so that the stress can move back a syllable:

ακού-ω (I hear)	κάν-ω (I do)
άκου-σ-α I heard [akoosa]	έκαν-α I did [ekana]
άκου-σ-ες you heard [akooses]	έκανες you did [ekanes]
άκου-σ-ε he/she heard [akooseh]	έκανε he/she/it did [ekaneh]
ακού-σ-αμε we heard [akoosameh]	εκάναμε we did [ekanameh]
ακού-σ-ατε you heard [akoosateh]	εκάνατε you did [ekanateh]
άκου-σ-αν they heard [akoosan]	έκαναν they did [ekanan]

The past tense of 'to be' and 'to have' is:

ήμουν I was [imoon]
ήσουν you were [isoon]
ήταν he/she/it was [itan]

ήμασταν we were [imastan]
ήσασταν you were [isastan]
ήταν they were [itan]

είχα I had [ikha]
είχες you had [ikhes]
είχε he/she/it had [ikheh]

είχαμε we had [ikhameh]
είχατε you had [ikhateh]
είχαν they had [ikhan]

πόσα χρήματα είχατε στην τσάντα σας;
posa khrimata ikhateh stin tsanda sas?
how much money did you have in your handbag?

επισκεφτήκατε το Αρχαιολογικό Μουσείο;
episkeftikateh to Arkheoloyiko Moosio?
did you visit the Archaeological Museum?

οι τιμές ήταν πιό φτηνές πέρυσι
i times itan pio ftines perisi
prices were cheaper last year

υπογράψατε στο βιβλίο;
ipograpsateh sto vivlio?
did you sign the book?

The Indefinite

The Greek indefinite form of the verb has no direct equivalent in English although its use often corresponds to the infinitive used after verbs such as 'to want', 'to be able to', 'can', etc, and has the following pattern:

να + basic form of verb + ending of the verb preceding it.

It must agree in person and number with the main verb preceding it:

θα μπορούσα να πληρώσω με επιταγή;
THa boroosa na pliroso meh epitayi?
could I pay by cheque?

The exception to this is the impersonal verb 'to have to', 'must' which always takes the same form πρέπει:

πρέπει να πηγαίνουμε τώρα
prepi na piyenoomeh tora
we must go now

Here is a list of some useful verbs with their indefinite and past simple in the first person:

present	indefinite	past simple	perfect
βλέπω see	να δω	είδα	έχω δει
vlepo	na tho	itha	ekho thi
βρίσκω find	να βρω	βρήκα	έχω βρει
vrisko	na vro	vrika	ekho vri
δίνω give	να δώσω	έδωσα	έχω δώσει
thino	na thoso	ethosa	ekho thosi
έρχομαι come	να έλθω	ήλθα	έχω έλθει
erkhomeh	na elTHo	ilTHa	ekho elTHi
κάνω do	να κάνω	έκανα	έχω κάνει
kano	na kano	ekana	ekho kani
λέω say	να πω	είπα	έχω πει
le-o	na po	ipa	ekho pi
μένω stay	να μείνω	έμεινα	έχω μείνει
meno	na mino	emina	ekho mini
παίρνω take	να πάρω	πήρα	έχω πάρει
perno	na paro	pira	ekho pari
πηγαίνω go	να πάω	πήγα	έχω πάει
piyeno	na pao	piga	ekho pa-i
πίνω drink	να πιώ	ήπια	έχω πιεί
pino	na pio	ipia	ekho pi-i
στέλνω send	να στείλω	έστειλα	έχω στείλει
stelno	na stilo	estila	ekho stili
τρώω eat	να φάω	έφαγα	έχω φάει
tro-o	na fa-o	efaga	ekho fa-i
ρωτώ ask	να ρωτήσω	ρώτησα	έχω ρωτήσει
roto	na rotiso	rotisa	ekho rotisi

αγοράζω buy	να αγοράσω	αγόρασα	έχω αγοράσει
agorazo	na agoraso	agorasa	ekho agorasi
κλείνω close	να κλείσω	έκλεισα	έχω κλείσει
klino	na kliso	eklisa	ekho klisi
κοιτάζω look	να κοιτάξω	κοίταξα	έχω κοιτάξει
kitazo	na kitaxo	kitaxa	ekho kitaxi
σταματώ stop	να σταματήσω	σταμάτησα	έχω σταματήσει
stamato	na stamatiso	stamatisa	ekho stamatisi
νομίζω think	να νομίσω	νόμισα	έχω νομίσει
nomizo	na nomiso	nomisa	ekho nomisi
γράφω write	να γράψω	έγραψα	έχω γράψει
grafo	na grapso	egrapsa	ekho grapsi

Future Tense

The simplest way to form the continuous future tense in Greek is to take the present tense forms and add the word θα in front of them:

I will be waiting	θα περιμένω	[THa perimeno]
you will ...	θα περιμένεις	[THa perimenis]
he/she will ...	θα περιμένει	[THa perimeni]
we will ...	θα περιμένουμε	[THa perimenoomeh]
you will ...	θα περιμένετε	[THa perimeneteh]
they will ...	θα περιμένουν	[THa perimenoon]

To form the simple future tense you use θα and the appropriate forms of the indefinite (without the να):

I will buy	θα αγοράσω	[THa agoraso]
you will ...	θα αγοράσεις	[THa agorasis]
he/she/it will ...	θα αγοράσει	[THa agorasi]
we will ...	θα αγοράσουμε	[THa agorasoomeh]
you will ...	θα αγοράσετε	[THa agoraseteh]
they will ...	θα αγοράσουν	[THa agorasoon]

θα σε δω το βράδυ
THa seh tho to vrathi
I'll see you tonight

Imperatives

The imperative form of the verb is used to give commands. To create the singular, familiar imperative, take the indefinite form of the verb (without the να) and change the final -ω to -ε:

κοίταξε εκεί!	πρόσεξε!
kitaxeh eki!	**pro**sexeh!
look over there!	watch out!

Polite and plural forms of the imperative are created by changing the final -ω of the indefinite form (without the να) to -ετε or -τε :

ρωτήστε τον αστυνόμο εκεί πέρα	υπογράψτε εδώ, παρακαλώ
rotisteh ton astin**o**mo eki **pe**ra	ipog**ra**psteh eth**o**, parakal**o**
ask the policeman over there	sign here, please

Negative imperatives are formed by placing μη or μην in front of the second person of the indefinite form (without the να) of the verb:

μην πάτε από αυτόν το δρόμο	μην πιείς αυτό το νερό
min **pa**teh ap**o** aft**o**n ton thr**o**mo	min pi-**is** aft**o** to ner**o**
don't go along this street	do not drink this water

Some common irregular imperatives are:

familiar	polite/plural
βρες find [vres]	βρείτε [vriteh]
δες see [thes]	δείτε [thiteh] or δέστε [thesteh]
πιές drink [pies]	πιείτε [pi-iteh] or πιέστε [pi-esteh]
πες say [pes]	πείτε [pesteh] or πέστε [pesteh]
ελα come [ela]	ελάτε [elateh]

Negatives

To form the negative, place the word δε or δεν in front of the verb:

δε μου αρέσει αυτό	δε μιλάω καλά Ελληνικά
theh moo a**re**si aft**o**	theh mil**a**-o kal**a** Elinik**a**
I don't like this	my Greek is not very good

δεν μπορώ να βρώ το ξενοδοχείο
then **boro** na vro to xenothokh**io**
I cannot find the hotel

Questions

The word order and intonation for questions in Greek are the same as in English:

πού είναι το γραφείο του ΕΟΤ, παρακαλώ;
poo **ineh** to graf**io** too **E**-OT, parakal**o**?
where is the tourist information office, please?

Note that in questions in Greek, a semi-colon is used instead of a question mark.

Dates

To say the date, take the ordinal number, then the genitive of the month. The exception is 'the first', when you should use the ordinal number:

σήμερα είναι εικοσιεφτά Φεβρουαρίου
simera **i**neh **i**kosi-ef**ta** Fevroo-ar**i**oo
today is the 27th of February

αύριο είναι πρώτη Ιουλίου
avrio **i**neh pro**ti** loo**li**-oo
tomorrow is the 1st of July

χθες ήταν τρεις Δεκεμβρίου
khThes **i**tan tris thekemvr**i**oo
yesterday was the 3rd of December

Πρωταπριλιά
protapril**ia**
1st of April

Πρωτομαγιά
protomay**a**
1st of May

Instead of saying 'nineteen ninety-five' you literally say 'one thousand, nine hundred, ninety five:

χίλια ενιακόσια ενενήντα πέντε
kh**i**lia eniak**o**sia enen**i**nda p**e**ndeh

Days

Monday i Theftera
Tuesday i Triti
Wednesday i Tetarti
Thursday i Pempti
Friday i Paraskevi
Saturday to Savato
Sunday i Kiriaki

Months

January o I-anooarios
February o Fevrooarios
March o Martios
April o Aprilios
May o Ma-ios
June o I-oonios
July o I-oolios
August o AvGoostos
September o Septemvrios
October o Oktovrios
November o No-emvrios
December o Thekemvrios

Time

what time is it? τί ώρα είναι; [ti **o**ra ineh?]
one o'clock μία η ώρα [mia i **o**ra]
two o'clock δύο η ώρα [thio i **o**ra]
it's one o'clock είναι μία η ώρα [ineh mia i **o**ra]
it's two o'clock είναι δύο η ώρα [ineh thio i **o**ra]
it's ten o'clock είναι δέκα η ώρα [ineh theka i **o**ra]
five past one μία και πέντε [mia keh pendeh]
ten past two δύο και δέκα [thio keh theka]
quarter past one μία και τέταρτο [mia keh tetarto]
quarter past two δύο και τέταρτο [thio keh tetarto]
twenty past ten δέκα και είκοσι [theka keh ikosi]
half past ten δέκα και μισή [theka keh misi]
twenty to ten δέκα παρά είκοσι [theka para ikosi]
quarter to two δύο παρά τέταρτο [thio para tetarto]
at half past four στις τέσσερις και μισή [stis teseris keh misi]
at eight o'clock στις οκτώ [stis okto]
14.00 δεκατέσσερις [theka-teseris]
17.30 δεκαεφτά και τριάντα [theka-efta keh trianda]
2 am δύο η ώρα το βράδυ [thio i **o**ra to vrathi]
2 pm δύο η ώρα το μεσημέρι [thio i **o**ra to mesimeri]
6 am έξι η ώρα το πρωί [exi i **o**ra to pro-i]
6 pm έξι η ώρα το απόγευμα [exi i **o**ra to apoyevma]
noon το μεσημέρι [to mesimeri]
midnight τα μεσάνυχτα [ta mesanikhta]

an hour η ώρα [i **o**ra]
a minute το λεπτό [to lepto]
one minute ένα λεπτό [ena lepto]
two minutes δύο λεπτά [thio lepta]
a second το δευτερόλεπτο [to thefterolepto]
a quarter of an hour ένα τέταρτο [ena tetarto]
half an hour μισή ώρα [misi **o**ra]
three quarters of an hour τρία τέταρτα της ώρας [tria tetarta tis **o**ras]

Numbers

0	μηδέν [mithen]
1	ένα [ena]
2	δύο [thio]
3	τρία [tria]
4	τέσσερα [tesera]
5	πέντε [pendeh]
6	έξι [exi]
7	επτά [epta]
8	οχτώ [okhto]
9	εννιά [enia]
10	δέκα [theka]
11	έντεκα [endeka]
12	δώδεκα [thotheka]
13	δεκατρία [theka-tria]
14	δεκατέσσερα [theka-tesera]
15	δεκαπέντε [theka-pendeh]
16	δεκαέξι [theka-exi]
17	δεκαεπτά [theka-epta]
18	δεκαοχτώ [theka-okhto]
19	δεκαεννιά [theka-enia]
20	είκοσι [ikosi]
21	εικοσιένα [ikosi-ena]
22	εικοσιδύο [ikosi-thio]
30	τριάντα [trianda]
31	τριανταένα [trianda-ena]
40	σαράντα [saranda]
50	πενήντα [peninda]
60	εξήντα [exinda]
70	εβδομήντα [evthominda]
80	ογδόντα [ogthonda]
90	ενενήντα [eneninda]
100	εκατό [ekato]
110	εκατό δέκα [ekato theka]

200	διακόσια [thiakosia]
300	τριακόσια [triakosia]
1,000	χίλια [khilia]
2,000	δύο χιλιάδες [thio khiliathes]
5,000	πέντε χιλιάδες [pendeh khiliathes]
10,000	δέκα χιλιάδες [theka khiliathes]
20,000	είκοσι χιλιάδες [ikosi khiliathes]
50,000	πενήντα χιλιάδες [peninda khiliathes]
100,000	εκατό χιλιάδες [ekato khiliathes]
1,000,000	ένα εκατομμύριο [ena ekatomirio]

Ordinals

Ordinal numbers decline like regular adjectives:

1st	πρώτος [protos]
2nd	δεύτερος [thefteros]
3rd	τρίτος [tritos]
4th	τέταρτος [tetartos]
5th	πέμπτος [pemptos]
6th	έκτος [ektos]
7th	έβδομος [evthomos]
8th	όγδοος [ogtho-os]
9th	ένατος [enatos]
10th	δέκατος [thekatos]

Conversion Tables

1 centimetre = 0.39 inches

1 metre = 39.37 inches = 1.09 yards

1 kilometre = 0.62 miles = 5/8 mile

1 inch = 2.54 cm

1 foot = 30.48 cm

1 yard = 0.91 m

1 mile = 1.61 km

km	1	2	3	4	5	10	20	30	40	50	100
miles	0.6	1.2	1.9	2.5	3.1	6.2	12.4	18.6	24.8	31.0	62.1

miles	1	2	3	4	5	10	20	30	40	50	100
km	1.6	3.2	4.8	6.4	8.0	16.1	32.2	48.3	64.4	80.5	161

1 gram = 0.035 ounces

1 kilo = 1000 g = 2.2 pounds

g	100	250	500
oz	3.5	8.75	17.5

1 oz = 28.35 g

1 lb = 0.45 kg

kg	0.5	1	2	3	4	5	6	7	8	9	10
lb	1.1	2.2	4.4	6.6	8.8	11.0	13.2	15.4	17.6	19.8	22.0

kg	20	30	40	50	60	70	80	90	100
lb	44	66	88	110	132	154	176	198	220

lb	0.5	1	2	3	4	5	6	7	8	9	10	20
kg	0.2	0.5	0.9	1.4	1.8	2.3	2.7	3.2	3.6	4.1	4.5	9.0

1 litre = 1.75 UK pints / 2.13 US pints

1 UK pint = 0.57 litre

1 US pint = 0.47 litre

1 UK gallon = 4.55 litre

1 US gallon = 3.79 litre

centigrade / Celsius

°C = (°F - 32) x 5/9

°C	-5	0	5	10	15	18	20	25	30	36.8	38
°F	23	32	41	50	59	64	68	77	86	98.4	100.4

Fahrenheit

°F = (°C x 9/5) + 32

°F	23	32	40	50	60	65	70	80	85	98.4	101
°C	-5	0	4	10	16	18	21	27	29	36.8	38.3